Informational Approaches to Regulation

Regulation of Economic Activity

General Editors

Nancy L. Rose and Richard Schmalensee, MIT Sloan School of Management

Informational Approaches to Regulation

Wesley A. Magat and W. Kip Viscusi

The MIT Press
Cambridge, Massachusetts
London, England

363.19
M18

This books was set in Times by Asco Trade Typesetting Ltd., Hong Kong and was printed and bound in the United States of America.

Library of Congress Cataloging-in-Publication Data

Magat, Wesley A.
   Informational approaches to regulation/Wesley A. Magat and W. Kip Viscusi.
    p.   cm.—(Regulation of economic activity; 19)
   Includes bibliographical references and index.
   ISBN 0-262-13277-X
   1. Consumer protection—United States. 2. Labels—United States. 3. Product safety—United States. 4. Consumer protection—Law and legislation—United States.
I. Viscusi, W. Kip. II. Title. III. Series.
HC110.C63M34   1992
363.19—dc20   91-29483
                                                   CIP

Contents

List of Tables and Figures

Tables

Figures

Series Foreword

Government regulation of economic activity in the United States has changed dramatically in this century, radically transforming the economic roles of government and business as well as relations between them. Economic regulation of prices and conditions of service was first applied to transportation and public utilities and was later extended to energy, health care, and other sectors. Competition in financial services was restricted in the name of stability. More recently social regulation grew explosively, focusing on workplace safety, environmental preservation, consumer protection, and related goals. Regulatory reform has occupied a prominent place on the agendas of recent administrations, and considerable economic deregulation and other reform has occurred. But the U.S. economy remains highly regulated, and the aims, methods, and results of many regulatory programs remain controversial.

The purpose of the Regulation of Economic Activity series is to inform the ongoing debate on regulatory policy by making significant and relevant research available to both scholars and decision makers. Books in this series present new insights into individual agencies, programs, and regulated sectors, as well as the important economic, political, and administrative aspects of the regulatory process that cut across these boundaries.

Economists generally assume that workers and consumers are supremely competent, unboundedly rational information processors. Accordingly, economists have long argued that if the government has a choice between banning a risky product or activity and providing information about the risks involved, it should choose information provision over regulation. And, for a variety of reasons, during the 1980s the federal government substantially increased its reliance on hazard warnings.

As noneconomists might suspect, however, analysis of these programs indicates that individuals' response to hazard warnings depends on exactly what information is provided and how effectively it is communicated. The medium matters, not just the message, narrowly defined. In this volume Wesley A. Magat and W. Kip Viscusi report on three careful studies of the effects of informational regulations. Their results shed light on individuals' response to risk information and suggest guidelines for designing information-based policies. The methods they develop and employ draw on a variety of disciplines and should be generally useful in the analysis of informational programs. This study should accordingly be of interest to economists and others concerned with consumer behavior as well as to scholars and policymakers concerned with public policy toward risky products and activities.

Nancy L. Rose
and
Richard Schmalensee

One of the major changes in the role of government in this country over the last decade has been the increasing reliance on information provision programs to alter economic behavior. Whether it be in the home, the workplace, or the supermarket, Americans are constantly confronting information mandated by various government laws and regulations.

As consumers, we are warned about the risks of pesticides and toxic chemicals, cautioned about the dangers of alcohol, cigarette, and drug consumption, informed about the energy efficiency of appliances and energy-saving investments in our homes, and admonished to safely use machines such as lawn mowers and chain saws. Soon we will find all packaged foods labeled for nutrients, and in the not so distant future we may be able to glean whether products are environmentally safe through "green" labeling. In our places of employment we are provided detailed information about pesticides and other hazardous chemicals. There is simply no escape from the onslaught of information provided to us by government programs aimed at changing our behavior.

Although much work, such as our recent book *Learning about Risks: Consumer and Worker Responses to Hazard Information,* has increased our understanding of information provision programs, we are only beginning to understand how to effectively use information policies in situations where consumers and workers lack adequate information. This book takes both a positive and a normative approach to the issue. Our research provides new insight into how people respond to risk information, and it suggests guidelines for designing information provision policies. In addition, we develop some promising methodologies for assessing the effects of information programs on consumer and worker behavior based on survey and experimental approaches. These methodologies can be used by other researchers and by industry and government professionals who design information programs.

Although the primary case study in this book examines the use of product labels to reduce the risks of using hazardous chemicals, our focus is broader than the labeling approach to information provision and broader than the concern with conveying information about products' hazards. The results and principles we discuss apply to all forms of information programs, and as the example of home energy audits in chapter 8 illustrates, they apply to any type of information that consumers or workers may be missing in their consumption and workplace decisions.

Our work draws upon previous work in the fields of economics, psychology, decision sciences, and marketing. The problem of effectively communicating information draws on insights from all of these fields. Indeed, it is the need to integrate the knowledge from so many diverse fields that makes the study of information programs so interesting and intellectually challenging. We envision that this book will be of interest to academics studying the design of regulations and information polices, as well as to practitioners in government and business responsible for the design and implementation of information programs in their organizations. It is written using the language of economics and statistics, but the main contributions are meant to be accessible to readers choosing to skip the more mathematical sections of the text.

The research reported in this book was funded by the U.S. Environmental Protection Agency and the North Carolina Energy Institute under contracts to Duke University and the Duke Center for the Study of Business, Regulation, and Economic Policy. We are particularly grateful to our EPA Project Officer, Alan Carlin, who provided ongoing advice and assisted us in gaining close cooperation with the agency. Ralph Luken and Albert McGartland, who were formerly at EPA, also provided valuable advice on the research. Bertrand Munier and his colleagues at the GRASCE research center in Aix-en-Provence, France, supplied Wesley Magat with a most supportive and pleasant environment to complete parts of the book.

Lester Lave read and provided many useful suggestions on the manuscript. We also benefited from many insights offered by Howard Kunreuther. At MIT Press, Terry Vaughn and Nancy Rose did an excellent job in expediting the review and production of this book. We would also like to thank Dana Andrus for her editing of the manuscript.

The research could not have been completed without the extensive work and close intellectual cooperation of our Duke colleague, Joel Huber, who is the coauthor of three of the chapters in the book. In all of our work on information and risk regulation, we have greatly benefited from the advice of another Duke colleague, John W. Payne. John was instrumental in the home energy audit research reported in chapter 8, which he coauthored. Two of our former graduate students, Anne Forrest and Peter F. Brucato, Jr., played central roles in the chemical labeling and the home energy audit studies, respectively. Anne is coauthor of chapter 4, and Peter is coauthor of chapter 8. Duke Economics Department graduate students Teresa Carroll and Jane Rosetti also provided excellent support in their work as research assistants on the chemical labeling study. Dr. Shirley Osterhaut, director of the Duke University Poison Control Central, again graciously assisted us in understanding the medical effects of exposure to the pesticide and chemical products involved in our research.

This book could not have been finished without the tireless, rapid, and always cheerful assistance of Anita Tapp, who typed the entire manuscript. We thank our families who have for many years strongly supported and encouraged our work.

Finally, we thank the publishers of the following journals which granted us permission to use some materials that appeared in previous publications: *Food Drug Cosmetic Law Journal, Journal of Policy Analysis and Management, Journal of Risk and Uncertainty,* and *The Rand Journal of Economics.*

Informational Approaches to Regulation

1

Introduction

One of the main shifts in risk regulation policies in the 1980s was the federal government's increased involvement in hazard warnings. In earlier decades the federal government had utilized warnings only in selected instances, namely, for cigarettes, saccharin, and particular product groups such as pesticides. The emergence of the right-to-know movement and the political support for regulations that were less obtrusive than the command-and-control regulations of the 1970s led to a proliferation of warnings efforts. Warnings now appear on alcoholic beverages and on a wide variety of consumer products. For food substances the formatting of nutritional labeling is still a matter of public debate, as is the desirability of indicating which products don't promote heart disease or which products are safe for the environment. Consumers entering the supermarket are now engulfed with risk information about the products they use. Workers are in a similar position in their jobs because of comprehensive safety training programs and chemical labeling programs that began in the 1980s.

Despite the substantial information available, the public is not always well equipped to make sound decisions about the risks addressed in the hazard warnings. One difficulty is that these warnings are not well coordinated. If everything in society receives a risk warning, then no distinctions among risks can effectively be made. In the absence of any clear criteria for when risk warnings should be used and when they should not, there is little to guide the labeling programs.

Even if a hazard warning is justified, the actual mode of expressing this warning may not be well chosen. Often the labeling efforts are developed by analogy. Policymakers, for example, may seek to replicate a cigarette-style warning in another context, and thus emulate both the format and the structure of the cigarette warning without questioning whether this type of warning will be effective in another instance. More fundamentally these framers of the warnings may have little knowledge of whether the original cigarette warnings were even effective.

A major focus of this book is on research that provides a scientific basis for the assessment and design of hazard warning efforts. Society should not provide warnings for all risks, particularly if the recommended course of action is not worthwhile. As with decisions about adopting other forms of regulation, a benefit-cost analysis is necessary. Hazard warning regulations should be adopted only if the benefits of the recommended precautions exceed their costs, and the net benefits of these regulations exceed those from other regulatory approaches.

consequences The economic costs of hazard warnings include the monetary costs of the warnings themselves, which in the case of product labeling include the costs of redesigning and printing labels, as well as disposing of or relabeling products in inventory. But perhaps a larger share of the costs is in the expenditures on protective equipment, any reductions in productivity due to adopting the recommended precaution behavior, and the disutility suffered by consumers and workers because they follow the precautions (a well-known example being the use of earphones and other personal protective equipment by industrial workers to guard against hearing loss).

The primary economic benefits from hazard warnings accrue from the reduced incidence of accidents and of adverse health effects. In this study we will explore how consumers value the risk reductions that induce them to avert behavior due to hazard warnings.

Of course benefits from reduced risk exposure only occur *if* people respond to a hazard warning by taking appropriate precautions. Thus a critical issue in evaluating the benefits of an information provision policy is the extent of the behavioral response to hazard warnings. This raises the question of the appropriate structure and content of the information provided, since people do not have unlimited information-processing capabilities. We all process information imperfectly and make flawed decisions, particularly under situations of uncertainty.

In exploring these limitations and the role that warnings play with respect to them, we will not only develop guidelines for the development of informational regulations but will also address a variety of decision-making phenomena that are becoming of increasing interest in the fields of economics, psychology, and decision sciences. A broad range of recent research has indicated that there are systematic ways in which individuals err in the decisions they make, particularly when these choices involve probabilistic elements. One can view an assessment of the role of hazard warnings as providing a case study of the manner in which individuals process and act upon the information they receive.

Even in situations *not* involving risk, information provision programs can be an effective policy response to improve decision errors due to lack of information or to lack of information-processing capabilities of consumers and workers. Information about the energy efficiency of appliances provides an instructive example. Buyers of infrequently purchased appliances, such as air conditioners, refrigerators, and freezers, generally bring little information about the energy efficiency of those appliances to the purchase decision. Thus, to the extent to which sellers do not provide easy-to-use comparative information, the buyers' decisions can be poorly informed. Federal regulations requiring energy efficiency labels on new air conditioners and refrigerators directly address consumers' information needs. The labels provide comparative information across different models and brands, as well as information about the expected energy costs of using the appliances.

Although this book will primarily rely upon examples of informational regulation directed to reduce accident and health *risks*, its purpose is more broadly to understand how to effectively use information provision programs in all situations where consumers and workers lack adequate information. One class of decision problems that are not risk related and that are particularly amenable to information provision solutions is that of complex but infrequent purchase decisions. In these situations consumers tend to have much less information about the goods or services under consideration than for frequently purchased items because they lack the information that can be learned from prior purchases. This lack of information is more likely to occur the more costly it is to acquire information and the less information there is relevant to their purchases that consumers can learn from the purchases of others. Chapter 8 analyzes a typical example of this type of infrequent purchase decision and a governmental information provision response—the use of home energy audits to better inform consumer decisions about the various energy conservation investment options available to them.

The findings from this book provide specific guidelines for when different types of information provision instruments are effective and when they are not, as well as which kinds of instruments will have the greatest impact. The experimental results are quite specific. They address such nuances as the choice of print size and the arrangement of information on product labels. By developing scientific criteria for the design of information provision programs—including warning labels against risk and benefit-cost reports for consumer decisions that are not risk related, this effort is intended to foster an improvement in the design of all information programs over current practice. The major task is to communicate information in an effective manner, and the primary resource that one can utilize in undertaking this effort will be knowledge of how individuals respond to the communication efforts.

1.1   Information as a Regulatory Tool

When government regulators are faced with a situation involving a risk, they have four policy options. The first is to do nothing, which is a desirable course of action in situations where the market functions effectively. The second option is to ban the product or activity generating the risk. The Food and Drug Administration, for example, screens new pharmaceutical products to ensure that drugs posing substantial risks are not marketed. Third, the government can undertake an action to directly alter the risk, as in the case of Occupational Safety and Health Administration regulations that control conditions of the workplace, or Environmental Protection Agency requirements on household pesticides that limit the potency of commercially marketed products.

A fourth option, which is a major focus of this volume, is to adopt a hazard-warning program. From a political standpoint this policy option is often viewed as a compromise between taking no action at all and taking an extreme form of action such as a product ban. As an intermediate policy option it has political appeal that is somewhat independent of its merits.

There are also sound economic reasons why such an intermediate course might be preferred. Informational programs often are potentially more effective than taking no regulatory action. Such programs can potentially remedy the informational inadequacies in markets. A major source of market failure that is often cited in the case of health and safety regulations is that if consumers and workers are not fully informed of the risks they face, market compensation for risk will not produce efficient safety incentives, thus leading to a justification for a government intervention. If these informational problems can be solved directly through informational regulation, more stringent forms of regulation will not be required, so the market outcome will be efficient.

Informational regulation also may be a more effective means of promoting safety than direct technological controls. Most accident situations are the result of two sets of influences: (1) the technological characteristics of the accident context, such as whether a lawn mower has an engine cutoff device, and (2) the role of the potential accident victim. The manner of operation of the lawn mower and the choice of which family member is to operate the mower play a potentially important role. In most instances consumer precautions are required for the amount and nature in which a product is used, as well as for particular precautions and precautionary equipment that should be employed. Once the role of individual action in contributing to risks is recognized, the potential role for regulatory intervention through an informational approach is apparent. Altering behavior may be a more effective regulatory strategy than is the technological approach that dominated the first decade of social regulation in the 1970s.

Partly in recognition of this role of individual behavior and partly because of the increasing cost of technological controls to reduce risk, the emphasis of health, safety, and environmental regulations in the 1980s became increasingly shifted toward informational regulations. In addition there has been increasing pressure to engage individuals in decisions about the risks they face by right-to-know activists.

A further argument for informational remedies, rather than command-and-central regulation, applies to informational problems prevalent in both risk and non-risk-related decisions. Consumer and worker preferences differ, as do the stocks of existing goods that they own, implying that the optimal regulation should differ across them. A product "improvement," such as a lawnmower engine cutoff system which makes the product safer but more costly, is more likely to be desired by consumers who are wealthy, risk averse, and careless than those with limited incomes who are risk prone and carefully operate the product. Similarly, a product requirement, such as the building code requiring adequate caulking around windows, is more likely to be desired by consumers who are wealthy and know little about new homes than those with less income who are well informed about building characteristics.

Although informational regulations have proliferated, they have not been without controversy. Informational regulations generally are not completely effective, and there are some circumstances in which they may not be effective at all. Not all people will read the information provided, and not all recipients of the information will act upon it. Perhaps the main difficulty is that informational regulations do not involve simple technological prescriptions to problems. There is an important human element involved in the processing of the information and in the decisions using the information, and one must take into account both this limitation and the decision-making orientation in which the information will be used. For informational regulations to be effective, they must provide new information that can potentially alter individual decisions. If the information cannot be processed reliably or is viewed as not contributing any new information or perspective on a decision, then the informational program will not be successful.

A natural starting point for developing guidelines for informational regulations is to assess the performance of past efforts of this type. The limitations of using such experiences are reflected in the studies that have been done on the cigarette and saccharin warning labels.[1] The first issue to address is whether the labels were effective in conveying the risk information needed for people to make sounder decisions with respect to these products. The most we have been able to glean from these experiences is considerably more limited than that. In particular, there was a significant drop in the consumption of soft drinks containing saccharin after the warnings were put in place, and there has been a substantial change in smoking patterns over the two decades in which we have had cigarette warnings. Unfortunately, in neither case can the effect of the informational regulation be distinguished from the broader publicity in the media concerning these two regulatory events. In the case of cigarettes, for example, one cannot distinguish the net impact of hazard warnings in 1964 from the series of Surgeon General's reports and the media coverage of cigarettes that appeared at roughly the same time. Since neither of these market experiments was a controlled experiment in which other forms of information were held constant, the experience has been sufficiently contaminated by other events that even with the aid of the usual multivariate statistical methods one cannot successfully disentangle the relationships.

Moreover, even if it were possible to do so, the information we would obtain from such an exercise would be quite limited. The result of a successful study of this type would be a conclusion such as the following: Saccharin labels reduced consumption of soft drinks by 2 percent, and 5 percent fewer of the American population smoked cigarettes as a result of the introduction of hazard warnings.

We do not know from such a result whether the informational program was a success. We know that effects have been observed, but the objective of such efforts is informed choice, not simply altered choice. It may be that the responses were generated by an excessively alarmist warnings policy that led individuals to respond too much to the new information. The opposite danger is also present, as existence of a statistically significant effect does not in any way imply that the impact is sufficiently large to indicate that optimal outcomes have been achieved.

A final restriction that is inherent in all studies based on actual informational regulations is that such studies are necessarily restricted to examining the regulations that have been implemented. Variations in the content and format of information provision mechanisms, such as warning labels and benefit-cost product reports, that have not yet been introduced consequently cannot be explored. In contrast, with the experimental methodology that we adopt in this book, it is possible to construct variations on alternative information provision instruments to ascertain the incremental differences attributable to variations in the format and content of the information.

Much of the work on label design has been developed by using the precedent of what we know about advertising and it effects on consumer behavior. Although this approach is potentially useful in the absence of any formal studies of labeling, it may not be a reliable guide, particularly in the case of hazard warnings. Even if we knew how individuals process different aspects of labels, the risk elements that become introduced within the context of hazard warnings raise a new class of issues. Choices involving risk and uncertainty are known to pose special problems for individual decision making and to require a separate analytical apparatus, wholly apart from any potential inadequacies that may arise with respect to the decisions.[2] One cannot simply apply previous results that abstract completely from the essential element of a hazard warning, which is that it addresses a risk.

The consensus in the early literature was that informational regulations were a failure.[3] Programs in education proved not to be successful, with perhaps the most noteworthy example being the poor performance of successive years of seatbelt campaigns. There is also a tendency to generalize from these disappointing educational efforts to conclude that informational regulations are not a viable policy alternative. Conclusions of this type are too hasty because they neglect the different circumstances under which informational regulations would be effective, and they fail to distinguish the difference between educational programs and programs that provide new knowledge and that are truly informational in nature. Programs of exhortation and policies that might be characterized more as browbeating (or as consumer reminders) have not been successful, but this does not imply that regulations that convey new information to assist in making decisions will not have a beneficial effect.

In our earlier work we have established that the effect of the regulation on risk perceptions and on attitudes toward job risks depends on the extent to which new knowledge is being provided.[4] In addition informational programs for consumers have an effect if the structure of the information can be readily processed by the individuals receiving it.[5] The existence of an effect does not imply that all individuals will take a particular precaution. Indeed, if that were our policy objective, we might wish to compel precautionary behavior, as in the case of mandatory seatbelt laws. Rather, informational efforts are most desirable in situations where there is an element of individual choice. Such regulations are particularly useful when individual behavior cannot be monitored and enforced. In addition circumstances in which a particular precaution may be warranted depending on one's particular risk and values also lend themselves to informational regulations.

A major practical problem is ensuring that individuals read the warning label or acquire information in some other form, since there is no general assurance that individuals will do so. The existing evidence on the extent to which people read patient package inserts or take advantage of point of-purchase displays reflect mixed findings, and as in the case of warning labels, no simple generalizations are possible.[6] The efficacy of the approach will depend in large part upon its prominence. Thus a hazard warning that is not in a prominent location on a product, or that ranks low in terms of the overall priority of the messages conveyed by the product label, is much less likely to be read than a warning that ranks high in this priority. Results reported later in this book will shed some light on how individuals process labeling information as well as on their cognitive limitations in doing so.

Overall, informational regulations are a viable policy alternative, but one must recognize the circumstances under which they will be effective. Not all situations lend themselves to informational regulations. One essential ingredient is that there must be some form of information gap that the regulation will alleviate. Once the information is provided, it must be received by an individual who controls the action to be influenced. The character of the information must be such that there must be some incentive for the party to alter the action depending on the information that is provided.

Although the results in this book will focus on two particular kinds of information—hazard warnings and energy audits—informational regulations are by no means limited to these two approaches.[7] A patient package insert is a simple variant on a product warning in situations where the warning information is too extensive to be included on the product. Similarly, as we will discuss with respect to California's carcinogenic food substances warnings, the message could be provided through an 800 number or through some other mechanism, such as a point-of-purchase display. In many other contexts involving substantial risk, different forms of media are used. To promote safe use of its lift trucks, for example, Caterpillar Tractor provides safety videos to lift truck dealers, extensive safety manuals to accompany each machine, and warning labels on the lift truck itself. Consequently the range of potential forms of information is quite extensive. Rather than focus on each, we explore economic and cognitive issues that pertain to all of these information transfer mechanisms.

The content of the information provided is also of substantial importance. Many hazard warning efforts that have been adopted on a large scale appear to have been drafted by lawyers who have perused a summary of scientific studies regarding the risk. There is even one notable instance of a patient package insert for a pharmaceutical product for which the wording was drawn from a court decision, thus increasing the likelihood that the firm would be able to fend off future claims against it.

The results that we provide in this book suggest that the skills needed to convey an adequate warning extend beyond knowledge of the scientific information regarding the risk and an ability to write clearly and logically. The format, prominence, structure, and the amount of the information provided are also of substantial import. Moreover the content of the informational regulation must continually be assessed with respect to our standard of judgment—informed choice—to ensure that we are succeeding in promoting this objective.

Our research findings can be used to assess informational regulations as well as to provide guidance with respect to their design formats. Thus in the case of warnings for chemical and pesticide products, we are concerned not only with the effect of these regulations on precautionary behavior but also on the consumers' valuations of the risks that are prevented. In the case of food cancer warnings our interests are not only on the effect of these warnings on the prices consumers are willing to pay for the products receiving the warnings but also on whether these warnings provide accurate information to consumers about the possible risks. Similarly, in the case of home energy audits, our objective is to assess whether benefit and cost information about energy efficiency improves the energy choices of the households receiving the energy conservation information.

1.2   Organization of the Volume

This book consists of research results regarding three studies of the effects of informational regulations. Two of them involve health risks addressed by product labels, and a third analyzes a difficult, non-risk-related decision, involving a large quantity of unfamiliar information, that some consumers make with the aid of a complicated report on the benefits and costs of the various choices available to them.

The primary case study is that of hazard warnings for pesticides and chemicals. Results from this field experiment provide the basis for assessing the appropriate design of hazard warnings, the effect of hazard warnings on precautionary behavior, and individual valuation of the losses that are prevented by these precautions. The second case study pertains to carcinogenic food substances warnings. We apply the insights developed from the pesticide and chemical warning analysis and provide new empirical results pertinent to consumers' interpretations of such warnings for food products. The final empirical study examines home energy audits and addresses the role of the structure of the energy efficiency information presented and its effect on consumer behavior. Although the focus of each is somewhat different, these studies share a concern with the importance of providing information in a manner that can be interpreted and acted upon in a rational manner.

Chapter 2 of the book introduces the major empirical study dealing with household pesticide and chemical warnings, the two main areas in which warnings are issued by the U.S. Environmental Protection Agency. The focus of the study was twofold. First, we addressed the extent to which hazard warnings affect precautionary behavior. Do people process the information about risks and precautions and act upon it in a reliable manner? The discussion includes ways to redesign warnings to enhance their efficacy as well as the effect of warnings as presently designed. The second focus concerns the economic benefits from the information regulations that are relevant to government policymakers assessing the merits of regulations. To assess each of these issues, the survey approach we used was a field experiment in which hundreds of consumers were shown alternative labels. On these alternative labels we altered one aspect of the warning (holding the other features constant) so that we could distinguish the incremental effect of changes in label design. This approach enabled us to run a purer labeling experiment than is possible with commercially available labels. Differences in the responses across treatment groups were used to assess the effect of the hazard warnings. These subjects also provided responses that could be used to assess their valuations of the health outcome. The sample consisted of consumers who use this class of products and were recruited in a shopping small and a hardware store in Greensboro, North Carolina.

The possibility of a beneficial effect of hazard warnings on precautionary behavior is not in and of itself a justification for such regulation. These warnings may be instructing consumers to undertake precautions that are not warranted. If hazard warnings simply provided information regarding the risks and payoffs associated with alternative forms of behavior, then individuals could undertake an internal calculation of the benefits and costs associated with an action and pursue only those precautions that were economically warranted. Hazard warnings are generally not of this innocuous informational nature. They tend to be more dictatorial in tone, exhorting consumers to undertake a particular precaution in using the product.

The key ingredient in such benefit-cost calculations is the value that the beneficiaries of the regulation place upon the risk reductions that are achieved. In particular, how much is it worth to prevent poisonings and other adverse health outcomes that are reduced through improved hazard warnings? Once this issue is resolved, policymakers can calculate the desirability of the warnings in a fairly straightforward manner, as the earlier analysis in Viscusi and Magat (1987) indicates.

The approach we used in chapter 3 to ascertain these values involves a series of survey questions that elicit dollar values that individuals attach to this risk reduction. In our past study we have shown that this methodology yields estimates comparable to those obtained using statistical estimations of wage premiums for job risks for labor market data. Moreover the results are similar to those obtained using conjoint analysis for assessing consumer valuations for health risks. In each case the validity of the survey approach was corroborated. Since market data are not available to assess implicit market prices for the risks examined in this book, we will report only survey results.[8]

The class of injuries being considered includes relatively minor injuries, such as hand burns and poisonings. The results in chapter 3 indicate that consumers' valuations of the pairs of injuries that were being prevented were generally on the order of $2,000 to $3,000—far below the risk-dollar trade-off for outcomes as severe as the standard job injury.

These values are of interest in their own right in that they establish a measure of the benefits achieved through risk communication efforts. Exploration of individuals' valuations is also of interest in that it indicates how people respond to different kinds of risks. The usual economic models indicate that ideally people should react in similar ways to small changes in riskiness that are of comparable magnitude but that may differ in some other respects. For example, if a risk change is very small, the amount that we need to compensate a consumer for bearing this additional risk should be roughly comparable to the amount that the consumer would pay for a comparably safer product. Similarly, if we were to reduce the risk posed by a consumer product by a very small amount, then the value consumers place on this increased safety should be fairly similar, whether the risk reduction is sufficient to eliminate all risk or whether it simply reduces an already high level of risk that one faces. There are of course ways in which economists would modify these results, but for very small changes in risk these two pairs of circumstances each yield analogous results.

The results in chapter 3 explore risk valuations such as these quite explicitly. They provide the striking finding that individuals respond in quite different ways to risk increases and risk decreases, and they regard risk changes that involve changes in the regime from the presence of a risk to complete elimination of a risk as being quite different from other variations of the risk.

Of perhaps greatest interest is the manner in which these values varied according to particular levels of the risk. Two extreme sets of responses were identified in the results in chapter 3. First, in situations in which a risk reduction would lead to complete elimination of a class of risks faced by consumers, there was a substantial jump in consumers' willingness to pay for this risk reduction. Thus consumers appear to place substantial value on certain elimination of the risks, perhaps in part because of the reduction in anxiety and decision making costs associated with zero risk levels. A second phenomenon is that the consumer participants in the study responded in an extreme fashion to increases in the risk above its current level, or what we term a "reference risk" effect. Modifications in a product that will raise the product risk are viewed with considerable alarm by consumers.

These reactions are quite consistent with observed behavior. For example, in 1989 the publication of information on poison residues in grapes imported from Chile and on Alar residues in apples led to dramatic consumer responses in each instance to their perceived increases in risk. There is no similar aversion to many other consumer risks of an equal or even greater magnitude, perhaps in part because these risks are at their customary levels and individuals have grown to accept these risks. Natural carcinogens, for example, evoke less concern than do man-made carcinogens.

The class of results pertaining to individuals' substantial evaluations of risk reductions that provide for complete safety also is consistent with observed behavior. Government policies have proliferated in recent years, where their focus has been on achieving complete elimination of all measurable risks or all risks found to be statistically significant. The usual assumption by economists is that such policies are irrational in that they do not reflect a careful balancing of the risks and benefits. Moreover the widespread support of such policies has remained a puzzle for those who believe that policies should ideally reflect the interests of those affected by them. What our results indicate is that the emphasis of government programs on providing complete elimination of risks, even when they may be miniscule, is not simply the result of an oversight by the drafters of the legislation that specifies these objectives. Rather, it reflects the character of individual attitudes toward risk, as individuals place a much greater value on policies that achieve complete safety than on those that will not. The reasons for this surprising result are explored in chapter 3 within the context of individual valuations of a reduction in the risks that will be most consequential for our hazard warning study.

A potential missing link in the benefit calculations is that health risks are accorded special status in our society. The promotion of individual health has been the object of a wide variety of government programs, ranging from Medicare for the aged to Medicaid for the indigent and tax deductions for health insurance fringe benefits for the entire population. The benefit value of risk reductions is consequently not limited to that of the individual directly affected by the risk reduction. Other individuals in society may also experience an altruistic benefit from the improved health and safety promoted by effective hazard warnings.

Chapter 4 reports on preliminary results that are intended to provide an assessment of the extent of this altruistic interest. Two contexts were explored. First, respondents were asked questions to elicit their altruistic interests in promoting health improvements in their home state. Second, they were then asked to extend these contributions to a nationwide basis. The survey results indicated that altruism did matter, as the altruistic valuations were even greater than the private valuations of the risk in the case of the within-state altruism. There was, however, no "deep pocket" for altruism, as the altruistic concern diminished substantially once one moved to a national as opposed to a within-state context.

Taken literally, these results suggest that altruism is an important benefit component, but that there is no "deep pocket" for altruism once one increases the scope of concerns for which respondents are asked to make an altruistic contribution. Limits on altruism suggest viewing these results with caution. In surveys it may be easy to elicit altruistic concern for any worthy cause, but the willingness to contribute to diminishes once the respondent is pressed to exhibit altruism across a broader range of worthy causes. The analysis in chapter 4 serves to highlight altruism as a potential benefit component, though the specific numerical estimates should be regarded as highly exploratory in nature.

In chapter 5 we present the first set of results on the effect of hazard warnings on precautionary behavior. We discuss the methodology used to assess the effect of warnings, using an open-ended memory recall technique. This innovative approach enabled us to assess not only the information that is acquired by the recipient of the hazard warning but also the prominence of the information in consumers' memories as well as the ordering and linkages of this information.[9] This memory recall technique indicated that provision of risk information in hazard warnings does have a substantial effect on consumers' precautionary intentions.

This technique led to several other striking findings as well. In particular, there is a trade-off in terms of how much information can be provided on a label. As the amount of hazard warning information is increased, consumer recall of other information on the product's label declines. A second striking result is that substantial increases in the amount of information included on a label decreases the performance of the hazard warning. Thus label clutter leads to problems of information overload that may actually reduce the efficacy of the hazard warning. Although this phenomenon has been raised previously in the literature, it has never been subjected to a refined experiment that tests the effect of information overload.

The information overload results are pertinent to the design of hazard warning labels and, in general, to an assessment of hazard warning efforts in other media. Over time there is a tendency for warnings to become increasingly complicated as we learn about more and more risks that may be posed by products. One reason for this rise in knowledge is not that the products themselves have become riskier. Rather, our ability to detect hazards has become greatly refined. For pesticide regulations, for example, the U.S. Environmental Protection Agency has found that its risk warnings have become increasingly lengthy—so lengthy that many agency officials fear that the warnings may not be accomplishing their intended objective.

The results presented here bear these fears out. In particular, they indicate that overwhelming consumers with a comprehensive recounting of all the potential risks will not be the most effective warnings effort. Our experimental results with respect to this effect are quite specific, as they indicate how many pieces of information individuals can recall reliably based on hazard warnings. In addition we indicate the manner in which individuals err once too much information has been provided, such as by ignoring information with respect to precautionary actions.

This same kind of result is more generally applicable to the societal choice of the role of warnings. Even if we restrict warnings for a product to an amount of information that can be processed reliably but inundate consumers with information across products, we run the danger of diluting our risk communication efforts and undermining the primary intent of across-product warnings, which is to foster distinctions among products of different riskiness.

Chapter 6 explores further the results on precautionary behavior to deal with the choice of format of the hazard warning. We found the manner and structure in which we presented the information to have a substantial effect on the amount of information that the subjects were able to recall. Among the variations that we examine are changes in print size, increases in the amount of warning information on the label, and restructuring of the information to make it more organized and easier to process. Although improved information formatting is beneficial, manipulations in label design such as increases in the size of lettering or in the hazard warning area appear to have diminishing returns. Eventually one reaches the point where no additional gains are achieved by altering the dimensions of the hazard warning. For example, increasing the percentage of the label devoted to risk information had no significant effect for the insecticide warning, where the initial amount of risk information was already substantial, but it was influential in the case of the warning for toilet bowl cleaner, where the baseline amount of risk information was not as great.

A fundamental question raised by field experiments is the extent to which experimental results convincingly correspond to actual behavior. No general answers to this question are possible since a broader interpretation of the experimental results depends in large part on the validity of the experiment's design. Poorly designed experimental settings that do not establish a meaningful warnings context are unlikely to yield results that can be used to assess the efficacy of hazard warnings.[10] Thus, even if there were a general finding in the literature that supported the use of experimental research, such as is widely practiced in the social sciences, one would not be able to utilize that result in justifying the validity of any particular experiment that was undertaken.

In an effort to corroborate our research results, we undertook a telephone survey of actual product usage patterns for a well-known toilet bowl cleaner and insecticide. This survey was product specific so that we could match the telephone responses for products with labels identical to those in the experimental study. In this way we could make a direct comparison between experimental and actual behavior. The results reported in chapter 7 show that the composition of the sample of actual product users closely paralleled the demographic mix of the experimental subjects. More important, the implications of the experimental study for precautionary behavior were similar to precautionary behavior reported in the telephone survey, with a reasonably close correspondence for all the major precautions that were the focus of the study.

Chapter 8 examines the use of home energy audits to promote energy conservation. With this study we shift our focus from informational regulations involving health risks to those involving only financial losses. The context in which informational regulations are potentially useful is not limited to the health area, although this has been the most frequent regulatory domain of informational regulations. Any situation in which information can be provided to improve decisions is a potential candidate for informational regulation. Home energy audits are a response to one important domain of informational regulation, that for infrequent purchase decisions involving many possible choices, with each choice differing along several dimensions which are unfamiliar to most consumers. In these cases information provision programs can serve two functions: They can provide missing information, and they can organize complicated information in ways easier for consumers to understand.

The findings in chapter 8 also show that the concerns about the format and structure of information which were found to be important in the design of hazard warnings are pertinent here as well. Moreover, since the financial resources of consumers vary considerably, financial constraints must be considered when developing informational programs that involve monetary decisions.

Chapter 9 turns to the case of labeling carcinogenic food substances in the wake of California's Proposition 65, which took effect in 1989. This rather sweeping measure requires that warnings be given to all consumers and workers in California who are exposed to significant risks of cancer or reproductive toxicity from products sold or used in the state. It encompasses food products, all household products such as chemicals, gasoline, products used in the workplace, and products served in restaurants. In effect, it covers all major product contexts in which individuals could be exposed to a risk.

The approach that has been taken under Proposition 65 is still being developed by the state of California. The implementers of the regulation have apparently used the cigarette warning example as their model, patterning the warning for low levels of carcinogenic risks after cigarette warnings. Since the food cancer warning threshold under the California system is lower than the probability of being struck by lightning, the task of conveying this low probability event to consumers was clearly difficult. The actual wording chosen for the warning did not convey the risk level involved. Experimental evidence in chapter 9 shows that consumers interpret the risk as being equivalent to a lifetime death risk in excess of one in ten, which dwarfs the actual risk posed by most of the products that will receive the warnings.

The results of chapter 9 provide a substantive extension of the earlier findings on precautionary behavior. The emphasis here is not on precautionary actions when the product is used but on apprising consumers of a risk prior to purchase so that they can make informed purchasing decisions. In this case the accuracy of risk assessments in response to warnings is of great concern. We report on a series of experimental results that provide evidence of the impact of different warnings on risk perceptions.

As these chapters and the concluding chapter 10 indicate, the design and implementation of a successful informational regulation is not a trivial undertaking. The first issue that is generally addressed is whether warning programs can potentially be effective. It is clear from our experimental results that when new hazard information is being provided to consumers or workers who must take a safety-enhancing action, there is a potential role for informational efforts to play.

The next policy choice that is involved is the content and manner of presentation of the information. Our results suggest that individual responses to warnings is much too subtle to adopt the same warning approach in all circumstances, or to simply convey all that is known about a risk and thus to inundate information recipients with extensive information.

Warnings information must assist consumers in making decisions. Consumers do not always respond rationally to both the information and the changes in risk levels. To be effective, information programs must convey information in a form that can be easily processed, and in an accurate and meaningful way that will enable individuals to make informed decisions.

I

HAZARDOUS CHEMICAL PRODUCT LABELING: METHODOLOGY

Methodology for the Consumer Surveys

Labeling is increasingly being used and considered as an alternative to more conventional approaches to regulation, such as standard setting and product bans (see Hadden 1985). In Viscusi and Magat (1986) we describe several examples of the use of product labeling, as well as the advantage of this over other approaches. There are two key research issues that must be addressed in a study of information provision programs for risks: How consumers value the adverse health outcome being communicated, and how to design the informational program to convey the precautionary information effectively. Each question hinges on appropriate research design. In the first case, which risks should one ask consumers to value, and how should the questions elicit these valuations? Our concern is with the social valuation of risk. In our study we address both the social valuation and the private valuation of risk. In the second case, the two experimental design questions are, which alternative labels does one test, and how does one best assess the precautions that changes in the label will induce?

We will address the two research issues using an experimental design that has been constructed to assess consumers' valuations of risks and their precautionary behavior. We chose the experimental approach over using data from previous warnings because detailed data for the broad range of issues we are addressing are simply not available. The existing data would have greatly restricted the scope of our research, completely eliminating the valuation segment of the study and greatly restricting the label designs that could be considered.

With regard to the first issue of how consumers value the avoidance of the risks that can be caused by hazardous chemicals, we focus on morbidity risks, extending our earlier study (Viscusi and Magat 1987) to the measurement of consumer preferences with respect to multiple risks. We also explore how the morbidity valuations are affected by factors such as the extent of risk reduction offered by safer products and whether the safer products eliminate all risks. The hypotheses we use have their roots in the economics and psychology of risk-taking behavior. In addition, by examining responses to two kinds of programs—one that reduces risks of injury to an individual and one that reduces injury risks to all product users in the state or country—we were able to draw some tentative conclusions about the effect of altruism on morbidity risk valuations. This result is useful from the standpoint of social benefit assessment.

On the second issue of how well consumers respond to information on chemical product labels, we address several specific questions. A natural first set of questions ascertains the base level of knowledge about the risks and precautions associated with the products before reading the labels. One can then assess the increase in understanding of risk and precautions due to reading the labels. We then explore how variations in the design and information of labels affect consumer responses to them, examining in particular the effects of information clutter and of a design format suggested by the literature on information-processing theory. In our study we utilize two different methodological approaches—an open-ended recall and a series of direct questions. We also measure variations in responses to product labels with differences in users' demographic characteristics, differences in the types of products and product uses, and differences in the precautions required for the products.

2.1 Selection of Products and Risks

We selected two household chemical products: a toilet bowl cleaner and an insect spray that is used primarily in the yard and garden. Both products are reasonably representative of chemical products used in and around the home, yet different enough from each other to allow some testing of whether variations in products and their associated risks affect responses to labels and risk valuations. The toilet bowl cleaner and the outdoor insect spray share a precautionary need to store the products out of children's reach, though many of the other precautions and risks differ. Both are frequently used products, and data from the Consumer Product Safety Commission and the U.S. Poison Control Centers indicate that a larger number of injuries are associated with them than with other household chemical products.

Since our study was funded by the U.S. Environmental Protection Agency (EPA), it was designed to also be responsive to the needs of the agency. Accordingly in our product selection we focused on morbidity losses rather than death because few household chemical and pesticide injuries are fatal. Likewise we chose to examine acute injuries created through short-term exposure, rather than chronic risks such as cancer, because this is the emphasis of the EPA labeling effort. The EPA was further interested in assessing consumer responses to chemical product labels that have gone through the EPA's formal label approval process, which is the case for both the toilet bowl cleaner and the insect spray.

Table 2.1   Assignment of risks to subjects in risk valuation study

Product risks	Group 1 (with children)	Group 2 (without children)	Group 3 (with children)	Group 4 (without children)
A. Toiler bowl cleaner				
Chloramine gas poisoning	×	×		
Eye burns		×		
Child poisonings	×			
B. Insect spray				
Skin poisoning			×	×
Inhalation poisoning				×
Child poisonings			×	

Notwithstanding these restrictions on the types of products we could selected, the labels on commercial brands of toilet bowl cleaner and outdoor
insect spray in our study differ considerably.

In our field work on the precautionary behavior induced by labels, we
measured the consumer responses to *all* the risks and the precautions that
are identified on the product labels. To simplify the morbidity risk valuation task of the study, however, we focused on three of the most common
risks associated with each of the two products. Table 2.1 summarizes the
design of the assignment of risks to subjects in the morbidity risk valuation
segment, where each subject considered only two risks associated with the
use of a single product. All subjects in groups 1 and 2 were asked to value
reductions in the rate of chloramine gas poisoning associated with mixing
toilet bowl cleaner with bleach or other household products. Subjects with
children under the age of five (group 1) were additionally asked to value
reductions in the rate of child poisoning caused by young children swallowing the cleaner, while those without young children (group 2) to value
reductions in eyeburns. Each of the subjects in groups 3 and 4 was asked to
value reductions in the rate of skin poisoning, which occurs when outdoor
insect spray is left on the skin for several hours. Subjects with children
under five years old (group 3) were also asked to value reductions in the
child-poisoning rate from insect spray, while those without small children
(group 4) to value reductions in the rate of inhalation poisoning.[1]

2.2   Sample Selection for Mall Intercept Study

We simulated a product usage environment to learn how consumers respond to the labels on hazardous chemicals and how they value reductions

in the morbidity risks associated with their usage. Interview specialists from a professional market research firm contacted purchasers of toilet bowl cleaners and outdoor insect sprays at a mall and a hardware store, invited them to sit down in a quiet location, presented them with a fictitious but realistic product, and asked them a series of carefully worded questions about how they would use the product and how much they would pay for a similar product that had different risk characteristics.

The use of surveys is particularly suited for detecting differences in behavior across different experimental treatments (in our case, labels), even when the absolute levels of responses are somewhat higher or lower than would be found in actual choice behavior. Nevertheless, one has to be careful in designing the choice environment and the survey questions to be as realistic as possible and to be unbiased (see Fischhoff and Furby 1988). The questionnaires of our surveys were administered by a survey research firm in Greensboro, North Carolina. The interviewers were instructed by a marketing professor (Joel Huber) affiliated with the project, and the interview process was monitored by two economics graduate students. For the toilet bowl cleaner survey we recruited 883 subjects who were presented with the product and an associated questionnaire. The 77 percent of this sample (group 2 in table 2.1) who had no children below the age of five were administered the questionnaire in appendix A, and the other 23 percent with small children in their households (group 1 in table 2.1) were asked a similar set of questions which differed only in the second risk (accidental swallowing by children instead of an eye burn). For the insecticide survey 893 other subjects were recruited. The 87 percent of this group with no children below five years old (group 4 in table 2.1) were given the questionnaire in appendix B, with the remaining group of subjects with small children (group 3 in table 2.1) asked questions that differed only in the second risk (accidental swallowing by children instead of skin poisoning). The samples used for the statistical analysis in the next chapter are somewhat smaller than the groups described above because some of the subjects' responses were incomplete or the treatments required breaking up the groups.

In chapter 5 we compare the demographic and product usage statistics for the two samples from at the mall intercept surveys with comparable statistics for random samples of consumers contacted by telephone. The mall samples of users of toilet bowl cleaner and insect spray users turned out to be reasonably representative of the populations of users of the two products in the Greensboro area.[2]

2.3   Methodology for Measuring the Behavioral Effects of Labels

For product users to respond to precautions on labels, they must first read and remember the precautions and then intend to follow them—and of course they must follow through on those intentions. If a field experiment could be implemented in which products with different labels were purchased for use in the home and then observations of differences in precautionary behavior recorded, that might provide the best predictor of labeling effects. However, besides being costly and time-consuming, it would still be impossible to measure consumers' precautionary behavior in an unbiased way. If product users are required to self-report precautionary actions, or if their behavior is observed by cameras or researchers in their homes, then their behavior could be biased toward more precaution taking. Accurate recall of the precautions taken also would be difficult, and the more often researchers asked for recall of behavior the greater would be the bias from the demand effect.

If demand effects could be eliminated, the next best approach to studying precautionary behavior would be to measure user *intentions* to take precautions, as in Viscusi and Magat (1987). This approach assumes that the link between intentions to take precautions and actual behavior does not differ systematically across labels. Because of the critical need to keep subjects unaware of the purpose of questions to avoid creating demand effects that cause them to overstate their true intentions, only a limited number of questions can be asked of each subject, and the questions must be carefully disguised. For example, in our previous study (Viscusi and Magat 1987) we employed this technique to find out whether subjects would store chemical products in a childproof location, but we approached the problem by first asking them where they would store the product and then probing indirectly until learning whether that location was safe from children.

In this study we measure unaided *recall* of precautionary information, rather than intentions to take precautions or actual precautionary use. This approach greatly reduces the potential demand effects, allows a more extensive set of questions to be asked, and provides for discrimination among the effectiveness of different warnings labels.

We measure the unaided recall of precautionary information through unstructured questions. This approach contrasts with the common use of structured questions and responses. Structured questions are easy to administer and analyze, and they provide easily communicated, reproducible results. However, in analyzing the impact of labels on memory, structured questioning may impose the questioner's structure on the memory recall and create demand effects. Avoiding demand effects is important in uncovering the hierarchical structure of information in memory, one of the purposes of the next chapter.

Despite the advantages of the memory recall approach, it assumes that differences in recall will translate into differences in precautionary behavior. We do not assume, however, that consumers follow all the precautions they recall from product labels, only that more recall leads to more precautionary use. While this assumption is well accepted in the literature, such as that on advertising effectiveness, we present evidence in chapter 5 that further supports its validity.

For the two products analyzed in this study, the toilet bowl cleaner and the garden insecticide, as well as other frequently used products whose hazards are not so severe as to cause undue concern, one would not expect consumers to reread risk information on the labels every time they use the products. Consumers who reread the labels to refresh their memories, would naturally recall more information.

To avoid the problems with structured questions about memory, we designed an open-ended question that elicited the subject's recall of the information on the product remembered and the order in which he or she recalled that information. Open-ended data, however, are notoriously difficult to decode and analyze (Kassarjian 1977). For recorded verbal responses transcripts need to be made and coded. Partially as a result of these difficulties, most studies using this approach have a small number of subjects, and this reduces the statistical power of the tests performed on the data.

To be able to handle free verbal responses from a large number of subjects, our interviewers directly coded the free-response data by placing the responses into categories as the interview progressed. This technique enabled us to carry out about 1,800 interviews at a reasonable cost. There were nevertheless a number of steps needed to develop a coding sheet and to train the interviewers how to use the technique.

The shoppers contacted in the shopping mall and a hardware store were first screened to ensure that they were over twenty-one years old, could read, and had used at least one of the two consumer chemical products under study in the past year. Then the interviewer showed them one of the two products in a container used for that type of product. On each container we glued a professionally prepared label analogous in design and color to those on similar products sold in stores. Although the product names were fictitious, all other aspects of the products, their containers and their labels closely matched their commercially available counterparts.

The subjects were asked to examine the new product for two minutes as if they were about to use it for the first time. With the product out of sight, they were asked "Suppose a friend of yours has never used this kind of product before. Explain to me the directions you would give to your friend about the proper use of (the product)." Further prompting was then limited to, "Are there any other instructions you would give to your friend?" Through extensive pretesting, we discovered that this question and the associated prompting worked well in eliciting recall of the information on the label.

The coding sheets are shown in appendix C. These forms began in substantially shortened form, only containing portions of the information on the labels. Through a series of pretests, new responses were added, and some others consolidated. The open-ended categories on the sheet permitted us to check for common responses and change the categories accordingly. Five categories of possible responses evolved: directions for use (uses), how can it hurt you? (hurts), actions to take (do's), actions to avoid (don'ts), and antidotes. All categories of responses other than those dealing with uses were risk related. The process of developing the coding sheet was not easy; it required about 100 interviews for each product class before we could settle on the final codes.

Interviewers were instructed to record the order number of the open-ended responses—1 for the first response, 2 for the second one, and so on. Because the interviewer was required to simultaneously record the response and its order, some training was necessary. The interviewers practiced interviews on each other until they were able to master the task.[3]

2.4   Label Design

To test our hypotheses about the effects of warnings labels, we randomly divided our mall sample of 1,776 subjects into nine groups of approximately equal size. Four of the groups were given the toilet bowl cleaner questionnaire, with each group receiving a different product label on an identical white bottle similar to those normally used for toilet bowl cleaners. The other five groups were assigned to the insect spray questionnaire, with each group receiving a different product label on an identical brown bottle supplied to us by an insecticide manufacturer.

The nine labels were designed to address the following five questions about the effects of labels on the extent to which product users take the recommended precautions: To what degree does the inclusion of risk and precautions information on the labels induce users to take the recommended precautions? Does adding additional information on a label unrelated to risks and precautions (e.g., about product usage) that clutters the label cause users to respond less to the risk and precautions information? Relative to the responses to existing labels formats, does rearranging the format of the information on the label into the "test" format suggested by the research reported in Viscusi and Magat (1987), without changing the content of the label, cause consumers to take more precautions? Does increasing print size lead to more precaution taking? What is the relationship between increasing the percentage of the label devoted to risk and precautions information and the extent of precaution taking? The results reported in chapter 5 address the first two questions, and the results in chapter 6 the last three questions. Tables 2.2 and 2.3 summarize the differences among the nine labels. The nine labels are presented in figures 2.1 through 2.9.

We will report several multivariate analyses in the following chapters in order to increase the power of the statistical tests. However, all of the research questions can be answered by making comparisons among two or

Table 2.2   Differences in information content and format of toilet bowl cleaner labels

Label number	Contains risk and precautions information	Percentage risk and percautions information	Format
1	No	0	Standard
2	Yes	37	Standard
3	Yes	55.5	Standard
4	Yes	55.5	Test[a]

a. Based on format suggested by Viscusi and Magat (1987).

Table 2.3   Differences in information content and format of insect spray labels

Label number	Contains risk and precautions information	Percentage risk and precautions information	Cluttered?	Risk information print size
1	No	0	No	Regular
2	Yes	44	No	Small
3	Yes	44	Yes	Small
4	Yes	44	No	Regular
5	Yes	66	No	Large

CHEMTECH

Zinbryl
Insect Spray

Kills Insects — Aphids, Red Spider Mites, Mosquitoes, Flies, Mealybugs and Scales

Active Ingredients	By Wt.
Zinbryl	50%
Xylene-Range Aromatic Solvent	33%
Inert Ingredients	17%

NET CONTENTS 1 QT.

CONTAINS SPREADER

DIRECTIONS: Spray thoroughly covering both upper and lower leaf surfaces or other infested plant parts. Repeat as necessary. Can be used up to 3 days of harvest for food crops unless otherwise specified. Make new dilution for each use. Use 2 teaspoonfuls per gallon of water unless otherwise specified.

ORNAMENTALS: Kills Aphids, Red Spider Mites, Spruce Mites, Mealybugs, Woolly Aphid, Whitefly, Thrips, Tarnished Plant Bug, Fourlined Leaf Bug, Bagworms, Rose Leafhopper, Japanese Beetle Adults, Box Elder Bugs, and Scales. Do not use on ferns.

FRUITS: Kills Aphids, Codling Moth, Tent Caterpillar, Red-Banded Leafroller, Plum Curculio, Bud Moth, Fruit Tree Leafroller, Strawberry Leafroller, Spittlebug, Red Spider Mites, Mealybugs, Woolly Aphid, Whitefly, Thrips, Tarnished Plant Bug, Fourlined Leaf Bug, Grape Leafhopper, Pear Psyllid, Japanese Beetle Adults, and Scale Crawlers.
ZINBRYL may cause injury to McIntosh and Cortland varieties of apples, to Bosc pears and Ribier grapes. Do not apply to Pears within 1 day of harvest or to Apricots and Peaches within 7 days of harvest.

CITRUS: Kills Aphids, Whiteflies, Black Scale, Purple Scale, Yellow Scale, Florida Red Scale, and Thrips. Do not apply during full bloom. Do not apply within 7 days of harvest.

VEGETABLES: Kills Aphids, Red Spider Mites, Mealybugs, Whitefly, Thrips, Tarnished Plant Bug, Fourlined Leaf Bug, Bean Leafhopper, Potato Leafhopper, and Japanese Beetle Adults. Do not apply to Broccoli and Peas within 3 days of harvest, and to Brussel Sprouts, Cabbage, Radish, Squash, Tomatoes, Head Lettuce, Cauliflower or Kale within 7 days of harvest. Use up to day of harvest on potatoes. Do not apply to Leaf Lettuce within 14 days of harvest.

FLEAS: (Dogs and Cats) Animal Quarters—10 Tablespoonfuls (5 oz.) per gallon of water. Spray kennels, pens, yards, lawns and under houses, at the rate of 1 gallon diluted spray in a tank type sprayer per 1,000 square feet.

Chemtech Labs, Inc.
Insect Spray Product Division
Clayton, N.J. 08312
Form 9399-R2 Product 8492 Made in U.S.A.

0 4711059

Figure 2.1 Label with no risk and precautions information, no clutter, regular print

ChemTech

Zinbryl
Insect Spray

Kills Insects — Aphids, Red Spider Mites, Mosquitoes, Flies, Mealybugs and Scales

Active Ingredients	By Wt.
Zinbryl	50%
Xylene-Range Aromatic Solvent	33%
Inert Ingredients	17%

Keep out of reach of children

WARNING
See side panel for additional precautionary statements.

NET CONTENTS 1 QT.

PRECAUTIONARY STATEMENTS

HAZARDS TO HUMANS & DOMESTIC ANIMALS

WARNING: Causes eye irritation. Harmful if swallowed. Do not get in eyes, on skin or on clothing. Avoid breathing vapors or spray mist. In case of eye contact, immediately flush eyes with fresh water for 15 minutes and get medical attention. If swallowed, promptly drink a large quantity of water and induce vomiting. Get medical attention immediately. Wash skin and hands thoroughly with soap and water after using and immediately in case of skin contact. Remove and launder contaminated clothing before reuse. **Note to Physicians:** Emergency information — call (800) 684-6671. This product contains a cholinesterase inhibitor. If signs and symptoms of cholinesterase inhibition are present, atropine is antidotal. 2-PAM may also be given in conjunction with atropine. Keep children and animals away from treated areas until these areas are dry.

PHYSICAL OR CHEMICAL HAZARDS
Do not use or store near heat or open flame.

READ ENTIRE LABEL. USE STRICTLY IN ACCORDANCE WITH LABEL PRECAUTIONARY STATEMENTS AND DIRECTIONS.

CONTAINS SPREADER

DIRECTIONS: Spray thoroughly covering both upper and lower leaf surfaces or other infested plant parts. Repeat as necessary. Can be used up to 3 days of harvest for food-crops unless otherwise specified. Make new dilution for each use. Use 2 teaspoonfuls per gallon of water unless otherwise specified.

ORNAMENTALS: Kills Aphids, Red Spider Mites, Spruce Mites, Mealybugs, Woolly Aphid, Whitefly, Thrips, Tarnished Plant Bug, Fourlined Leaf Bug, Bagworms, Rose Leafhopper, Japanese Beetle Adults, Box Elder Bugs, and Scales. Do not use on ferns.

FRUITS: Kills Aphids, Codling Moth, Tent Caterpillar, Red-Banded Leafroller, Plum Curculio, Bud Moth, Fruit Tree Leafroller, Strawberry Leafroller, Spittlebug, Red Spider Mites, Mealybugs, Woolly Aphid, Whitefly, Thrips, Tarnished Plant Bug, Fourlined Leaf Bug, Grape Leafhopper, Pear Psyllid, Japanese Beetle Adults, and Scale Crawlers. ZINBRYL may cause injury to McIntosh and Cortland varieties of apples, to Bosc pears and Ribier grapes. Do not apply to Pears within 1 day of harvest or to Apricots and Peaches within 7 days of harvest.

CITRUS: Kills Aphids, Whiteflies, Black Scale, Purple Scale, Yellow Scale, Florida Red Scale, and Thrips. Do not apply during full bloom. Do not apply within 7 days of harvest.

VEGETABLES: Kills Aphids, Red Spider Mites, Mealybugs, Whitefly, Thrips, Tarnished Plant Bug, Fourlined Leaf Bug, Bean Leafhopper, Potato Leafhopper, and Japanese Beetle Adults. Do not apply to Broccoli and Peas within 3 days of harvest, and to Brussel Sprouts, Cabbage, Radish, Squash, Tomatoes, Head Lettuce, Cauliflower or Kale within 7 days of harvest. Use up to day of harvest on potatoes. Do not apply to Leaf Lettuce within 14 days of harvest.

FLEAS: (Dogs and Cats) Animal Quarters—10 Tablespoonfuls (5 oz.) per gallon of water. Spray kennels, pens, yards, lawns and under houses, at the rate of 1 gallon diluted spray in a tank type sprayer per 1,000 square feet. Remove animals before treatment, putting in fresh bedding after treatment.

STORAGE AND DISPOSAL
Store in a cool, dry place. When container is empty, immediately wash thoroughly and destroy. Do not store diluted spray.

Chemtech Labs, Inc.
Insect Spray Product Division
Clayton, N.J. 08312
Form 9899-RZ Product 8492 Made in U.S.A.

EPA Reg. No.978-725-ZX
EPA Est. 978-CA-6,978-NJ-6,978-MO-6
Superscript used is first letter of lot number.

4711059

Figure 2.2 Label patterned after Ortho Malathion brand label without clutter, small print

Figure 2.3 Label patterned after Ortho Malathion brand label with clutter, small print

CHEMTECH

Zinbryl
Insect Spray

Kills Insects — Aphids, Red Spider Mites, Mosquitoes, Flies, Mealybugs and Scales

Active Ingredients	By Wt.
Zinbryl	50%
Xylene-Range Aromatic Solvent	33%
Inert Ingredients	17%

Keep out of reach of children

WARNING

See side panel for additional precautionary statements.

NET CONTENTS 1 QT.

PRECAUTIONARY STATEMENTS

HAZARDS TO HUMANS & DOMESTIC ANIMALS

WARNING: Causes eye irritation. Harmful if swallowed. Do not get in eyes, on skin or on clothing. Avoid breathing vapors or spray mist. In case of eye contact, immediately flush eyes with fresh water for 15 minutes and get medical attention. If swallowed, promptly drink a large quantity of water and induce vomiting. Get medical attention immediately. Wash skin and hands thoroughly with soap and water after using contaminated clothing before reuse. **Note to Physicians:** Emergency information—call (800) 684-6671. This product contains a cholinesterase inhibitor. If signs and symptoms of cholinesterase inhibition are present, atropine is antidotal. 2-PAM may also be given in conjunction with atropine. Keep children and animals away from treated areas until these areas are dry. Food utensils such as teaspoons and tablespoons should not be used for food purposes after use with pesticides.

ENVIRONMENTAL HAZARDS

This product is toxic to fish, shrimp, crabs and other aquatic organisms. Keep out of lakes, streams, ponds, tidal marshes and estuaries. Do not apply where runoff is likely to occur. Do not apply when weather conditions favor drift from areas treated. Do not contaminate water by cleaning of equipment or disposal of wastes.

This product is highly toxic to bees exposed to direct treatment or residues on crops. Protective information may be obtained from your Cooperative Agricultural Extension Service.

PHYSICAL OR CHEMICAL HAZARDS

Do not use or store near heat or open flame.

DIRECTIONS FOR USE

It is a violation of Federal law to use this product in a manner inconsistent with its labeling.

READ ENTIRE LABEL. USE STRICTLY IN ACCORDANCE WITH LABEL PRECAUTIONARY STATEMENTS AND DIRECTIONS.

CONTAINS SPREADER

DIRECTIONS: Spray thoroughly covering both upper and lower leaf surfaces or other infested plant parts. Repeat as necessary. Can be used up to 3 days of harvest for food crops unless otherwise specified. Make new dilution for each use. NOTE: 3 teaspoonful = 1 Tablespoonful = ½ oz.

ORNAMENTALS (Roses, Camellias, Azaleas, Stocks, Chrysanthemums, Evergreens)—Aphids: 2 teaspoonfuls to 1 gal. water. **Red Spider Mites, Spruce Mites, Mealybugs, Woolly Aphid, Whitefly, Thrips, Tarnished Plant Bug, Fourlined Leaf Bug, Bagworms, Rose Leafhopper, Japanese Beetle Adults, Box Elder Bugs:** 1 Tablespoonful (½ oz.) per gal. water. **Scales (Black Scale, Soft Brown Scale, Oyster Shell Scale):** 1½ to 2 Tablespoonfuls per gal. water. Do not use on Boston, Maidenhair, and Pteris ferns, Canaerti Juniper and some species of Crassula (example: Jade Plant).

FRUITS (Apples, Pears, Grapes, Apricots, Cherries, Peaches, Strawberries)—Aphids: 2 teaspoonfuls to 1 gal. water. **Codling Moth, Tent Caterpillar, Red-Banded Leafroller, Plum Curculio, Bud Moth, Fruit Tree Leafroller, Strawberry Leafroller, Spittlebug, Red Spider Mites, Mealybugs, Woolly Aphid, Whitefly, Thrips, Tarnished Plant Bug, Fourlined Leaf Bug, Grape Leafhopper, Pear Psyllid, Japanese Beetle Adults:** 1 Tablespoonful (½ oz.) per gal. water. **Scale Crawlers:** 1½ to 2 Tablespoonfuls per gal. water. ZINBRYL may cause injury to McIntosh and Cortland varieties of apples, to Bosc pears and Ribier grapes. Do not apply to Pears within 1 day of harvest or to Apricots and Peaches within 7 days of harvest.

CITRUS (Oranges, Tangerines, Grapefruit, Lemons, Limes)—Aphids, Whiteflies, Black Scale, Purple Scale, Yellow Scale, Florida Red Scale, Thrips: 2 teaspoonfuls per gal. water. Thorough coverage of branches and upper and lower leaf surfaces is necessary to control insects. Do not apply during full bloom. Do not apply within 7 days of harvest.

VEGETABLES (Broccoli, Brussel Sprouts, Cabbage, Cauliflower, Kale, Beans, Fleas, Potatoes, Lettuce, Radish, Squash, Tomatoes)—Aphids: 1¼ to 2 teaspoonfuls to 1 gal. water. **Red Spider Mites, Mealybugs, Whitefly, Thrips, Tarnished Plant Bug, Fourlined Leaf Bug, Bean Leafhopper, Potato Leafhopper, Japanese Beetle Adults:** 1 Tablespoonful (½ oz.) per gal. water. Do not apply to Broccoli and Peas within 3 days of harvest, and to Brussel Sprouts, Cabbage, Radish, Squash, Tomatoes, Head Lettuce, Cauliflower or Kale within 7 days of harvest. Use up to day of harvest or potatoes. Do not apply to Leaf Lettuce within 14 days of harvest.

FLEAS: (Dogs and Cats) Animal Quarters—10 Tablespoonfuls (5 oz.) per gallon of water. Spray kennels, pens, yards, lawns and uncier houses, at the rate of 1 gallon diluted spray in a tank type sprayer per 1,000 square feet. Remove animals before treatment, putting in fresh bedding after treatment.

HOUSE FLIES: Around Dwellings (outside only). Outbuildings, Chicken Houses, Stables, Dog Kennels, Patios, Garbage Containers—SPRAY APPLICATON: 6 Tablespoonfuls (3 oz.) to 1 gal. water. Spray around house foundation under porches along fences, shrubbery and other infested areas. Use 1 gal. diluted spray to 1000 sq. ft. area. **DO NOT APPLY THIS DOSAGE TO ANIMALS.** Maintain sanitary conditions around barns, outbuildings and other areas to prevent fly breedings.

HOUSEHOLD PESTS: Clover Mites around outside dwellings and lawns—2 teaspoonfuls per gal. water. Spray lower foundation of house as well as ground lawns and plants in the area 10 ft. wide along side of house. Repeat as necessary. **Outdoor residual adult Mosquito control—**9 Tablespoonfuls (4½ oz.) per gal. water. Spray foundation of houses and lawn areas. Repeat as necessary.

STORAGE AND DISPOSAL

Keep pesticide in original container. Do not cut concentrate or dilute into food or drink containers. Store in a cool, dry place. When container is empty, immediately wash thoroughly and destroy. Do not store diluted spray. Do not reuse empty container. Wrap container and put in trash collection.

NOTICE: Buyer assumes all responsibility for safety and use not in accordance with directions.

Chemtech Labs, Inc.
Insect Spray Product Division
Clayton, N.J. 08312
Form 9699-R2Product 8492 Made in U.S.A.
EPA Reg No.976-725-ZX
EPA Est. 976CA-6,976NJ-6,976-MO-6
Superscript used is first letter of lot number.

CHEMTECH
Zinbryl
Insect Spray

Kills Insects — Aphids, Red Spider Mites, Mosquitoes, Files, Mealybugs and Scales

Active Ingredients		By Wt.
Zinbryl		50%
Xylene-Range Aromatic Solvent		33%
Inert Ingredients		17%

Keep out of reach of children

WARNING

See side panel for additional precautionary statements.

NET CONTENTS 1 QT.

PRECAUTIONARY STATEMENTS
HAZARDS TO HUMANS & DOMESTIC ANIMALS

WARNING: Causes eye irritation. Harmful if swallowed. Do not get in eyes, on skin or on clothing. Avoid breathing vapors or spray mist. In case of eye contact, immediately flush eyes with fresh water for 15 minutes and get medical attention. If swallowed, promptly drink a large quantity of water and induce vomiting. Get medical attention immediately. Wash skin and hands thoroughly with soap and water after using and immediately in case of skin contact. Remove and launder contaminated clothing before reuse. **Note to Physicians:** Emergency information—call (800) 684-6671. This product contains a cholinesterase inhibitor. If signs and symptoms of cholinesterase inhibition are present, atropine is antidotal. 2-PAM may also be given in conjunction with atropine. Keep children and animals away from treated areas until these areas are dry.

PHYSICAL OR CHEMICAL HAZARDS
Do not use or store near heat or open flame.

READ ENTIRE LABEL. USE STRICTLY IN ACCORDANCE WITH LABEL PRECAUTIONARY STATEMENTS AND DIRECTIONS.

CONTAINS SPREADER

DIRECTIONS: Spray thoroughly covering both upper and lower leaf surfaces or other infested plant parts. Repeat as necessary. Can be used up to 3 days of harvest for food crops unless otherwise specified. Make new dilution for each use. Use 2 teaspoonfuls per gallon of water unless otherwise specified.

ORNAMENTALS: Kills Aphids, Red Spider Mites, Spruce Mites, Mealybugs, Woolly Aphid, Whitefly, Thrips, Tarnished Plant Bug, Fourlined Leaf Bug, Bagworms, Rose Leafhopper, Japanese Beetle Adults, Box Elder Bugs, and Scales. Do not use on ferns.

FRUITS: Kills Aphids, Codling Moth, Tent Caterpillar, Red-

Banded Leafroller, Plum Curculio, Bud Moth, Fruit Tree Leafroller, Strawberry Leafroller, Spittlebug, Red Spider Mites, Mealybugs, Woolly Aphid, Whitefly, Thrips, Tarnished Plant Bug, Fourlined Leaf Bug, Grape Leafhopper, Pear Psyllid, Japanese Beetle Adults, and Scale Crawlers.

ZINBRYL may cause injury to McIntosh and Cortland varieties of apples, to Bosc pears and Ribier grapes. Do not apply to Pears within 1 day of harvest or to Apricots and Peaches within 7 days of harvest.

CITRUS: Kills Aphids, Whiteflies, Black Scale, Purple Scale, Yellow Scale, Florida Red Scale, and Thrips. Do not apply during full bloom. Do not apply within 7 days of harvest.

VEGETABLES: Kills Aphids, Red Spider Mites, Mealybugs, Whitefly, Thrips, Tarnished Plant Bug, Fourlined Leaf Bug, Bean Leafhopper, Potato Leafhopper, and Japanese Beetle Adults. Do not apply to Broccoli and Peas within 3 days of harvest, and to Brussel Sprouts, Cabbage, Radish, Squash, Tomatoes, Head Lettuce, Cauliflower or Kale within 7 days of harvest. Use up to day of harvest on potatoes. Do not apply to Leaf Lettuce within 14 days of harvest.

FLEAS: (Dogs and Cats) Animal Quarters—10 Tablespoonfuls (5 oz.) per gallon of water. Spray kennels, pens, yards, lawns and under houses, at the rate of 1 gallon diluted spray in a tank type sprayer per 1,000 square feet. Remove animals before treatment, putting in fresh bedding after treatment.

STORAGE AND DISPOSAL
Store in a cool, dry place. When container is empty, immediately wash thoroughly and destroy. Do not store diluted spray.

Chemtech Labs, Inc.
Insect Spray Product Division
Clayton, N.J. 08312
Form 9899-RZ Product 8492 Made in U.S.A.

EPA Reg No.978-725-ZX
EPA Est. 978-CA-6 978-NJ-6 978-MO-6
Superscript used is first letter of lot number.

0   4 7 1 1 0 5 9

Figure 2.4 Label patterned after Ortho Malathion brand label without clutter, regular print

CHEMTECH

Zinbryl

Insect Spray

Kills Insects — Aphids, Red Spider Mites, Mosquitoes, Flies, Mealybugs and Scales

Active Ingredients	By Wt.
Zinbryl	50%
Xylene-Range Aromatic Solvent	33%
Inert Ingredients	17%

Keep out of reach of children

WARNING

See side panel for additional precautionary statements.

NET CONTENTS 1 QT.

PRECAUTIONARY STATEMENTS

HAZARDS TO HUMANS & DOMESTIC ANIMALS

WARNING: Causes eye irritation. Harmful if swallowed. Do not get in eyes, on skin or on clothing. Avoid breathing vapors or spray mist. In case of eye contact, immediately flush eyes with fresh water for 15 minutes and get medical attention. If swallowed, promptly drink a large quantity of water and induce vomiting. Get medical attention immediately. Wash skin and hands thoroughly with soap and water after using and immediately in case of skin contact. Remove and launder contaminated clothing before reuse. **Note to Physicians:** Emergency information—call (800) 684-6671. This product contains a cholinesterase inhibitor. If signs and symptoms of cholinesterase inhibition are present, atropine is antidotal. 2-PAM may also be given in conjunction with atropine. Keep children and animals away from treated areas until these areas are dry.

PHYSICAL OR CHEMICAL HAZARDS

Do not use or store near heat or open flame.

READ ENTIRE LABEL. USE STRICTLY IN ACCORDANCE WITH LABEL PRECAUTIONARY STATEMENTS AND DIRECTIONS.

CONTAINS SPREADER

DIRECTIONS: Spray thoroughly covering both upper and lower leaf surfaces or other infested plant parts. Repeat as necessary. Can be used up to 3 days of harvest for food crops unless otherwise specified. Make new dilution for each use. Use 2 teaspoonfuls per gallon of water unless otherwise specified

ORNAMENTALS: Kills Aphids, Red Spider Mites, Spruce Mites, Mealybugs, Woolly Aphid, Whitefly Thrips, Tarnished Plant Bug, Fourlined Leaf Bug, Bagworms, Rose Leafhopper, Japanese Beetle Adults, Box Elder Bugs, and Scales. Do not use on ferns.

FRUITS: Kills Aphids, Codling Moth, Tent Caterpillar, Red-Banded Leafroller, Plum Curculio, Bud Moth, Fruit Tree Leafroller, Strawberry Leafroller, Spittlebug, Red Spider Mites, Mealybugs, Woolly Aphid, Whitefly Thrips, Tarnished Plant Bug, Fourlined Leaf Bug, Grape Leafhopper, Pear Psyllid, Japanese Beetle Adults, and Scale Crawlers. ZINBRYL may cause injury to McIntosh and Cortland varieties of apples, to Bosc pears and Bibier grapes. Do not apply to Pears within 1 day of harvest or to Apricots and Peaches within 7 days of harvest.

CITRUS: Kills Aphids, Whiteflies, Black Scale, Purple Scale, Yellow Scale, Florida Red Scale, and Thrips. Do not apply during full bloom. Do not apply within 7 days of harvest.

VEGETABLES: Kills Aphids, Red Spider Mites, Mealybugs, Whitefly, Thrips, Tarnished Plant Bug, Fourlined Leaf Bug, Bean Leafhopper, Potato Leafhopper, and Japanese Beetle Adults. Do not apply to Broccoli and Peas within 3 days of harvest, and to Brussel Sprouts, Cabbage, Radish, Squash, Tomatoes, Head Lettuce, Cauliflower or Kale within 7 days of harvest. Use up to day of harvest on potatoes. Do not apply to Leaf Lettuce within 14 days of harvest

FLEAS (Dogs and Cats) Animal Quarters—10 Tablespoonfuls (5 oz.) per gallon of water. Spray kennels, pens, yards, lawns and under houses, at the rate of 1 gallon diluted spray in a tank type sprayer per 1,000 square feet. Remove animals before treatment, putting in fresh bedding after treatment.

STORAGE AND DISPOSAL

Store in a cool, dry place. When container is empty, immediately wash thoroughly and destroy. Do not store diluted spray.

Chemtech Labs, Inc.
Insect Spray Product Division
Clayton, N.J. 08312
Form 9899-KZ Product 8492 Made in U.S.A.

EPA Reg. No. 978-725-ZX
EPA Est. 978-CA-6,
978-NJ-6,978-MO-6
Superscript used is first letter of lot number.

4711059
0

Figure 2.5 Label patterned after Ortho Malathion brand label with increased area devoted to risk and precautions information, no clutter, large print

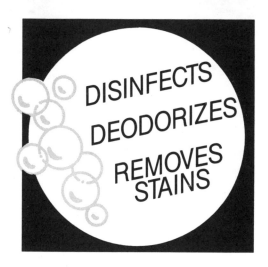

Figure 2.6 Label with no risk and precautions information

CONQUER

TO DISINFECT AND CLEAN: Raise toilet seat. Direct CONQUER inside bowl, including under the rim, on the sides, and into the water. To kill household germs, including staph and strep, use at least 4 oz. (squeeze approximately 15 seconds). Leave CONQUER in bowl for 10 minutes, then brush and flush. Rinse bowl brush in fresh water after use.

TO REMOVE STUBBORN STAINS: For hard water stains, follow directions above. Then apply more product directly to stained areas. Let CONQUER stand at least 15 minutes, brush and flush. Repeat if necessary.

Regular use of CONQUER keeps toilet bowls sparkling white. CONQUER is excellent for brightening colored toilet bowls. Harmless to plumbing and septic tanks.

Active Ingredients:
Hydrogen Chloride 9.25%
n-Alkyl (60%C14,30%C16,5%C12,5%C18)
  dimethyl benzyl ammonium chloride 0.30%
n-Alkyl (50%C12,30%C14,17%C16,3%C18)
  dimethyl ethylbenzyl ammomium
  chloride 0.30%
1-(2-Hydroxyethyl)-2 heptadecenyl
  imidazolinium chloride 1.60%
Inert Ingredients 88.55%

© 1975-1983
Brampton Products
Marshfield, Wisconsin 54449
U.S.A. Distributor
Questions about CONQUER? Toll Free 1-800-684-6671

CONQUER
LIQUID DISINFECTANT
TOILET BOWL CLEANER

DISINFECTS
DEODORIZES
REMOVES STAINS

NET 32 FL. OZ. (1 QT.)

DANGER: KEEP OUT OF REACH OF CHILDREN.
READ PRECAUTIONS ON REAR PANEL.

Figure 2.7   Label patterned after Vanish brand label

CONQUER

DIRECTIONS FOR USE: It is a violation of Federal Law to use
this product in a manner inconsistent with its labeling.

TO DISINFECT AND CLEAN: Raise toilet seat. Direct CONQUER inside bowl, including
under the rim, on the sides, and into the water. To kill household germs, including staph
and strep, use at least 4 oz. (squeeze approximately 15 seconds). Leave CONQUER
in bowl for 10 minutes, then brush and flush. Rinse bowl brush in fresh water after use.

TO REMOVE STUBBORN STAINS: For hard water stains, follow directions above. Then
apply more product directly to stained areas. Let CONQUER stand at least 15 minutes,
brush and flush. Repeat if necessary.

Regular use of CONQUER keeps toilet bowls sparkling white. CONQUER is excellent for
brightening colored toilet bowls. Harmless to plumbing and septic tanks.

CONQUER should be used only for toilet bowls.

STORAGE & DISPOSAL: Store out of reach of children. Clean up spills right away.
When bottle is empty, rinse and discard.

PRECAUTIONARY STATEMENTS

DANGER: MAY BE FATAL IF SWALLOWED. DO NOT BREATHE VAPOR OR
FUMES. MAY PRODUCE CHEMICAL BURNS TO SKIN AND EYE DAMAGE.
DO NOT GET IN EYES, ON SKIN, OR ON CLOTHING. CORROSIVE TO METAL.
PHYSICAL & CHEMICAL HAZARDS: NEVER USE WITH CHLORINE
PRODUCTS . . . can react to give chlorine gas. If gas forms, flush toilet to remove
chemicals and leave area. Do not return for half hour . . . ventilate if possible.
Never use or mix with other cleaners and chemicals.
IMMEDIATELY GIVE FIRST AID: **THEN** CALL PHYSICIAN.
IF SWALLOWED: Rinse mouth. Drink one glass of milk or water. DO NOT
INDUCE VOMITING.
EYES & SKIN: Flush with water for 15-30 minutes.

Active Ingredients:

Hydrogen Chloride 9.25%

n-Alkyl (60%C14,30%C16,5%C12,5%C18)
dimethyl benzyl ammonium chloride 0.30%

n-Alkyl (50%C12,30%C14,17%C16,3%C18)
dimethyl ethylbenzyl ammomium
chloride 0.30%

1-(2-Hydroxyethyl)-2 heptadecenyl
imidazolinium chloride .1.60%

Inert Ingredients 88.55%

EPA REG. NO. 9879-89   EPA EST. 8798-WI-2

© 1975-1983
Brampton Products
Marshfield, Wisconsin 54449
U.S.A. Distributor

Questions about CONQUER? Toll Free 1-800-684-6671

CONQUER
LIQUID DISINFECTANT
TOILET BOWL CLEANER

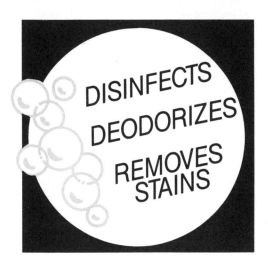

DISINFECTS

DEODORIZES

REMOVES
STAINS

NET 32 FL. OZ. (1 QT.)

DANGER: KEEP OUT OF REACH OF CHILDREN.
READ PRECAUTIONS ON REAR PANEL

Figure 2.8   Label with increased area devoted to risk and precautions information

CONQUER

DIRECTIONS FOR USE: It is a violation of Federal Law to use this product in a manner inconsistent with its labeling.

TO DISINFECT AND CLEAN: Raise toilet seat. Direct CONQUER inside bowl, including under the rim, on the sides, and into the water. To kill household germs, including staph and strep, use at least 4 oz. (squeeze approximately 15 seconds). Leave CONQUER in bowl for 10 minutes, then brush and flush. Rinse bowl brush in fresh water after use.

TO REMOVE STUBBORN STAINS: For hard water stains, follow directions above. Then apply more product directly to stained areas. Let CONQUER stand at least 15 minutes, brush and flush. Repeat if necessary.

Regular use of CONQUER keeps toilet bowls sparkling white. CONQUER is excellent for brightening colored toilet bowls. Harmless to plumbing and septic tanks.

CONQUER should be used only for toilet bowls.

STORAGE & DISPOSAL: Store out of reach of children. Clean up spills right away. When bottle is empty, rinse and discard.

PRECAUTIONARY STATEMENTS

DANGER: MAY BE FATAL IF SWALLOWED. DO NOT BREATHE VAPOR OR FUMES. MAY PRODUCE CHEMICAL BURNS TO SKIN AND EYE DAMAGE. DO NOT GET IN EYES, ON SKIN, OR ON CLOTHING. CORROSIVE TO METAL.

PHYSICAL & CHEMICAL HAZARDS: NEVER USE WITH CHLORINE PRODUCTS . . . can react to give chlorine gas. If gas forms, flush toilet to remove chemicals and leave area. Do not return for half hour . . . ventilate if possible. Never use or mix with other cleaners and chemicals.

IMMEDIATELY GIVE FIRST AID: **THEN** CALL PHYSICIAN.
IF SWALLOWED: Rinse mouth. Drink one glass of milk or water. DO NOT INDUCE VOMITING.

EYES & SKIN: Flush with water for 15-30 minutes.

Active Ingredients: ·
Hydrogen Chloride..............................9.25%
n-Alkyl (60%C14,30%C16,5%C12,5%C18)
   dimethyl benzyl ammonium chloride.............0.30%
n-Alkyl (50%C12,30%C14,17%C16,3%C18)
   dimethyl ethylbenzyl ammomium
   chloride....................................0.30%
1-(2-Hydroxyethyl)-2 heptadecenyl
   imidazolinium chloride......................1.60%
Inert Ingredients 88.55%

EPA REG. NO. 9879-89   EPA EST. 8798-WI-2

Bramptom Products   © 1975-1983
Marshfield, Wisconsin 54449
U.S.A. Distributor
Questions about CONQUER? Toll Free 1-800-684-6671

CONQUER
LIQUID DISINFECTANT
TOILET BOWL CLEANER

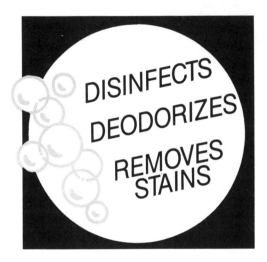

DISINFECTS
DEODORIZES
REMOVES
STAINS

NET 32 FL. OZ. (1 QT.)

DANGER: KEEP OUT OF REACH OF CHILDREN.
READ PRECAUTIONS ON REAR PANEL.

Figure 2.9 Test label

CONQUER

DIRECTIONS FOR USE: It is a violation of Federal Law to use this product in a manner inconsistent with its labeling.

TO DISINFECT AND CLEAN: Raise toilet seat. Direct CONQUER inside bowl, including under the rim, on the sides, and into the water. To kill household germs, including staph and strep, use at least 4 oz. (squeeze approximately 15 seconds). Leave CONQUER in bowl for 10 minutes, then brush and flush. Rinse bowl brush in fresh water after use.

TO REMOVE STUBBORN STAINS: For hard water stains, follow directions above. Then apply more product directly to stained areas. Let CONQUER stand at least 15 minutes, brush and flush. Repeat if necessary.

Regular use of CONQUER keeps toilet bowls sparkling white. CONQUER is excellent for brightening colored toilet bowls. Harmless to plumbing and septic tanks.

PRECAUTIONARY STATEMENTS

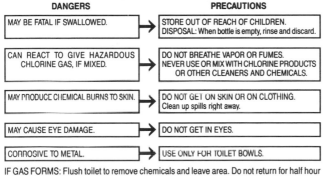

DANGERS	PRECAUTIONS
MAY BE FATAL IF SWALLOWED.	STORE OUT OF REACH OF CHILDREN. DISPOSAL: When bottle is empty, rinse and discard.
CAN REACT TO GIVE HAZARDOUS CHLORINE GAS, IF MIXED.	DO NOT BREATHE VAPOR OR FUMES. NEVER USE OR MIX WITH CHLORINE PRODUCTS OR OTHER CLEANERS AND CHEMICALS.
MAY PRODUCE CHEMICAL BURNS TO SKIN.	DO NOT GET ON SKIN OR ON CLOTHING. Clean up spills right away.
MAY CAUSE EYE DAMAGE.	DO NOT GET IN EYES.
CORROSIVE TO METAL.	USE ONLY FOR TOILET BOWLS.

IF GAS FORMS: Flush toilet to remove chemicals and leave area. Do not return for half hour . . . ventilate if possible.

IMMEDIATELY GIVE FIRST AID: THEN CALL PHYSICIAN.

IF SWALLOWED: Rinse mouth. Drink one glass of milk or water. DO NOT INDUCE VOMITING.

EYES & SKIN: Flush with water for 15-30 minutes.

Active Ingredients:
Hydrogen Chloride. 9.25%
n-Alkyl (60%C14,30%C16,5%C12,5%C18)
    dimethyl benzyl ammonium chloride 0.30%
n-Alkyl (50%C12,30%C14,17%C16,3%C18)
    dimethyl ethylbenzyl ammomium
    chloride. 0.30%
1-(2-Hydroxyethyl)-2 heptadecenyl
    imidazolinium chloride 1.60%
Inert Ingredients 88.55%

EPA REG. NO. 9879-89   EPA EST. 8798-WI-2

Bramptom Products   © 1975-1983
Marshfield, Wisconsin 54449
U.S.A. Distributor
Questions about CONQUER? Toll Free 1-800-684-6671

three labels. As table 2.3 indicates, comparing the insect spray label 1 with label 4 responses allows a direct test of the effect of adding risk and precautions information to labels, for all other characteristics of the two pairs labels are the same. Insect spray labels 2 and 3 directly test the clutter hypothesis because they differ only in this dimension. Toilet bowl cleaner labels 3 and 4 differ only in the format used to portray the information on the labels, thus allowing for a direct test of the reformatting hypothesis. The responses to insect spray labels 2 and 4 allow for a test of the effect of print size on consumer responses to labels because the other three characteristics of these two labels are equal. Finally, toilet bowl cleaner labels 2 and 3 and insect spray labels 4 and 5 allow for testing the effect of increasing the percentage of the label devoted to risk and precautions information, although there is a minor difference in the label percentage and print size dimensions for the insect spray labels.

2.5   Morbidity Valuation Approach

As mentioned earlier in this chapter, the methodology for the morbidity valuation portion of the study involved describing product risks to subjects and measuring their willingness to pay to reduce the levels of those risks. For this purpose the mall sample was divided into the four groups described in table 2.1, with each subject asked questions about two risks from either a toilet bowl cleaner or an outdoor insect spray. Since the leading hazard from both products—child poisoning—is not pertinent to households without children, the risks to be valued by each subject depended on whether there were young children in the household. For households with young children, the questionnaire focused on the risks of child poisoning and chloramine gas poisoning from the toilet bowl cleaner and the risks of skin poisoning and child poisoning from the insecticide. For households without young children, the child-poisoning risk was replaced by the risk of eyeburns from the toilet bowl cleaner and the risk of inhalation poisoning from the insecticide.

The interviewer showed each respondent a card describing the health implications of each risk. The risk that is perhaps most unfamiliar is that of chloramine gassing. If toilet bowl cleaner is mixed with products containing bleach, then chloramine gas forms, possibly causing lung damage and other potentially serious consequences. Excepting suicidal and accidental drug overdoses, chloramine gassing is the leading cause of poisoning among adults.

Each consumer was asked to consider only one product. For that product he or she was told the current price per bottle ($10 for insecticide and $2 for toilet bowl cleaner) and the current risk level (15 injuries for each of the two types of risks per 10,000 bottles sold). The subject was then asked his or her willingness to pay for a safer product. The following instructions given by the interviewer for the insect spray questionnaire for consumers without children illustrate the procedure.

Suppose that you currently use an insect spray that costs you $10.00 per bottle, and it results in 15 inhalation poisonings and 15 skin poisonings for every 10,000 bottles of insect spray that are used. (Show current insect spray card and point to numbers on the card.)

6.1   I want you to think about a new formulation of insect spray that a manufacturer might develop that is as effective as your current product but eliminates all chance of inhalation poisonings. The number of skin poisonings caused by the product remains the same. (Show last card. Point to card but cover the number of inhalation poisonings with finger.) Would you be willing to pay more than what you currently pay to reduce this risk of injury to your household?

Yes _____   No _____
          (put $0 in 6.2a and to go to 6.3)

6.2a What is the most over current costs that you would be willing to pay to avoid this risk of inhalation poisoning?

$_____ more per bottle to reduce the risk of inhalation poisoning to zero.

This set of questions produced willingness-to-pay estimates for the total elimination of the inhalation-poisoning risk of 15/10,000, holding constant the skin-poisoning risk at 15/10,000. The other questions asked elicited valuations for eliminating the skin-poisoning risk, for eliminating both risks, and for partially reducing both risks. A similar set of questions was posed to subjects in the other three groups, in each case keeping the base level of each risk constant at 15 injuries per 10,000 bottles.

To avoid confounding the private valuations of risk reduction with values generated by an altruistic concern for others, the respondents were then asked whether they assumed that fewer injuries would occur to *other* households if *they* purchased the product (e.g., through reductions in sales to other households). If they thought other households would be affected, they were told that this was not the case, and the valuation question was repeated. After eliciting these private valuations, we further explored altruistic valuations of risk reduction through another set of questions. Chapter 4 reports the results of this inquiry.

2.6 Mall Intercept and Telephone Questionnaires

Each of the four groups identified in table 2.1 was given one of the four mall intercept questionnaires (see appendixes A and B for the questionnaires given to respondents without children). These questionnaires follow the same structure, although some of the questions vary by product and by whether the subject lives in a household with small children. Each question was carefully pretested in the interviews of consumers at the mall before we arrived at the final wording.

The experiment using these questionnaires was divided into seven stages. Appendix C describes each of the seven stages in detail. Chapter 7 uses the telephone questionnaire given in appendix D to compare the answers to the same questions on the mall intercept questionnaire. This enabled us to identify subjects who were over 20 years old and had used a similar product in the last year. They were asked questions about product usage and precautions, and then a set of demographic questions.

The next two chapters show how we developed our methodology to elicit willingness-to-pay values for reducing the risks associated with exposure to hazardous pesticides and chemicals.

II

HAZARDOUS CHEMICAL PRODUCT LABELING: RISK VALUATION

3

Risk Valuations and the Rationality of Consumer Behavior

A key policy issue for regulatory agencies implementing informational regulations is what benefit valuations should be attached to risk reductions. During the past decade economists have devoted considerable attention to assessing the nature of individuals' risk–dollar trade-offs, particularly in the labor market (e.g., Thaler and Rosen 1976; Viscusi 1979, 1986; Smith 1979). At the core of these analyses is Adam Smith's theory of compensating differentials for labor market risks. This generalizes quite easily to other choices, such as those involving product safety.

Because of their dependence on market data—primarily data from the labor market—past studies have been restricted to analyzing only the most fundamental aspects of economic behavior with respect to broad risk categories.[1] The chief relationship that has been examined is the existence of a positive trade-off between wage rates and job risks where the two major risk groups are fatalities and job injuries involving lost workdays. Studies of compensating differentials have provided perhaps the strongest empirical evidence in support of rational decisions under uncertainty. Nevertheless, these studies provide little guidance for EPA benefit valuation for health outcomes, such as child poisonings and skin burns. Are these outcomes more or less severe than a typical job injury, and what is the extent of the difference? Ultimately EPA needs the capability to go beyond labor market studies if it is to attach meaningful benefit values to its policies.

A second line of research in psychology, and more recently in economics, has explored the rationality of individual choices under uncertainty and its implications.[2] These analyses have primarily relied on experimental evidence and some survey data to assess the reliability of individuals' formations of probabilistic perceptions and the consistency of their behavior under uncertainty. In some instances analysts have observed deviations from rational behavior in the sense of being inconsistent with the predictions of the subjective expected utility model.[3] Although most of these studies have not been directed at obtaining risk valuation estimates, they are nevertheless pertinent to that issue because they indicate potential distortions in observed risk–dollar trade-offs due to cognitive factors.

The net impact of these research findings is unclear. The studies of actual market behavior are broadly consistent with rational behavior, whereas direct experimental evidence often is not. Testing the competing theories has been difficult since there has been little overlap in the range of economic behavior analyzed by the two sets of studies. Moreover from the standpoint of EPA benefit valuation we would like to know the character of the irrational aspects of behavior and the underlying valuations of the risks once we control for these factors.

In this chapter we analyze the results of our consumer survey to determine whether individual behavior is consistent with the major predictions of an optimizing economic framework. The structure of our survey permits us to examine whether this same behavior is consistent with features of cognitive processes that are not generally explored in standard economic models. Variations in risk valuations with the probability of the adverse outcome will be of particular concern.

The structure of the study permits us not only to examine simultaneously these two general classes of concerns but to extend them. In terms of predicted economic behavior, we go beyond examining issues such as the existence of positive risk—dollar trade-offs to consider influences such as the dependence of the rate of trade-off on the extent of risk reduction. In so doing, we extend the forms of nonrational behavior to address some concerns about multiple risks that have not yet been examined in the literature.

Section 3.1 presents the theoretical underpinnings of our analysis. We analyze the determinants of the risk–dollar trade-off when there are multiple risks and briefly discuss two possibly influential cognitive factors—certainty premiums and "reference risk" effects. In section 3.2 we discuss the nature of our sample and the survey instrument. Section 3.3 reports means effects of different risk changes on consumers' product valuations. As we observe in section 3.4, our results provide some support for a more diverse set of predictions of a model of rational economic choice than have heretofore been examined. In addition they reveal substantial departures from the model's predictions that are consistent with other "nonrational" features of cognitive processes.

3.1 The Theory of Consumer Choice Involving Multiple Risks

Before considering some of the cognitive factors that influence consumer valuations of risk avoidance, we develop a formal economic model of utility-maximizing behavior that serves as a point of reference for our empirical study.

Economic Framework

Consider consumers who maximize their expected utility when making choices among potentially hazardous products, where their preferences can be characterized by von Neumann-Morgenstern utility functions indexed by different health states. Whereas the standard compensating differential literature focuses on individual selling prices for increases in risk, our focus is on buying prices for reductions in risk. For sufficiently small changes in risk, the results for buying and selling prices reflect the same rate of trade-off.

We consider two different health risks, although the results generalize directly to any finite number of risks. This is the class of economic issues most directly related to benefit valuation. For simplicity, we model consumer decisions in terms of purchase of a single product, where the influence of other purchases has been subsumed into the relation between income and utility. The basic issues are how much the consumer should be willing to pay for a safer product and what the determinants of this amount are.

The consumer has an income Y, of which he spends C on a particular risky product. This product poses a chance p_1 of injury 1 occurring alone and p_2 of injury 2 occurring alone. Since we assume that the two risks are independent, they both occur with probability $p_1 p_2$, and $(1 - p_1)(1 - p_2)$ is the probability of no injury. For the three injury states and the healthy state the consumer has a state-dependent utility function defined on his income net of the purchase price of the risky good, which we denote by x.[4]

The restrictions on individual preferences are quite minor. The consumer would rather be healthy than not.

ASSUMPTION 1   For all x, $U^0(x) > U^1(x)$, $U^0(x) > U^2(x)$, and $U^0(x) > U^3(x)$, where the superscripts index the health states (0 = healthy, 1 = only injury 1, 2 = only injury 2, and 3 = both injuries).

We assume that utility with both injuries can be no higher than utility with either injury by itself.

ASSUMPTION 2   For all x, $U^1(x) \geq U^3(x)$ and $U^2(x) \geq U^3(x)$.

In addition, for any given level of consumption, the marginal utility of consumption is positive and greater when the consumer is healthy than not healthy.[5]

ASSUMPTION 3   For all x, $U_x^0 > U_x^1 > 0$, $U_x^0 > U_x^2 > 0$, and $U_x^0 > U_x^3 > 0$.

Thus adverse health impacts lower one's welfare and one's marginal utility of consumption, which is an effect quite different from equating injuries to monetary losses.[6] Finally, marginal utility decreases with consumption.

ASSUMPTION 4 $U_{xx}^0, U_{xx}^1, U_{xx}^2,$ and $U_{xx}^3 < 0.$

The two injuries are not necessarily ordered in terms of their severity. Moreover an injury may affect both the level of utility and one's marginal utility in a complex fashion so that, for example, injury 1 may result in a lower level of utility than injury 2, but the marginal utility at one's current consumption level may be greater for injury 1.

Suppose that the consumer can reduce each of the risks through some additional expenditure for a safer product. Let the risk reduction be α for p_1 and β for p_2. The willingness to pay for this reduction is V, which is the maximum premium the consumer would spend to leave him just indifferent between the original version of the product at price C and the safer version at price $C + V$. To make the notation below more compact, we define $A \equiv Y - C$ and $B \equiv Y - C - V$. The consumer's willingness to pay V for a safer product satisfies

$$(1 - p_1)(1 - p_2)U^0(A) + p_1(1 - p_2)U^1(A) + p_2(1 - p_1)U^2(A) + p_1 p_2 U^3(A)$$

$$= (1 - p_1 + \alpha)(1 - p_2 + \beta)U^0(B) + (p_1 - \alpha)(1 - p_2 + \beta)U^1(B)$$

$$+ (p_2 - \beta)(1 - p_1 + \alpha)U^2(B) + (p_1 - \alpha)(p_2 - \beta)U^3(B). \qquad (1)$$

In appendix G we prove the following three properties of the willingness to pay measure V for the multiple product risk situation: As in the single-risk case, there is a positive incremental willingness to pay for greater risk reduction,

$$\frac{\partial V}{\partial \alpha} > 0 \quad \text{and} \quad \frac{\partial V}{\partial \beta} > 0. \qquad (2)$$

This is the product market variant of Adam Smith's compensating differential result. In the empirical analysis we test whether this result is present for consumers' use of risky products.

The second relationship that we investigate is whether there is any variation in the risk–dollar trade-off as the extent of the risk reduction is increased.[7] In particular, will consumers' risk–dollar trade-off be the same, higher, or lower if they are purchasing larger reductions in risk? The model implies that the trade-off diminishes with the extent of risk reduction, or that

$$\frac{\partial^2 V}{\partial \alpha^2} < 0 \quad \text{and} \quad \frac{\partial^2 V}{\partial \beta^2} < 0. \qquad (3)$$

The risk–dollar trade-off diminishes for two reasons. First, as an individual purchases successively larger reductions in risk, he becomes poorer, and this wealth effect diminishes his willingness to pay for further reductions. Second, larger risk reductions increase the probability of being in more desirable states.

The final issue we examine is the influence of a simultaneous reduction in both risks by equal amounts. Consider the case of infinitesimally small risk reductions γ, with $\alpha = \beta = \gamma$. The model implies that

$$\frac{\partial V}{\partial \gamma} = \frac{\partial V}{\partial \alpha}\bigg|_{\alpha=\gamma} + \frac{\partial V}{\partial \beta}\bigg|_{\beta=\gamma} > 0. \tag{4}$$

That is, for equal incremental reductions in risk, the sum of the marginal valuations for each risk equals the value the consumer places on eliminating both risks simultaneously.[8] The various consumer product risks that we consider experimentally tend to be small in terms of the associated probabilities and involve fairly minor health losses. As a first approximation, then, one would expect the sum of the marginal willingness to pay for each risk reduction to equal the willingness to pay for reducing both risks together.

The Role of Cognitive Processes

In making decisions under uncertainty, individuals may be affected not only by the economic parameters of the problem but also by the manner in which complex probabilistic information is processed and acted on. In the simplest case, the role of cognitive processes will be an intervening mechanism that has no influence on the predicted outcomes from the preceding model of rational economic behavior. At the other extreme, if individuals are unable to make logical judgments under uncertainty and are unresponsive to changes in risks, then none of the economic predictions may hold. Here we focus on two hypotheses regarding information processing—certainty premiums and reference risks.

CERTAINTY PREMIUMS   Certainty premiums exist if, for any given risk change, individuals place an added value on the elimination of risk.

In our empirical analysis we provide not only the first quasi-market test of certainty premiums but also the first investigation of certainty premiums in a multiple-risk context. The analytical basis for the premium individuals are willing to pay for the elimination of risk can be traced to the Russian roulette paradox, originally formulated by Richard Zeckhauser. Consider the following two situations: In each case one has the option to purchase back one bullet from a loaded gun in Russian roulette. In one situation there are three bullets left in the gun, and one must ascertain how much making the gun completely risk free is worth. In general, respondents tend to place a greater value on buying back the bullet that leads to elimination of the risk than they do on purchasing the first of the three remaining bullets.

This is the same phenomenon that will be apparent in the consumer responses to successive reductions in risk. The major difference in our case is that the risk reductions were handled incrementally until complete certainty was achieved, whereas in the Zeckhauser paradox there was a pairwise comparison of two alternative risk reduction situations. In each case the mechanisms driving the behavior are the same.

Certainty premiums may arise for three reasons. First, eliminating all the risk from a product reduces both the anxiety associated with uncertainty and any decision-making costs associated with thinking about a probabilistic outcome.[9] Anxiety effects for uncertainties resolved over time are quite consistent with rational behavior.

Second, the value of a risk reduction that eliminates all residual risk is greater to the extent that individuals overassess small probabilities. If they overestimate the initial risk but accurately assess the terminal risk (because all risk is eliminated), they overestimate the magnitude of the risk reduction. Thus in this case consumers attach a higher value to the risk reduction than they would if they had correctly assessed the initial risk.[10]

The prospect theory developed by Kahneman and Tversky (1979) provides a third reason that consumers may overvalue risk reductions that completely eliminate risk. According to their theory, individuals place decision weights on probabilities. Because these decision weights exceed the probability values for low probabilities but equal zero for zero-probability events, consumers would tend to overvalue risk reductions that eliminate all risk from products.

REFERENCE RISKS   A phenomenon that we will designate as "reference risks" arises because the value of any given risk reduction may depend upon the level of risk usually borne by the consumer in using the product.

In particular, we consider the importance of departures from the reference point of the initial level of the risk before the consumer was asked to consider possible risk changes. Is the consumer's risk–dollar trade-off sensitive to whether the change in the risk raises or lowers his risk level? Our hypothesis is that individuals exaggerate the magnitude of any *increases* in risk from levels to which they have become accustomed. Thus, if a product poses a risk of 15/10,000 and the risk is increased to 16/10,000, the implied risk–dollar trade-off will be much greater than if consumers were asked to purchase a risk reduction from 16/10,000 to 15/10,000. Even for very small changes in risk for which buying and selling prices for risk should be identical, the compensation required to accept an increase in risk will be much greater if there is a reference risk effect.

Several authors have theorized about the role of reference points in analyses of cognitive processes in the risk area. Kahneman and Tversky (1979) and Tversky and Kahneman (1981), for example, incorporate reference effects into their prospect theory of decisions under uncertainty. In their case, however, the reference points pertain to payoffs, not probabilities. Consequently individual utility is based on the utility implied by the effect of a lottery on the change in the individual's income. Our reference points are the probabilities of the outcomes rather than the payoffs, and the mechanism of reference risk effects is the perception of the probability rather than the utility of the payoff.[11]

Our reference risk effect also is analogous in spirit to a related class of phenomena that have since been identified by Samuelson and Zeckhauser (1988). What they showed is that in a wide variety of situations, some of which involve certainty and some of which do not, individuals display a substantial aversion to departing from the current status quo situation. In contexts of decision making under uncertainty, the reference risk level in effect defines the status quo, and as our results indicate, there is a substantial reluctance on the part of consumers to incur increases in risk levels from their accustomed level.

3.2   The Sample and Experimental Design

Ideally, one would like to obtain market data that are sufficiently rich to explore the hypotheses raised above. Unfortunately, market data that permit investigation of multiple risks that take on different values are not available. The alternative approach we adopted was to construct a hypothetical market situation in which we questioned individuals about economic decisions involving health risks.

Specially, we explore differences in consumer valuations for changes in two risks from the two products in our consumer study, the toilet bowl cleaner and insecticide. By replicating our experiments on four different risk-product pairs, we are able to generalize more confidently our findings about the properties of consumer risk valuations, as well as to check the consistency of the valuations of more serious injuries relative to the valuations of less serious ones.

In framing the study in terms of a marketing survey directed toward potential consumers of the products, we attempted to replicate the outcomes that would occur if we could observe a market in which there were risk–dollar trade-offs. There is ample precedent for this approach in the economics literature. Viscusi and O'Connor (1984) analyzed chemical workers' wage-and-quit responses to a job hazard labeling experiment using an approach similar to this consumer risk study. They found levels of risk–dollar trade-offs and structures of wage-and-quit equations that were similar to those obtained with market data. Similarly, in an earlier consumer study reported in Viscusi and Magat (1987), we found that our overall approach to eliciting the risk–dollar trade-offs yielded results that were similar to those obtained with the conjoint analysis technique used in the marketing field. The reliability of using this survey approach was also corroborated by examining consumers' responses to a set of questions on precautionary behavior, which we report in chapter 5. The reliability of any such study stems from establishing a realistic context.

While the psychology and marketing literatures contain large numbers of experimental findings that have been replicated in field studies, it is important to recognize that the primary purpose of experiments is to test causal hypotheses. For our purposes we use the approach to test the hypotheses outlined in the previous section. The consumers' responses in our experiment may accurately reflect those that would be given in actual choice situations, but our study was not designed to make population estimates of the magnitudes of consumer risk valuations.

Subjects

All of the participants in the consumer sample participated in a valuation segment of the survey pertinent to their product and their family characteristics (i.e., whether they have children under the age of five). The sample for analyzing the toilet bowl cleaner responses consisted of 551 respondents without children under five years old and 183 respondents with children under the age of five. For the insecticide survey the sample comprised 672 respondents without children under five and 113 respondents with children under five. The age five cutoff provided a useful basis for segmenting each sample because it is for the cohort below this that the frequency of child poisonings from both products is most prevalent.

After the interviewer asked the subject a series of questions about how to use the test product and the frequency of product use, the interviewer informed the subject that all toilet bowl cleaners (or insecticides) can cause injuries if misused. The interviewer then explained that a recent newspaper article had identified two particularly serious injuries from misuse.

For households with children, the interviewer focused on the risks of child poisoning and eyeburns from the toilet bowl cleaner and the risks of inhalation and child poisoning from the insecticide. For households without children, the child-poisoning risk was replaced by the risk of chloramine gassing for the toilet bowl cleaner and the risk of skin poisoning for the insecticide.

The interviewer then showed each subject a card describing the health implications of each risk. The consequences and the baseline risk levels for the injuries were explained in detail to the consumer after the consumer read about them on the card. Depending on the sample group, the cards included two of the following three injury descriptions:

Inhalation poisoning
If a large amount of insect spray is inhaled, it can cause tearing, salivating, coughing, and difficulty in breathing, sometimes followed by muscle twitching, feelings of weakness, headaches, nausea, stomach pains, and diarrhea. Hospitalization may be required. Recovery usually occurs within a day but may extend beyond a week if the dose is unusually large. There are 15 inhalation poisonings for every 10,000 bottles of insect spray that are used.

Skin poisoning
If insect spray is left on the skin for several hours, it can cause muscle twitching, feelings of weakness, headaches, nausea, stomach pains, and diarrhea. Hospitalization may be required. Recovery usually occurs within a few hours but may take over a week if the dose is unusually large. There are 15 skin poisonings for every 10,000 bottles of insect spray that are used.

Child poisonings
If children drink insect spray, it can cause nausea, stomach pains, diarrhea, headaches, blurred vision, coughing, weakness, and, for some children, seizures. Hospitalization may be required. Recovery time varies from a few hours in most cases to several weeks for children who drink large doses of the insect spray. There are 15 child poisonings for every 10,000 bottles of insect spray that are used.

The risk that is perhaps most unfamiliar is that of chloramine gassing. If a toilet bowl cleaner is mixed with products that contain bleach, chloramine gas forms. Chloramine gas can cause lung damage and other potentially serious conditions.

Each consumer considered only one product. The interviewer told the subject the current price per bottle ($10 for insecticide and $2 for toilet bowl cleaner) as well as the current risk level of 15 injuries of each type per 10,000 bottles sold. The subject was then asked his willingness to pay for a safer product according to the contingent valuation approach, a standard nonmarket methodology for eliciting estimates of willingness to pay. The survey focused on the appropriate economic matter of concern, which is the incremental willingness to pay for an incremental change in the risk. The following instructions given by the interviewer for the insecticide questionnaire for consumers without young children illustrate the procedure:

Suppose that you currently use an insect spray that costs you $10.00 per bottle and it results in 15 inhalation poisonings and 15 skin poisonings for every 10,000 bottles of insect spray that are used. (Show current insect spray card and point to numbers on the card.)

3.1   I want you to think about a new formulation of insect spray that a manufacturer might develop which is as effective as your current product but eliminates all chance of inhalation poisonings. The number of skin poisonings caused by the product remains the same. (Show last card. Point to card but cover the number of inhalation poisonings with finger.) Would you be willing to pay more than what you currently pay to reduce this risk of injury to your household?

Yes ____   No ____
(put $0 in 3.2a and to 3.3)

3.2   What is the most over current costs that you would be willing to pay to avoid this risk of inhalation poisoning?

$____ more per bottle to reduce the risk of inhalation poisoning to zero.

Experimental Design

Each subject answered a series of six valuation questions about changes in the two primary risks associated with product usage. To simplify the task, we held the starting risk constant at 15 injuries per 10,000 bottles for both of the risks faced by every subject.[12] Table 3.1 summarizes the risk changes presented in the six questions using the notation (c, d) to refer to a *change* in the first risk of c injuries per 10,000 bottles and a change in the second risk of d injuries per 10,000 bottles. For example, in the first question $(-15, 0)$ the first risk was reduced from 15 injuries per 10,000 to 0 injuries per 10,000 bottles, while the second risk was not changed from its initial level of 15 injuries per 10,000 bottles.[13]

The final column in table 3.1 summarizes the relationship between each question and the hypotheses derived in section 3.1. The first five questions allow us to test whether consumers are willing to pay positive amounts to decrease product risks, while the sixth question provides a test of whether

Table 3.1   Design of risk valuation experiment

Question number	Change in risk[a]		Hypotheses
	Risk 1(c)	Risk 2(d)	
1	−15	0	Positive valuation of risk reduction, certainty premium
2	0	−15	Positive valuation of risk reduction, certainty premium
3	−15	−15	Positive but diminishing valuation of risk reduction, certainty premium
4	−5	−5	Positive valuation of risk reduction
5	−10	−10	Positive but diminishing valuation of risk reduction
6	+1	+1	Negative valuation of risk increases, reference risk effects

a. Risk is measured in units of 1/10,000 per container of product used, with a starting risk of 15/10,000.

they must be compensated to accept risk increases. The final question also allows us to test for the existence of reference effects caused by focusing on the base risk of 15 injuries per 10,000 bottles and then increasing rather than decreasing the risk levels. The responses to questions 4, 5, and then 3 allow us to determine whether there are diminishing valuations to additional reductions in risk. Comparing the responses to questions 3 and 5 provides a test of whether there is a certainty premium associated with reducing both risks to zero that exceeds the effect of the diminishing marginal valuation of risk reduction. Finally, questions 1, 2, and 3 test the additivity of the valuations of eliminating individual risks separately in contrast to eliminating both risks at the same time, that is, contrasting the sum of the values of $(-15, 0)$ and $(0, -15)$ to the value of $(-15, -15)$.

3.3   Experimental Results

Risk Reductions

Table 3.2 summarizes the mean responses for the five sets of risk reduction questions. These figures reflect the additional amounts that consumers are willing to pay for safer products. In each panel the question 3 responses for eliminating both risks produced the largest values. On average, consumers with young children indicated that they would be willing to increase their insecticide purchase price from $10.00 to $18.09 for a completely safe product and that they would be willing to pay $4.22 instead of $2.00 for a toilet bowl cleaner without any risk of injury. Consumers without small children

Table 3.2 Risk valuations for reductions in injuries

Risk change		Mean willingness to pay ($/bottle)	Standard error of mean ($/bottle)
Risk 1	Risk 2		
A. Subjects without young children: insecticide[a]			
−15	0	2.05	0.13
0	−15	1.85	0.15
−15	−15	3.78	0.18
−5	−5	1.04	0.09
−10	−10	1.37	0.11
B. Subjects with young children: insecticide[a]			
−15	0	2.69	0.31
0	−15	4.29	0.48
−15	−15	8.09	1.13
−5	−5	1.84	0.35
−10	−10	2.38	0.37
C. Subjects without young children: toilet bowl cleaner[b]			
−15	0	0.91	0.07
0	−15	0.91	0.05
−15	−15	1.67	0.11
−5	−5	0.65	0.04
−10	−10	0.84	0.05
D. Subjects with young children: toilet bowl cleaner[b]			
−15	0	0.92	0.11
0	−15	1.52	0.20
−15	−15	2.22	0.22
−5	−5	0.99	0.15
−10	−10	1.23	0.15

a. Risk 1 = inhalation, risk 2 = skin poisoning.
b. Risk 1 = gassings, risk 2 = eyeburns.

would be willing to pay an average of $3.78 more for the completely safe insecticide and $1.67 more for the toilet bowl cleaner that eliminated all risks of injury.

To obtain mean implicit values for avoiding an expected injury, we first divided the values from questions 1 and 2 in table 3.2 by the 15-injury risk reduction level, giving average values per injury avoided per 10,000 bottles, and we then multiplied by the number of bottles (10,000). Table 3.3 lists these implicit values, which range from $610 to $2,860. These implicit value estimates can serve as the basis for EPA benefit valuations. Since both subjects with and without children were asked to value reductions in the risk of insecticide inhalation and toilet bowl cleaner gassing, for these two

Table 3.3   Mean values of statistical injury reduction

Product/injury	Mean value ($)
Insecticide	
Skin poisoning	1,233
Inhalation	1,428
Child poisoning	2,860
Toilet bowl cleaner	
Gassing	612
Eyeburn	610
Child poisoning	1,010

injuries we calculated the weighted averages of the responses to question 1, where the weights were the fractions of subjects with and without small children.

All of the more serious insecticide injuries have higher values than the less serious toilet bowl cleaner injuries. This pattern is to be expected in view of the injury descriptions that the subjects had been given. For example, people are willing to pay almost three times as much on average to avoid the more hazardous child poisonings from insecticide than from the less hazardous toilet bowl cleaner. For both products the child-poisoning injury is valued more than either of the adult injuries. This probably reflects the severity of child-poisoning injuries and a strong degree of parental altruism. In all cases the valuations are well below the estimated implicit value of $20,000 to $30,000 for lost-workday job injuries obtained from labor market data—an expected result since reported job injuries tend to be more severe. Unfortunately, there are no more specific benchmarks that can provide a basis of comparison.

Consider each of the behavioral hypotheses presented in section 3.1. First, the responses to the first five questions reflect a positive and statistically significant valuation of risk reduction, which is to be expected. Second, the economic prediction that the willingness to pay per unit of risk reduction decreases with the extent of the risk reduction is supported by the difference between the question 4 $(-5, -5)$ and question 5 $(-10, -10)$ responses.

This diminishing willingness to pay is reflected in the first two rows of table 3.4, which provide the marginal valuations in risk reduction for different increments of five injuries of each type. The first row summarizes the $(-5, -5)$ responses, and the second row gives the incremental risk valuation for eliminating an additional five injuries of each type, that is, the

Table 3.4   Marginal valuations of reducing both risks by 5/10,000

Starting risk (injuries/10,000 bottles)	Incremental willingness to pay ($/bottle)			
	Inhalation–skin poisoning	Inhalation–child poisoning	Gassing–eyeburn	Gassing–child poisoning
15	1.04	1.84	0.65	0.99
10	0.34	0.54	0.19	0.24
5	2.41	5.71	0.83	0.99

difference between the $(-10, -10)$ and $(-5, -5)$ responses. For all four injury pairs there is a substantial and significant drop in the rate of consumer willingness to pay, which is consistent with the economic prediction in inequality (3).

An alternative perspective on this relationship is provided by an analysis of the individual responses. Columns 2 through 4 of panel A in table 3.5 summarize the relationship between the marginal valuations of reducing both risks by 5/10,000 when the starting risk is 10/10,000 as compared with the results when the starting risk is 15/10,000. As these data indicate, for all four injury pairs most of the subjects valued the risk reduction from 15/10,000 to 10/10,000 at least as much as the risk reduction from 10/10,000 to 5/10,000. In all cases fewer than 20 percent of the subjects indicated increasing marginal valuations, with the number showing diminishing marginal valuations almost three times the number of subjects showing increasing marginal valuations. Thus both the across-subject means reported in table 3.4 and the within-subject comparisons reported in panel A of table 3.5 are consistent with the hypothesis of diminishing marginal valuations of risk reduction.

The existence of a strong certainty premium is apparent from the third row of table 3.4. The incremental willingness to pay for a risk reduction from question 5 $(-10, -10)$ to question 3 $(-15, -15)$ does not decline, as predicted by the rational choice model in section 3.2, but instead rises to the highest levels observed in the table. There is striking evidence of the existence of a certainty premium that more than compensates for the decline in the willingness to pay that the rational economic model predicts should occur as the extent of the risk reduction increases.

A similar pattern is borne out in the individual responses in panel B of table 3.5. For all four injury pairs at most 11 percent of the subjects stated a marginal value for the 10/10,000 to 5/10,000 risk reduction that was greater than their value for the 5/10,000 to 0/10,000 risk reduction, and the large majority expressed a lower value for the first risk reduction than for the

Table 3.5 Breakdown of individual risk valuation responses

Injury pair	% marginal valuation at 15/10,000 ___ Marginal valuation at 10/10,000		
	Less than	Equal to	More than
A. Comparison of marginal valuations of reducing both risks by 5/10,000, evaluated at starting risks of 15/10,000 and 10/10,000			
Inhalation–skin poisoning	13	57	29
Inhalation–child poisoning	18	42	40
Gassing–eyeburn	15	38	47
Gassing–child poisoning	13	30	57

Injury pair	% marginal valuation at 10/10,000 ___ Marginal valuation at 5/10,000		
	Less than	Equal to	More than
B. Comparison of marginal valuations of reducing both risks by 5/10,000, evaluated at starting risks of 10/10,000 and 5/10,000			
Inhalation–skin poisoning	65	30	6
Inhalation–child poisoning	75	19	6
Gassing–eyeburn	59	31	11
Gassing–child poisoning	61	30	9

Injury pair	% with $[(-15, 0) + (0, -15)]$ ___ $(-15, -15)$		
	Less than	Equal to	More than
C. Difference between sum of the values of eliminating each risk individually and value of simultaneously eliminating both risks			
Inhalation–skin poisoning	33	46	21
Inhalation–child poisoning	35	29	35
Gassing–eyeburn	28	37	35
Gassing–child poisoning	26	37	38

second. In other words, with few exceptions consumers attach a strong certainty premium to the total elimination of risk from a product that more than compensates for the effect of diminishing marginal valuations described above. The existence of this certainty premium is supported by both the mean values in table 3.4 and the within subject comparisons in panel B of table 3.5.

The final hypothesis tested concerns whether consumers attach a certainty premium for eliminating both risks above and beyond the sum of the certainty premiums for eliminating each risk individually. The economic model of section 3.2 predicts that for a sufficiently small risk reduction, the sum of the individual risk reduction valuations should equal their valuation for eliminating both risks. For nonincremental risk reductions, however, the relation becomes ambiguous. Consideration of the certainty premiums that most consumers attach to total risk avoidance might sug-

Table 3.6 Tests of the additivity of multiple risks

	$\{[(-15, 0) + (0, -15)] - (-15, -15)\}^{a}$	
Injury pair	Mean ($/bottle)	Standard error of mean ($/bottle)
Insecticide		
Inhalation–skin poisoning	0.12	0.27
Inhalation–child poisoning	−1.11	1.27
Toilet bowl cleaner		
Gassing–eyeburn	0.15	0.14
Gassing–child poisoning	0.22	0.69

a. Measures the difference between the sum of the values of eliminating each risk individually and the value of simultaneously eliminating both risks.

gest that some consumers would be willing to pay an additional certainty premium to eliminate both risks beyond what they would pay to eliminate each of them separately. Because on theoretical grounds we cannot support a hypothesis that consumers will pay more for total risk avoidance, we turn to experimental evidence to see whether the data reveal any tendencies toward either subadditivity or superadditivity of risk valuations.

Table 3.6 lists the mean values of the difference between the sum of the responses to questions 1 and 2 [(−15, 0) and (0, −15)] and the response to question 3 (−15, −15) for all four injury pairs. Although three of the four mean differences show positive values and thus suggest subadditivity, none of the mean differences is statistically significant at the 5 percent level. Furthermore panel C of table 3.5 shows no strong patterns for the within-subject comparisons. Two of the injury pairs show more subjects with subadditivity than with superadditivity, one of the pairs shows an equal percentage, and one of the pairs has fewer subjects with subadditivity than superadditivity. Thus there is no apparent evidence of either superadditivity or subadditivity in consumers' values for multiple risks.

Risk Increases

Ascertaining consumers' responses to valuations of risk increases posed considerable practical difficulties. For risk increases on the order of (+5, +5) examined in the pretesting, almost all consumers refused to purchase the product at any price. For the very modest risk increases in question 6 of (+1, +1), up to three-fourths of all consumers said that they would refuse to buy the product at any discount below its purchase price, as is summarized in table 3.7.

Table 3.7   Responses to risk increase $(+1, +1)$ valuation questions

	Percentage for whom products is too risky to purchase	Mean value of positive responses ($/bottle)
Inhalation–skin poisoning	77.2	2.86
Inhalation–child poisoning	68.1	3.19
Gassing–eyeburn	61.5	5.52
Gassing–child poisoning	74.3	1.28

Note: This question asked subjects what price discount they would require on the new product to accept an additional risk of 1/10,000 for both injuries, starting with risks of 15 injuries per 10,000 bottles sold for both injuries.

The dramatic response to risk increases occurred despite the attempts of the interviewers to help consumers discover their rates of trade-off between higher risks and more disposable income. If a consumer's initial response to question 6 was that the product was too risky to purchase even with a discount large enough to reduce the net purchase price to zero, he was then asked how much he would have paid to use the product. The results in table 3.7 reflect the willingness to accept risk valuations when we take into account whether such a follow-up question was used.

Even for the segment of consumers willing to express a finite risk–dollar trade-off, the valuations of an injury pair are extraordinarily high. On the basis of the question 4 $(-5, -5)$ responses, the average willingness to pay per bottle per injury avoided ($\times 10^{-4}$) reaches a peak of $0.368 ($=$1.84/5$) for the inhalation–child-poisoning injury pair (see panel B of table 3.2), which is a factor of almost 9 below the rate of trade-off of $3.19 for a risk increase of the same magnitude (see table 3.7). The narrowest relative gap is for the gassing–child-poisoning injury pair, for which the question 4 $(-5, -5)$ response of $0.198 ($=$0.99/5$) per injury pair is only a factor of 6 below the trade-off reflected in the question 6 $(+1, +1)$ responses. Although past interview studies of nonrisk attributes, such as by Knetsch and Sinden (1984), have identified similar asymmetries between willingness-to-pay and willingness-to-accept values, the relative disparity in this case greatly exceeds the gaps observed in certainty contexts.

Both the large proportion of subjects unwilling to accept any finite payment to purchase and use the products and the large injury pair valuations expressed by those subjects willing to accept a payment indicate that the risk–dollar trade-offs applicable to risk decreases are poor predictors of behavior involving risk increases. The strong reference risk effects suggest that when individuals assess the implications of increases in risk from their current level, they act as if they possess a much higher rate of trade-off of risk for money than for decisions involving risk decreases.

These research findings point out the need for further exploration of the reasons for the large reference risk effects. In particular, further experimental research should address the question of whether the high implied trade-offs are caused by misperceptions of the magnitude of the risk increase being valued. It may be that consumers do not perceive risk increases and risk decreases of comparable magnitudes as changing their probabilities of injury by an equal amount.

3.4 Conclusions

These results have several implications for the nature of consumer choice under uncertainty. First, they bear out many of the most salient predictions of economic theory. Not only do individuals display a positive valuation of risk reduction, as expected, but the valuation per unit of risk reduction declines with the extent of the risk reduction, provided that the risk is not totally eliminated. This diminishing risk–dollar trade-off accords with the predictions of a model of rational risk-taking behavior, which is a key issue from the standpoint of establishing EPA benefit values.

Second, for probability increments near the zero-risk level, the nature of individuals' processing of risk information is of considerable consequence and perhaps even of dominant concern. For risk reductions that lead to elimination of risk, consumers are willing to pay extremely large premiums. However, there does not appear to be any additional premium offered for the elimination of multiple risks above the sum of the premiums for individual risks, which suggests that the anxiety and decision-making costs posed by the presence of multiple risks are not instrumental. Rather, the driving force appears to be factors pertinent to the particular risk, such as the overestimation of low probabilities.

Risk reference points were found to be a second class of influential cognitive effects. Consumers in our sample exhibited what appears to be an excessive reaction to increases in the risk of a product from its current level. Since this overreaction is consistent with frequently observed responses to newly discovered hazards on the part of both individuals and regulatory agencies, this finding may be a fundamental aspect of behavior toward risks.

Overall, our results provide some evidence in support of the more refined predictions of a rational model of risk bearing developed in section

3.1, although alternative models are also consistent with these findings. There are, however, substantial departures from the model's predictions that appear attributable to the influence of cognitive factors lying outside economists' traditional sets of concerns.

4

Altruistic and Private Components of Risk Valuation

Although the appropriate valuation of risk reduction benefits has long been a matter of controversy, the methodological basis for analysis is relatively clearcut. The general principle for valuing the benefits in other policy contexts also applies to valuing risk reduction—one should assess society's willingness to pay for the reduced risk.[1] Consequently benefits consist of two components: the private valuation consumers attach to their own health, plus the altruistic valuation that other members of society place on their health.

Although altruism is recognized as being a pertinent consideration, the magnitude of such effects has never been estimated reliably. In practice, benefit assessment of risk reduction policies focuses exclusively on the private valuations. Indeed, the role of altruism is seldom even mentioned as a potentially important factor. Likewise altruism is generally ignored in analyses of health risk reduction policies.

The research effort reported here provides an exploratory analysis of the role of altruism with respect to morbidity risk reduction. The specific policy context is consumers' valuation of the risks associated with an insecticide product. Since implicit market values of risk derived from studies of labor markets and other markets capture only private valuations, we employed an interview approach based on a quasi-market context. Thus, we have amended the standard risk interview study, such as the important early investigation by Acton (1973), to consider responses of consumers made in a simulated market setting.

Section 4.1 outlines our methodological approach and discusses the makeup of our sample, which consisted of 785 consumers. Section 4.2 summarizes the private valuations of reduced morbidity risk, thus establishing the baseline of comparison for the altruism results. In section 4.3 we present the altruism responses, both with respect to other individuals in the respondent's home state and the rest of the United States. The empirical determinants of these altruistic responses, such as the size of the private risk valuations, are explored in section 4.4. As we indicate in the concluding section, consumers do not appear to have a "deep pocket" for altruistic efforts, but the role of altruism may be sufficiently consequential to give it a dominant rather than subsidiary role in policy analyses.

4.1   Methodology and Sample Characteristics

The dominant empirical approach that has been used to attach values to risk reduction has been labor market studies of the wage premiums workers require to incur job risks. Analysis of the decisions that are made in the marketplace provides information on the trade-offs workers actually make between dollars and risk.

Two inherent limitations of the labor market studies are fundamental to assessing altruistic valuations.[2] First, the scope of the analysis is constrained to risks captured in published data series (fatal and nonfatal injury risks) and other job risks that can be assessed by a worker responding to a survey. Risks outside the workplace and other market contexts cannot be examined since there is no market experiment that can be observed. What, for example, is the value of reducing genetic damage or eliminating risks from nuclear reactors?

A second shortcoming of market experiments is that generally they reflect the valuation or the risk only to the individual bearing the risk. In some cases these private valuations may capture altruistic elements. For example, a head of household may attempt to take into account the loss that will be experienced by her family if she is killed on the job. Even in this case, however, it is not clear the extent to which workers take into account such altruism in their labor market decisions. Nor is it possible to distinguish which private valuations fully reflect the altruistic concerns and which only capture altruism partially.

As a result, if one's focus is on risks for which informative experiments are not available, then other techniques to assess these risks must be utilized. Our approach is the same as that which we took in chapter 3; that is, we elicit these values from individuals through interviews. In particular, we establish a quasi-market context to make the scenario as realistic as possible and to promote thoughtful responses by the subjects. To the extent that we engage consumers in a meaningful market experiment, we are able to replicate the behavior that would be observed if such a market experiment had taken place and could be observed.

Although the use of an interview approach to elicit risk valuations has not been the dominant methodology in the risk valuation literature, it has received considerable attention. The approach has been used for over a decade in a variety of major studies, such as those by Acton (1973), Jones-Lee (1976), Viscusi and O'Connor (1984), Jones-Lee, Hammerton, and Philips (1985), and Viscusi and Magat (1987). Outside of the risk area, interview studies have long been used to value amenities such as recreation benefits for water resources projects. A sizable literature on survey procedures for valuing environmental amenities has arisen under the heading of "contingent valuation," that is, survey valuations that are contingent upon certain hypothetical scenarios.[3]

Although interview approaches to benefit assessment are not entirely new, a long-standing issue has been the extent to which their results reflect those that would be obtained if we could observe an actual market rather than a simulated one. In an earlier study of labor market risks, Viscusi and O'Connor (1984) found that hypothetical risks generated in a chemical labeling experiment yielded wage-and-quit rate equations that closely paralleled those obtained with market data. The risk–dollar trade-offs were quite similar to these.

In the precursor to this study—Viscusi and Magat (1987)—we found that eliciting consumer valuations of risk through direct price-risk questions that parallel those employed here produced results very close to those obtained using conjoint analysis. The conjoint analysis technique is widely employed in the marketing literature. In our study we presented consumers products with different price-risk combinations. Based on consumers' rankings of the products, we inferred the risk–dollar trade- off.[4]

A final check on the validity of the results concerns the extent to which consumers responded in a meaningful manner to the survey instrument used. Although there is no feasible market check on the risk valuation responses, we were able to explore the consistency of the stated precautions for the hypothetical products considered as part of our survey with the precautions induced by actual consumer products. For the products with labels that had risk warnings identical in content to those on nationally marketed brands, the stated precautionary intentions were similar to those reported in a telephone survey of actual usage patterns for a (different) group of consumers. Chapter 7 describes this consistency check in more detail.

The sample included 672 respondents without children under five and 113 respondents with children under five. Table 4.1 summarizes the sample characteristics, which are generally representative of the adult consumer population.

The second section of the survey addressed consumers' valuations of the health risks. The interviewer informed the consumer that product misuse could result in injuries. To motivate this section of the survey, the interviewer explained that a recent newspaper article had identified two particularly serious injuries from misuse.

Table 4.1   Sample characteristics

	Mean (standard deviation)
Age	45.83
	(14.30)
Male (%)	63.61
	(48.14)
Black (%)	13.87
	(34.58)
Married (%)	78.54
	(41.08)
Five	0.17
	(0.49)
Education	13.40
	(2.54)
Income	36,520
	(18,855)

Table 4.2   Summary of injury categories

Subsamples	Injury Pairs
Without young children	Inhalation–skin poisoning
With young children	Inhalation–child poisoning

Table 4.2 summarizes the injury pairs presented to each subsample, which are the same as in chapter 3: All subjects considered inhalation risks, but the second risk was varied, and respondents without young children considered risks of skin poisoning, while respondents with young children considered child-poisoning risks. These injuries comprise the major risks from using insecticide products.

After informing respondents of the risk and showing them a card describing the injury (see appendix F), the interviewer told the subject the current price of the product. The interviewer then asked the respondent a series of questions designed to elicit his private and altruistic valuations.

4.2   Private Valuations of Risk

The Survey Instrument
The survey addressed a variety of issues pertaining to each individual's valuation of risk reductions for his or her own household. The private valuation questions discussed in chapter 3 were designed to ascertain, for example, how consumer valuations of risk reductions differed and whether

consumers would be willing to pay a premium over their value of risk avoidance to have a product that was completely safe. One of the questions asked the subjects to value the same risk reduction amounts that we subsequently addressed in our altruism questions. Thus its purpose was to establish a baseline private risk valuation level that could then be compared with the altruistic responses.

Let's recall the context of the study and examine the private valuation question reference point. Each consumer considered a single product, which had an initial price per bottle of $10 and a current poisoning rate of 15 poisonings per 10,000 bottles sold for each of the two poisoning categories (see table 4.2). The interviewer then told the consumer that the product could be reformulated to make the product safer:

6.1 I want you think about a new formulation of insect spray that a manufacturer might develop which is as effective as your current product but eliminates all chance of inhalation poisonings.

This question provided a scenario by which the product's risk would be reduced but its efficacy not affected. The consumer was then asked a series of questions about how much he or she would be willing to pay to eliminate each risk separately, as well as both risks combined. The respondent then considered the key private valuation question to be used as a comparison with the altruism responses:

6.5 Unfortunately, it is not always possible to develop a product that reduces the risks of all injuries to zero. You indicated that you would be willing to pay $____ (take from 6.4) more a bottle to reduce *both* risks from 15 injuries to zero for every 10,000 bottles used. What is the most you would be willing to pay for a smaller reduction, say, to reduce risks of *both* inhalation poisoning and child poisoning from 15 to 10 for every 10,000 bottles used? (Show card. Cover the number of inhalation poisonings and child poisonings with finger and say, "These numbers both become 10.")

($____ more per bottle to reduce both risks to 10/10,000 bottles used.)

(Cue with: Would you pay $10, $5, $2, $1, 50 cents, 25 cents, 10 cents, 5 cents, 1 penny?)

By this stage of the survey a cue was seldom needed since the respondents had become familiar with the valuation task.

A potential difficulty in answering such questions is that the consumer may not know whether purchasing the safer product for one's own household will reduce risks to other households as well by make the product safer. Such a spillover effect would presumably enhance consumers' willingness to pay for a safer product. To avoid contamination of the private valuations with such altruistic concerns, the first risk valuation question was followed by the following clarifying comment.

In asking this question, I didn't intend for you to assume that fewer inhalation poisonings would occur to other households if you purchased the insect spray.

Respondents who did have this confusion received the following clarification before the question was repeated:

Now consider the value of the safer new insect spray to your household, recognizing that your response and purchase decision have *no effect* on the number of injuries incurred by other households.

Mean Effects

The willingness-to-pay amounts for the private valuations (per 5 injury pairs avoided per 10,000 bottles of product sold) ranged from an average of $1.04 per bottle for inhalation and skin poisoning to an average of $1.84 per bottle for inhalation and child poisoning, as is indicated by the summary of the key results in table 4.3. In each case the largest valuations were for the risk pairs involving child poisoning. Based on the injury descriptions, this concern with the well-being of children is reasonable since these injuries have the greatest potential for prolonged medical treatment. Another contributing factor may be that parents are willing to pay a greater amount to prevent an injury to a child that has the same severity as an injury to themselves. While this hypothesis is quite plausible, it was not explicitly tested in our study.

The final column of table 4.3 presents the mean valuations associated with eliminating one injury pair. The implicit value of an injury pair is calculated as follows:

$$\text{Implicit value of an injury pair} = \frac{\text{willingness to pay per bottle}}{\text{risk reduction achieved}},$$

where the risk education achieved was 5/10,000. Thus, to calculate the implicit value per injury pair, one simply multiplies the willingness to pay per bottle by 2,000.

Table 4.3   Private risk valuation responses for reduction of five injury pairs per 10,000 bottles used

Injury pair	Mean willingness to pay ($/bottle)	Standard error of mean	Mean implicit value of risk pair
Inhalation–skin poisoning	1.04	0.09	$2,080
Inhalation–child poisoning	1.84	0.35	$3,680

As is standard in the literature on the value of life and health, this measure focuses on the value of a statistical injury, or in this case a pair of injuries. The value of eliminating the risk of such injuries represents the rate of trade-off between money and injury risk; it does not indicate how much the respondent would be willing to pay to eliminate certain injuries of this type.

The general order of magnitudes of these valuations appears to be reasonable. The implicit value of the injury pairs averaged $2,080 and $3,680. Although use of the implicit value of life as a reference point is not particularly instructive, the implicit value of nonfatal injuries based on actual wage-risk trade-offs is pertinent. The value of job injuries tends to be in the $20,000 to $30,000 range,[5] and recent evidence suggests that roughly half of this amount is wage loss and the other half represents nonmonetary loss.[6] Since the average injury (for the survey year considered) lasted roughly 12 weeks in terms of the period lost from work, the value of the health loss per week is on the order of $1,000. Most of the consumer injuries considered in our survey had one week as the usual upper bound for recovery time. As a result the estimates we obtained in the consumer study are at least generally consistent with what one would expect given available market data. There is, however, a broad range of responses that one might consider to be reasonable.

In chapter 3 we described the use of additional survey questions to distinguish the separate valuations of the risks in the risk pairs. This task will not be our concern here since the subsequent altruism questions focused on joint reduction of both risks. We adopted this approach on the belief that by measuring altruistic values, we could establish more credible scenarios for reducing both risks instead of just one risk. The public policy actions we envisioned would affect both risks, whereas a firm's reformulation of the product could have a more targeted influence.

4.3 Altruism for Morbidity Risks

The Survey Approach
The set of questions we developed to determine the altruistic concern of consumers was designed to ascertain how much a respondent would be willing to contribute to an advertising campaign that would reduce each of two risks to the average user from 15 to 10 injuries per 10,000 bottles. By this stage the respondent had acquired substantial information about the precautions necessary to avoid injuries from previous questions about precautionary behavior. Thus showing these advertisements presumably

would have little or no private value to them as new information. If there were such a value, the altruism results would overstate the true magnitude of the altruism values. It should also be noted that many respondents who are willing to pay a positive amount for a safer product were not willing to contribute to the advertising program, which is consistent with the program being viewed as an altruistic venture. In each case the product and the risk pair corresponded to those presented earlier in the questionnaire: Respondents with children answering the insecticide questions considered the risks of inhalation and child poisoning; those without children focused on the risks of inhalation and skin poisoning.

The questionnaire first addressed respondents' willingness to pay for an advertising program within their own state, North Carolina, by a private organization and not a state agency (in order that consumers would not believe that their taxes had already paid for the program). The wording of the question clearly stated the magnitude of the risk reductions in terms of absolute numbers of injuries, thus eliminating the task for the respondent to calculate these numbers. Had we not done this, additional error might have been introduced because of both the subjects' imperfect knowledge of the state's size and the difficulty of carrying out such large calculations mentally. The next questions were:

6.8   The number of injuries from insect spray misuse can also be reduced
      through a public advertising program. A nonprofit organization in North
      Carolina is considering running a public advertising program about insect
      spray safety. To be effective, the program needs to be administered once a
      year. The advertising campaign will reduce the risks of both inhalation
      poisonings and child poisonings from 15 to 10 injuries for every 10,000 bottles
      of insect spray used. This means that the number of both types of injuries for
      the 2 million household bottles used in North Carolina would drop from
      3,000 to 2,000. Suppose the sponsoring organization asked *you* and others in
      the state to contribute to this advertising program. Although in this interview
      I will *not* ask you for money, would you contribute to the program?

      ____ Yes   ____ No

      (If yes continue. If no, proceed to 6.10).

6.9   What is the *very most* you would contribute this year to support this public
      advertising program?

      $____ per year contribution to NC advertising campaign

      (Cue with: Would you contribute S5x. $25, $10, $5, $2, $1?)

After addressing the willingness to pay for this reduced rate of risk in North Carolina, the survey ascertained the willingness to pay for the same rate of risk reduction for the entire U.S. population. The U.S. altruism questions were as follows:

6.10   Suppose that the advertising campaign included the rest of the United States. Would you contribute anything (more)?

_____ Yes   _____ No

6.11   How much *more* would you contribute?

$_____ more per year contribution to U.S. advertising campaign.

(Cue with: Would you contribute $50, $25, $10, $5, $2, $1?)

A respondent's altruistic value for the U.S. population should not simply equal the altruistic value for North Carolina multiplied by the ratio of the U.S. to the North Carolina population. We would expect consumers to have a willingness to pay for altruistic causes that diminishes with the level of risk reduction expenditures. In addition they are likely to have family members and friends within the state. As a result the contrast between the North Carolina and the U.S. responses captures both the difference in the nature of the relationships with the beneficiaries of the program and the diminishing willingness to pay for altruism.

Ideally, we would have liked to have separated out the first change in the relationship issue from the second absence of a "deep pocket" hypothesis. One approach to making this distinction would have been to ask respondents for their willingness to pay for risk reduction in some state other than North Carolina where they resided. In pretesting of the questionnaire, we asked respondents their willingness to pay for risk reduction in Missouri. An additional group of subjects were as asked for their willingness to pay for risk reduction in the state of Georgia, which should have had more regional appeal. In each instance, the respondents indicated that they did not believe that a contribution to some other state's problems was appropriate. "It's their problem" was the most frequent response. The reactions were so strong that including such a question in the survey threatened the viability of the rest of the questionnaire by casting doubt upon the seriousness of our exercise. As a result the survey moves directly from North Carolina to the entire U.S. population for which the precedent of federal income taxes establishes the plausibility of the respondent's broader interests.

Mean Effects

Table 4.4 reports the altruistic results for each of the risk pairs considered. The first two columns give the overall means and standard errors for con-

Table 4.4 Summary of altruistic responses

Injury Pair	Contribution level (dollars)		Probability of contributing		Conditional contribution (dollar)	
	North Carolina	United States	North Carolina	United States	North Carolina	United States
Inhalation– skin poisoning	5.01 (0.35)	1.72 (0.33)	0.57 (0.02)	0.14 (0.01)	8.75 (0.55)	12.13 (2.01)
Inhalation– child poisoning	9.06 (1.27)	2.39 (0.74)	0.79 (0.04)	0.21 (0.04)	11.53 (1.51)	11.14 (2.83)

Note: Standard errors of means in parentheses.

tributions to reduce injuries in North Carolina and in the United States. Since not all individuals were willing to contribute to the risk reduction, the third and fourth columns summarize the fraction of respondents willing to make a nonzero contribution to reduce injuries in the two situations. The fifth and sixth columns give the contribution levels conditional upon making a nonzero contribution.

The additional amount that individuals are willing to spend to extend this rate of injury reduction nationally averages around $2 per respondent in both cases (see column 2 of table 4.4). This dropoff in valuations reflects both the diminishing altruism for additional health risk reduction as well as the more remote nature of the respondents' ties to individuals outside the state. The lower willingness to pay for a U.S. contribution was not greatly affected by whether one had contributed to the North Carolina injury reduction effort. In particular, we generated an additional set of statistics (not shown) to analyze the level of the U.S. contribution contingent on making a positive contribution to injury reduction in North Carolina. The differences between the full sample's U.S. altruism and the altruism toward the Untied States of those willing to make a North Carolina contribution averaged under $1. For example, the entire sample was willing to contribute an average of $2.39 for a U.S. injury reduction effort, and the sample that had made a positive contribution to the North Carolina advertising program was willing to contribute $2.78.

In all instances a substantial portion of the population had no altruistic interests in reducing risks outside the household (see column 3 of table 4.4). In the case involving child poisonings in the respondent's state, about three-fourths of the respondents indicated a positive willingness to pay, whereas for the injury pairs not involving children just over half of the respondents indicated a willingness to make a positive contribution for statewide injury reduction. The relative patten is similar to the probability of contributing to U.S. risk reduction (see column 4 of table 4.4), except

Table 4.5 Summary of implicit altruistic values in willingness to pay per injury pair prevented (dollars)

	North Carolina		Rest of United States	
	Per household (1)	Collective (2)	Per household (3)	Collective (4)
Inhalation–skin poisoning	5.01×10^{-3}	1.00×10^4	3.91×10^{-5}	3.07×10^3
Inhalation–child poisoning	9.06×10^{-3}	1.81×10^4	5.43×10^{-5}	4.26×10^3

that the frequency of positive contributions is much less (21 percent and 14 percent for the two injury pairs). Viewed somewhat differently, about 80 percent of the population was unwilling to contribute to a risk reduction effort outside their state. If the remaining 20 percent reflects in part a floor effect of the survey approach rather than the respondent's actual willingness to pay, the fraction who would make positive contributions if actually called upon to do so may be less.

Columns 5 and 6 of table 4.4 summarize the level of the contribution, given that one is made. It is striking that these conditional contribution levels do not differ greatly whether the population being considered is the state of North Carolina or the U.S. population. The source of the overall differences in the average North Carolina and U.S. contributions stems from the differing frequency of making a contribution rather than its magnitude. Once committed to making a contribution, the respondents generally have a willingness to pay of about $10.

The contribution amounts in columns 1 and 2 of table 4.4 can be translated into implicit values per injury pair, as in the case of the private valuation statistics in table 4.3. Two different measures are of potential interest. First, how much is the consumer willing to pay per injury prevented outside his household? Second, how much are all consumers collectively willing to pay for such a risk reduction? These two measures are given for both the North Carolina and U.S. valuations in table 4.5.

Calculating the value the particular household places on each pair of injuries reduced is straightforward. In the case of the North Carolina altruism scenario, 1,000 injury pairs would be prevented by the advertising program. For concreteness, consider the inhalation–skin-poisoning results. The average consumer is willing to pay $5.01 to reduce 1,000 injury pairs so that the willingness to pay per pair of injuries avoided is 5.01×10^{-3}, or $.0051. Assuming that this response represents the response for the entire household, we have the result that the average North Carolina household would be willing to contribute half a cent for each inhalation and skin poisoning prevented in the state. Similarly, on average, households in North Carolina are willing to pay slightly less than one cent for each inhalation and child poisoning presented in the state. A similar calculation yields the household's valuation of each injury pair prevented in the country, except that the number of injuries involved is considerably larger. As a result the per household willingness to pay per injury avoided ranges from only 3.91×10^{-5} to 5.43×10^{-5}, or under one-hundredth of a cent per injury pair avoided.

The second set of statistics of interest represents the collective willingness to pay of society to reduce injuries. In the case of North Carolina, we multiply the value per household of each injury pair prevented by the number of households in the state, which was 2.0 million in 1980.[7] Even if each household is willing to contribute under a penny per injury pair prevented, the altruistic effect is substantial. The values per injury pair range from $10,000 for inhalation and skin poisoning to $18,100 for inhalation and child poisoning.

Two considerations must be taken into account when interpreting these calculations. First, even very small altruistic concerns of under a penny per household will generate altruism benefit measures that far exceed the private valuations. Second, the precision of the willingness-to-pay estimates becomes a substantial concern when these numbers are extrapolated to the population at large. Before such numbers are utilized in an actual policy evaluation, we suggest that their robustness be explored with respect to different risk reduction increments, other wordings and formats for the questions, different interview contexts, and any other pertinent factors likely to influence the responses.

In the case of altruism toward the entire country, the collective willingness-to-pay figures relative to the North Carolina willingness-to-pay responses tend to follow the relative pattern of the mean values per bottle in table 4.4. This correspondence reflects the fact that as the total number of households contributing increases, the number of injuries prevented by the altruistic contribution increase as well. Thus the value *per injury* will be determined by these two offsetting influences. If the U.S. contributing population were to exceed the North Carolina contributing population by the same ratio as the overall U.S. number of injuries prevented exceeds the number of injuries prevented in North Carolina, the collective willingness to pay for the country would lead to results that are below the North Carolina altruism figures by the same ratio as is implied by comparing columns 1 and 2 in table 4.4.

The specific procedure that was utilized to capture the national injury valuation was the following: To calculate the household's willingness to pay per U.S. injury prevented, we divided the willingness-to-pay responses by the total reduction in the U.S. injuries. For instance, suppose that the U.S. injury reduction relative to North Carolina follows the ratio of the two populations, so that the advertising campaign would reduce an additional 44,000 injuries. If the values per within state injury pair prevented averaged under a cent, the value per out-of-state injury pair prevented was under a hundredth of a cent.

Even very small altruistic amounts are consequential when taken on a collective basis. Suppose that each household outside of North Carolina is willing to pay the amounts in column 3 of table 4.5 to prevent each such injury pair in North Carolina. Then the out-of-state benefit tally for the 78.4 million households[8] in the rest of the country would range from $3,070 for inhalation and skin poisoning to $4,260 for inhalation and child poisoning. The U.S. valuation numbers are smaller than the within-state collective altruism because the increase in the number of contributors is offset by the dampening of the willingness to pay per injury pair prevented.

4.4   Altruism Regression Results

From an economic standpoint one would expect the altruistic responses to vary systematically across the population. Two classes of factors should be particularly instrumental. First, households with large private valuations should be willing to contribute more for the altruistic cause to the extent that this private valuation reflects a higher private risk-to-dollar trade-off. It may be the case, however, that households have higher willingness to pay for safer products not because they regard the health outcome as being more severe, but because they consider their households to be above average in risk. Thus, though the correlation between private and altruistic valuations will not be perfect, one might expect a higher private valuation to boost the size of the altruistic contribution. The individual's private valuation amount can thus be included as a principal variable that is likely to affect altruistic behavior.

The second class of concerns pertains to individual wealth. If altruism is a normal good, then richer consumers should be more likely to contribute to charitable causes. The most refined measure of household wealth that we will include is household family income. In addition several of the demographic variables are also related to wealth. These include the respondent's age (positive effect on wealth early in the life cycle, negative effect later), race (blacks tend to be less wealthy), and years of schooling (positive lifetime wealth effect).

Table 4.6 Maximum likelihood estimates of the probability of contributing to injury reduction in North Carolina

| Independent variable | Coefficients (asymptotic standard errors) | | | |
| | Inhalation–skin poisoning | | Inhalation–child poisoning | |
	(1)	(2)	(1)	(2)
Intercept	1.528	1.786	0.815	3.997
	(0.625)	(0.596)	(1.326)	(1.891)
Private valuation	0.238	0.090	0.026	0.081
	(0.105)	(0.022)	(0.093)	(0.051)
Family income	−5.74E-6	3.29E-6	6.70E-6	2.34E-5
	(5.83E-6)	(4.89E-6)	(1.22E-5)	(1.93E-5)
Age	−0.021	−0.020	0.012	−0.054
	(0.004)	(0.006)	(0.027)	(0.032)
Male	−0.310	−0.436	−1.673	0.308
	(0.258)	(0.175)	(0.480)	(0.550)
Black	0.172	0.315	0.669	−0.111
	(0.220)	(0.256)	(0.417)	(0.593)
Married	0.082	0.311	—	—
	(0.197)	(0.207)		
Children under five	—	—	0.109	−0.208
			(0.317)	(0.432)
Years of schooling	−0.015	−0.074	−0.037	−0.142
	(0.037)	(0.036)	(0.075)	(0.135)
−2 log likelihood	651.8	860.1	199.6	104.6

In addition several demographic variables were also included to capture other differences in the willingness to contribute to altruistic causes. These variables were the respondent's sex, marital status, and whether the respondent had children under the age of the age of five in the household. Because of the strong positive correlation of marital status and children under the age of five in the household, both variables were not simultaneously included in the regressions.

Tables 4.6 through 4.9 include four sets of regressions. Tables 4.6 and 4.8 report the logit equation estimates for the probability that the respondent was willing to make a positive contribution to North Carolina and U.S. injury prevention, respectively. Thus the dependent variable has been transformed to reflect the log of the relative odds of making a contribution. This procedure ensures that the estimation technique will not lead to predicted values of probabilities that lie outside of the range from 0 to 1. Tables 4.7 and 4.9 report the regressions for the amounts of such contributions, conditional on making a nonzero contribution.

Since the expected signs are the same across equations, we will discuss the results variable by variable rather than equation by equation. In each

Table 4.7   Regression estimates of the magnitudes of nonzero contributions to injury reduction in North Carolina

	Coefficients (asymptotic standard errors)			
	Inhalation–skin poisoning		Inhalation–child poisoning	
Independent variable	(1)	(2)	(1)	(2)
Intercept	12.387	−2.659	8.708	5.305
	(12.133)	(3.846)	(8.052)	(11.858)
Private valuation	4.795	0.680	0.301	0.172
	(1.709)	(0.102)	(0.551)	(0.117)
Family income	1.81E-4	7.17E-5	1.30E-4	1.81E-4
	(1.08E-4)	(3.09E-5)	(0.76E-4)	(1.04E-4)
Age	−0.101	0.023	0.013	0.034
	(0.135)	(0.039)	(0.168)	(0.213)
Male	−0.836	0.233	0.149	1.530
	(4.904)	(1.064)	(4.350)	(3.412)
Black	−2.877	0.632	3.483	−3.498
	(3.967)	(1.501)	(2.433)	(3.937)
Married	−2.837	0.747	—	—
	(3.608)	(1.314)		
Children under five	—	—	0.542	−0.445
			(1.964)	(2.496)
Education	−4.408	0.292	−0.465	−0.205
	(0.733)	(0.236)	(0.479)	(0.860)
R^2	0.04	0.14	0.03	0.09

case two sets of equations (where the differences stem from the nature of the private valuation variable) are reported. Equation (1) results pertain to the private valuation analog of the altruism variable—the private value of reducing injuries from 15 to 10 injury pairs per 10,000 bottles. Equation (2) results utilize a somewhat different private valuation variable—the valuation of reducing the risk level from 15 injury pairs per 10,000 bottles to zero. Because the results of equation (2) are typically much stronger, this private valuation variable may be a superior measure of the respondent's private risk–dollar trade-off.

The private valuation variable has the expected positive coefficient in all cases considered, and it is statistically significant (at the 5 percent level) in two cases in table 4.6, two cases in table 4.7, two cases in table 4.8, and two cases in table 4.9. Because included variables other than the private valuation may capture some of this variable's influence, these results may understate the variable's actual impact. When these other variables are omitted and only a constant term and the private valuation variable are included, there are ten statistically significant private valuation coefficients (two more than in tables 4.6 through 4.9).

Table 4.8   Maximum likelihood estimates of the probability of contributing to injury reduction in United States

Independent variable	Coefficients (asymptotic standard errors)			
	Inhalation–skin poisoning		Inhalation–child poisoning	
	(1)	(2)	(1)	(2)
Intercept	−0.672	−0.622	0.180	2.846
	(0.729)	(0.844)	(1.355)	(1.977)
Private valuation	0.304	0.082	0.091	0.015
	(0.096)	(0.020)	(0.085)	(0.021)
Family income	7.4E-7	7.93E-6	−1.98E-5	4.53E-5
	(6.6E-6)	(6.45E-6)	(1.39E-5)	(1.96E-5)
Age	−0.000	−0.016	−0.011	−0.018
	(0.008)	(0.009)	(0.028)	(0.031)
Male	0.038	−0.483	0.095	−0.181
	(0.300)	(0.236)	(0.518)	(0.555)
Black	−0.391	0.320	0.450	2.161
	(0.270)	(0.323)	(0.382)	(0.596)
Married	−0.126	0.362	—	—
	(0.228)	(0.296)		
Children under five	—	—	0.024	0.388
			(0.328)	(0.432)
Education	−0.052	−0.086	−0.051	−0.349
	(0.043)	(0.052)	(0.077)	(0.159)
−2 log likelihood	503.9	513.1	194.3	93.4

Particularly when compared with the other patterns in the tables, there is very strong evidence that high private valuations of risk are positively associated with individuals' altruistic tendencies. Both the probability of contributing and the contribution amount are affected. The greatest difference in the results is that the inhalation–skin-poisoning results are more likely to be statistically significant than the inhalation–child-poisoning results. This discrepancy may stem from sample-size differences, as the inhalation–skin-poisoning sample is considerably larger (672, as compared with 113).

The second key variable of interest is family income, which has the expected positive sign in 12 of 16 cases and is negative (but not statistically significant) in the other instances. Only one of the positive family-income variables is statistically significant in the probability of contributing equations (tables 4.6 and 4.8), but five of the positive family-income coefficients in the contribution-amount equations (tables 4.7 and 4.9) are statistically significant. In the case of the insecticide-contribution results (table 4.7), the family-income variable is positive and statistically significant in all but one instance. Stronger results, consistent with the hypothesized direction of

Table 4.9   Regression estimates of the magnitudes of nonzero contributions to injury reduction in United States

| Independent variable | Coefficients (asymptotic standard errors) | | | |
| | Inhalation–skin poisoning | | Inhalation–child poisoning | |
	(1)	(2)	(1)	(2)
Intercept	−1.834	−12.766	14.663	−1.173
	(11.227)	(15.720)	(10.174)	(15.121)
Private valuation	2.250	0.567	0.287	1.300
	(1.410)	(0.282)	(0.476)	(0.358)
Family income	1.24E-4	3.42E-4	−1.65E-5	−1.20E-4
	(0.94E-4)	(1.06E-5)	(2.39E-4)	(2.15E-4)
Age	0.034	0.128	−0.088	−0.117
	(0.107)	(0.164)	(0.229)	(0.203)
Male	−0.891	−1.104	−1.216	−8.213
	(4.254)	(3.997)	(4.200)	(4.692)
Black	−5.441	4.428	−0.508	0.013
	(3.838)	(5.366)	(3.013)	(5.628)
Married	1.358	−3.891	—	—
	(3.160)	(5.268)		
Children under five	—	—	−1.465	−1.722
			(2.746)	(3.431)
Education	0.351	0.446	−0.181	−1.199
	(0.721)	(0.944)	(0.613)	(0.984)
R^2	0.08	0.20	0.03	0.62

influence, are apparent for the equations pertaining to the total amount of the contribution.

The demographic variables other than household income are inconsequential. Three of these variables—marital status, children under the age of five, and years of schooling—are never statistically significant, and the race of the respondent variable is statistically significant in only one case. The age and sex variables are occasionally statistically significant with a negative sign for older consumers and male consumers. Both the elderly and male respondents appear to have lower altruistic interests, but this effect is relatively inconsequential when compared with the more consistent results for the private valuation and family income variables.

The weak influence of the demographic variables and the somewhat poor overall fit of some of the equations does not imply that altruistic concerns are random and unpredictable. Omitted variables such as religious affiliations and participation in charitable activities may be influential. The results suggest that the private valuations and household income follow theoretical predictions but should not be regarded as the sole driving force behind the altruism responses.

4.5   Conclusion

The results for the two pairs of morbidity effects suggest that consumers have a significant private valuation of health outcomes, averaging $2,080 for inhalation and skin poisoning and $3,680 for inhalation and child poisoning. Although altruistic valuations per household are smaller, the collective altruistic valuations are considerable. For inhalation-skin poisoning the within-state collective altruism is $10,000 and the altruism from individuals outside the state is $3,070, for a combined altruistic amount of $13,070. For inhalation-child poisoning the within-state collective altruism is $18,000, and the out-of-state collective altruism is $4,260, leading to a total altruistic value of $22,360. These response patterns suggest that there does not appear to be a "deep pocket" for altruism since consumers are willing to contribute only modest additional amounts for injury prevention outside of their home states. However, the principal determinants of variations in the altruistic contributions among the population follow the expected patterns, with the private valuations of the risk and household income being most instrumental.

Although our results suggest that altruism values may comprise an important component of the benefits from risk reduction programs, we must not overlook the limitations of our study. The interviewed consumers stated willingness-to-pay values but were not required to make actual contributions. The caveats that we placed on our results at various junctures in the chapter become especially important when one extrapolates to the collective willingness-to-pay values. Yet the fundamental implications of our results are clearcut. The stated willingness to pay for altruistic concerns exceeded the stated willingness to pay for private risk reduction. Even if some experimental bias exists, if the bias affects both private and altruistic responses similarly, then the relative importance of altruism will not be affected.

Of course altruism will not necessarily play the same role in other risk contexts. One should not, for example, use the ratio of our altruism–private valuation numbers to scale up the value of other classes of risk reduction benefits. The altruism–private valuation relationship is not a universal constant. Additional studies are needed to explore the role of altruism in a variety of policy contexts. Altruism does nevertheless appear to be of sufficient consequence to emerge from the regulatory analysis footnotes and become an integral part of such policy analyses.

III

HAZARDOUS CHEMICAL PRODUCT LABELING: COGNITIVE PROCESSES AND BEHAVIOR

5

Consumer Responses to Risk Information

A common source of market failure in product markets and job markets is that individuals do not have full information about the risks they face. In product markets this inadequacy creates two principal problems. First, inadequate information distorts the mix and amount of products that consumers purchase, which in turn affects firms' incentives to produce safe products. Second, after purchasing the product, consumers may not take the appropriate precautionary actions. It is this latter impact of imperfect information that will be our focus in this chapter.

A natural remedy for imperfect knowledge is to provide consumers with additional pertinent information. This remedy holds considerable appeal among economists since it addresses the source of the market failure directly, while at the same time preserving the constructive aspects of markets. Government agencies have also displayed increasing reliance on information as a regulatory alternative since labeling is a less obtrusive action than a product ban.

Information policies represent the efficient solution to problems of inadequate information only if the informational inadequacy stems from shortcomings in the information provided to the individual, rather than limitations on his or her ability to process and act on the information. The standard economic model assumes that consumers are fully rational and that they possess all the relevant information about products, including the risks of using them. An alternative possibility is that consumers are not fully rational. In its most extreme form, their actions may be unaffected or even adversely affected by additional risk information, and they are less able to process the hazard warnings reliably or make sound decisions.

In an earlier field experiment reported in Viscusi and Magat (1987), we found that properly designed labels boost consumers' intentions to take safety precautions, which is consistent with the hypothesis that hazard-warning programs can alleviate market failures due to informational inadequacies. In this study we use memory recall techniques to explore the cognitive processes that were not measured in the earlier study.

This approach does more than provide an alternative perspective on the information-precautions linkage. The memory recall methodology enables us to explore an additional class of issues that arise because of limitations in human-processing capabilities. Our experimental results will suggest that hazard information warning programs convey risk information, but at a cost. Consumers in our study traded off increased recall of risk information for decreased recall of product usage information. Overloading consumers with risk information obscured the underlying message of the hazard warning.

Our recognition of the importance of cognitive factors in analyzing economic behavior has a number of precedents. It is now well accepted that people have limits on the amount of information that they can process. Thirty-five years ago Simon (1957) theorized that individuals possess "bounded rationality." More recently, Bettman (1979, 177) concluded in his review of the relevant literature that, "In general, consumers do not have the resource or the abilities necessary to process the total amount of information which might potentially be available for making any particular choice.... Consumers have limited processing capacity."

The literature on information processing identifies the presence and extent of external memory, or information outside consumer's memories, as an important characteristic of consumer choice tasks (Bettman 1979). Labeling can provide an important source of external memory in situations where inefficient consumer decisions are caused by lack of adequate information about products, rather than problems in processing information. Even in situations where information processing limitations create the inefficiencies, external sources of information can help by formatting information in ways that make processing easier for the consumer.[1]

We focus on product labels because they represent an important and frequently used class of information policies and because there is evidence that their effectiveness can be significantly improved.[2] Examining product labels also allows us to test hypotheses about consumer responses to information provision, and this is relevant to most other information policies, such as safety training programs and public service advertisements.

As described in chapter 2, we conducted our study by sampling the information recall of consumers for labels on hazardous products, and we found that their recall of warnings information was highly sensitive to the amount, type, and structure of the information on product labels. We premised this methodology on the notion that differences in memory recall translate into differences in indicated precautionary behavior. This allowed us to test the relative effectiveness of different labels in influencing economic behavior toward risk.

To explore the role of cognitive factors in detail, we applied the unstructured memory recall approach to three research questions. First, what is the structure of consumer memory with respect to the information on existing consumer product labels? The labels we used in the analysis of our fictitious toilet bowl cleaner and garden insecticide were patterned after those of two existing hazardous chemical products. We measured the amount of information the consumers recalled with and without prompting and the kind of information that they remembered (e.g., how to use the product, or what precautions to take in using it). We also measured the order in which information was recalled, such as which kinds of information are recalled early and which kinds late, and what types of responses were triggered by the recall of other material. These data allowed us to infer how product information is stored in memory. This knowledge about the structure of memory should be useful in the design of effective labels (see Bettman 1979, 223).[3]

The second research question we posed has two parts. In reading labels, do consumers learn about the risks of product use and the precautions they should take? If so, by what magnitude does their recall of risk and precautions information increase from reading the labels? Because most consumers either regularly use or have heard of the hazardous chemicals in products such as toilet bowl cleaners and insect sprays, we would expect them to know many of the risks and precautions associated with the products even without providing any information about risks and precautions. To measure the effect of labeling information, we had to first establish this level of baseline knowledge and then examine the incremental increase in knowledge above the baseline.

The third research question was, How can existing labels be made more effective? We wanted to learn whether adding a large amount of information to a label can cause consumers to recall less of the information on the label. Academics have long theorized about the contexts in which information overload can occur, and in recent years several tests of the hypotheses have been carried out (Gaeth and Shanteau 1984). Manufacturers of consumer products are also concerned with the possibility of information overload because regulatory agencies are requiring them to include increasingly more information on labels, a practice they fear will make the labels less effective. By comparing recall of information from two labels that differ only in the amount of information they contain, we test this clutter hypothesis.

The next section reviews the literature on the phenomenon of information overload. Section 5.2 briefly summarizes the methodology and data used in the study. In section 5.3 we analyze the responses to labels patterned after those on existing products in order to understand the hierarchy consumers use to recall information on hazardous chemical labels.

Section 5.4 examines the differences in the amount and type of recall from several alternative labels on two chemical products. These comparisons address the question of how much recall of risk and precautions is improved by placing it on product labels, as well as the question of whether cluttering labels with large amounts of information of minor importance to consumers contributes to information overload.

5.1   Information Overload

As noted earlier, informational remedies to information-based market failures will only be effective if the inefficient decisions made by consumers are due to lack of adequate information rather than their inability to process it. This distinction is particularly important for the design of product labels because if processing limitations create the problem, then adding additional information to labels may worsen rather than improve the situation.

Some authors have theorized that due to these processing limitations, consumers may become overloaded with information and respond to the additional information by making worse decisions. Jacoby, Speller, and Kohn (1974) and Jacoby, Speller, and Berning (1974) presented the first set of empirical results which, they claimed, demonstrated the existence of information overload.

Several authors immediately challenged these findings, both in terms of the study design and the interpretation of the data.[4] More recently Malhotra (1982) reported a new study of housing choices designed to overcome the major conceptual and methological criticisms made of the Jacoby et al. studies. Malhotra found significant evidence of information overload when consumers were provided with an excessive number of alternatives (10 or more) in their choice set, or given an excessive number of product attributes (15 or more). Grether and Wilde (1983) reported a study that asked students to select among lotteries, which, they claim, is analogous to choosing among products with multiple attributes. The majority were able to select undominated lotteries, even when the number of alternatives was large and attributes of each lottery (i.e., possible outcomes) were numerous. Grether and Wilde, however, found evidence of poor decision making when their subjects were required to *use* a large amount of information. In contrast, when given unnecessary or unwanted information, subjects were able to ignore it. Grether, Schwartz, and Wilde (1985) concluded that consumers often use familiar, simplifying strategies for overcoming task-choice problems, and thus that information overload is a myth that should be irrelevant to public policy concerns.

By contrast, work in psychology (see Gaeth and Shanteau 1984) has found that irrelevant information increases the time required to do tasks and that there are strong differences between individuals in their ability to correctly cope with irrelevant information. The idea that irrelevant information increases the time to do the task is important because it suggests that under a time constraint tasks with irrelevant information will be done less accurately. The finding of Gaeth and Shanteau (1984) that individual differences matter indicates that the negative impact of labels with irrelevant information will fall disproportionately on those members of society who are least able to process information.

Given the contradictory nature of the results reported above, Keller and Staelin (1987) designed a new study based on a new measure of consumer decision-making ability which they call *decision effectiveness*. This variable measures the difference between the utility of the consumer's ideal choice and the utility of his actual choice, given the limited information environment. Keller and Staelin also distinguish between the *quantity* of information available to a consumer and the *quality* of that information, hypothesizing that a higher quantity of information affects decision effectiveness adversely while higher information quality improves decision effectiveness. Using a sample of job choices by MBA students, they offer empirical evidence that supports both of these hypotheses.

Note that in all of these studies the ability of consumers to recall information was not at issue because all the information provided in the experiments was permanently available to subjects. Certainly accurate recall of information is helpful for making good decisions. Thus one reason for the degradation in the ability of consumers to make good purchase- and product-use decisions may be their difficulties with recalling information from memory, independent of any problems with processing that information. Even if one agrees with the findings of Grether, Schwartz, and Wilde (1985)—that excessive information does not generally overload consumers when that information is made easily available to them—information overload can still occur because of recall problems. In addition the optimistic results of Grether, Schwartz, and Wilde may be attributable to the use of more structured experimental stimuli than what is encountered in actual information transfer situations. We have designed an experiment related to the actual forms of information consumers see on products in order to test whether clutter on product labels can adversely affect their ability to recall important information from the labels. Thus, although our study represents a survey experiment, it was undertaken using a market-based approach that considers the actual type of information provided on a class of products, and as well as using regular consumers of those products. We can consequently be more confident when making inferences about actual economic behavior than if our study had been based on student responses to a more hypothetical task.

5.2   Methodology and Data

As we mentioned in chapter 2, the subjects in our study received either the toilet bowl cleaner or the outdoor insect spray. Although the brand names and labels on the products were fictitious, the information on the labels was patterned after the Vanish brand of toilet bowl cleaner and the Ortho Malathion brand of outdoor insect spray.

Tables 2.2 and 2.3 describe the differences between the two toilet bowl cleaner labels (numbers 1 and 2) and the three insect spray labels (numbers 1, 2, and 3) used in this portion of the study. Figures 2.1, 2.2, 2.3, 2.6, and 2.7 show the toilet bowl cleaner and insect spray labels.

The differences in the five labels addressed the following two questions about the extent to which product users take the recommended precautions and use the products correctly: To what degree does the inclusion of risk and precautions information on the labels induce users to remember to take the recommended precautions? Does adding to a label information that is unrelated to risks and precautions (e.g., about product usage) and that clutters the label cause users to overlook the critical information on labels? The responses to toilet bowl cleaner labels 1 and 2 and to the insect spray labels 1 and 3 allowed us to test the effectiveness of adding risk and precautions information to the labels. Insect spray labels 2 and 3 provided a test of the clutter hypothesis. The cluttered insect spray label 3 was patterned after the current Ortho Malathion label. In this way, if experimental results indicated an adverse effect of clutter, the current labeling efforts could be improved.

In designing our experimental labels, we considered the hierarchical structure of product information memory. The structure changed very little from label to label, but it was helpful in explaining the pattern of responses, as we will see in section 5.4.

5.3   Hierarchical Structure of Product Information Memory

The most effective labels on hazardous chemicals are likely to be those that reinforce the structure of processing information from labels that most consumers already use, or those that restructure the information in such a way that consumers can recall it more easily from their long-term memories. An advantage of the open-ended approach is that it allows us to infer the hierarchical order of information in long-term memory as well as the relative importance of different pieces of information. This section explores how consumers recall the information on existing labels for toilet bowl cleaners and insect sprays.[5] With minor variations across the two products, consumers first tend to recall product usage information, or information about product usage and the "Do" precautions (i.e., positive actions that they should take to avoid injury). Then they tend to recall both types of suggested precautions, the positive Do's and the negative Don'ts (i.e., actions not to take). However, the injury risks did play a critical role in that once recalled, the consumer tends to immediately associate the products with the precautions recommended to avoid injuries. Antidotes were recalled last, if at all.

Of the two products in our study, the toilet bowl cleaner label for the existing product (label 2) devotes a smaller fraction of its space, 37 percent, to information about precautions and risks (Do's, Don'ts, and Hurts) than does the insecticide label on the existing product (label 3), which allocates 44 percent. The toilet bowl cleaner is of course a less hazardous product than the outdoor insect spray, so the insect spray label contains more information about precautions. For all these reasons we would expect the insect spray label to induce a higher proportion of precautions and risk responses, and a lower fraction of use responses, than the toilet bowl cleaner label.

As discussed below, this was the very pattern to emerge in the responses to the labels on the two products. With one exception both labels elicited a similar pattern of responses from the open-ended question. When asked to describe how to use the product to a friend (in order of importance to the user), consumers generally started by recalling Uses or Uses and Do's, then they might recall Do's and Don'ts, then Hurts, which evoke mostly other Hurts, Don'ts, and Do's, and finally they would mention antidotes. This pattern of recall generally accords with what we expected. People tend to recall the overall function and manner of use of objects, and then they recall the risks and the associated precautions.

Table 5.1   Mean percentages of first responses classified by categories of responses (%)

Response category	1: No risk information on label		2: Risk information on label	
	First	First two	First	First two
A. Toilet bowl cleaner				
Uses	83.2	85.7	74.5	77.6
Don'ts, Hurts, Do's	16.8	14.1	25.5	22.4
Don'ts	1.9	1.7	3.2	4.2
Hurts	0	0.5	1.4	2.6
Do's	14.9	11.9	20.9	15.6
Antidotes	0	0.2	0	0
N	214	410	220	427

Response category	1: No risk inform-ation on label		2: Risk inform-ation on label		3: Risk information plus clutter on label	
	First	First two	First	First two	First	First two
B. Insect spray						
Uses	46.4	55.1	36.2	37.7	24.3	28.4
Don'ts, Hurts, Do's	53.6	44.9	63.5	62.3	75.7	71.0
Don'ts	4.2	6.1	8.4	13.2	16.9	20.4
Hurts	3.0	3.0	2.8	4.2	5.1	6.5
Do's	46.4	35.8	52.3	44.9	53.77	44.1
Antidotes	0	0	0	0	0	0.6
N	168	296	178	332	177	324

To discover this pattern of recall, we analyzed the responses to the existing labels (toilet bowl cleaner label 2 and insect spray label 3) in several ways. Table 5.1 reports the means of the first response when divided into the five categories, as well as the means of the first two responses. For the toilet bowl cleaner, consumers generally recall the Uses first (74.5 percent of the first response and 77.6 percent of the first two responses, respectively), followed far behind by Do's (20.9 and 15.6 percent), whereas for insect spray consumers first recall both the Do's (53.7 percent and 44.1 percent) and the Uses (24.3 and 28.4 percent).

Table 5.2 provides a similar classification, splitting the total set of responses into those in the first half of a subject's responses and those given in the second half of the responses. Again the first responses for the existing toilet bowl cleaner product (label 2) are dominated by Uses (82.7 percent), with Do's a distant second (9.7 percent). For the existing insect spray (label 3) both the Uses (29.6 percent) and the Do's (36.1 percent) dominate the first-half responses. The dampened role of Use information for insect spray indicates the greater prominence of the hazard warnings for this risky

Table 5.2 Mean percentages of responses divided into total, first half and second half and classified by categories of responses (%)

Response category	1: No risk information on label			2: Risk information on label		
	Total	1st	2nd	Total	1st	2nd
A. Toilet bowl cleaner						
Uses	45.3	89.7	58.3	61.5	82.7	36.6
Don'ts, Hurts, Do's	23.9	10.3	39.8	34.2	16.7	54.9
Don'ts	8.79	1.66	17.23	16.78	5.40	30.27
Hurts	2.29	0.50	4.41	2.68	1.60	3.91
Do's	12.82	8.13	18.24	14.74	9.74	20.75
Antidotes	0.82	0	1.80	4.26	0.58	8.5
N	1092	598	494	1269	485	584

Response category	1: No risk information on label			2: Risk information on label			3: Risk information plus clutter on label		
	Total	1st	2nd	Total	1st	2nd	Total	1st	2nd
B. Insect spray									
Uses	50.0	57.4	39.8	30.7	36.8	23.0	25.9	29.6	21.1
Don'ts, Hurts, Do's	50.0	42.6	60.2	63.7	59.8	68.7	68.6	66.2	71.1
Don'ts	13.1	8.1	20.1	22.2	19.5	25.7	26.2	23.8	29.2
Hurts	3.0	2.4	3.7	4.2	3.9	4.6	7.4	6.3	8.9
Do's	33.9	32.1	36.4	37.3	36.4	38.4	35.0	36.1	33.6
Antidotes	0	0	0	5.6	3.5	8.4	5.5	4.2	7.1
N	640	371	269	832	462	370	547	432	336

product. The results in these two tables suggest that consumers follow a recall pattern beginning with Uses, or with both Uses and Do's.

In the second half of the responses for the existing labels, the Uses diminish markedly, and the Don'ts increase but are mixed with Do's. Thus the role of risk-related responses increases greatly for the second half of the responses. For toilet bowl cleaner the second-half responses in table 5.2 (label 2) show that the Uses fall from 82.7 to 36.6 percent, while the Don'ts (30.3 percent) overtake the Do's (20.7 percent). For the insect spray (label 3) the Uses fall off from 29.6 to 21.1 percent, and the Don'ts increase from 23.8 to 29.2 percent, with the Do's declining slightly to 33.6 percent. Interestingly the Hurts percentage increases only slightly from the first-half responses to the second-half responses, an observation that is consistent with their central role as a referral response which will be discussed below.

Table 5.2 also suggests that Antidotes tend to be noted in the later stages of the memory recall, if at all. For toilet bowl cleaner label 2 the percentage of Antidotes jumps from 0.6 to 8.5 percent from the first- to second-half responses. Similarly, for insect spray label 3 the antidotes jump from 4.2

percent in the first-half responses to 7.1 percent in the second-half responses. These results suggest that after starting with Uses and Do's,
consumer recall moves to Do's and Don'ts, which are finally followed by
Antidotes, with the Hurts mixed fairly evenly throughout the responses.
This is sensible in the case of the Antidotes section since consumers can
refer to the label after the adverse outcome has occurred rather than
before.

Examining the transitions from one category of responses to another in
tables 5.3 and 5.4 provides a second test of the hierarchy of information
recall. By transitions we mean the relationship between the categories of
the successive responses given by consumers. Again we focus on the existing, toilet bowl cleaner (label 2) and insecticide (label 3). Table 5.3 gives the
recall percentages of each of the five categories of responses in terms of the
previous response. For example, for toilet bowl cleaner label 2, 87.5 percent
of the Uses responses were followed by another Uses response. Table 5.4
normalizes the percentages in these transition matrices by the percentage
of each category of subsequent response in the total sample, as listed in
table 5.2. This normalization allows us to compare the percentages in table
5.3 with those that would occur if there were no relationship between successive responses. Numbers greater than one indicate that the chance of the
subsequent response occurring is increased. Again, using toilet bowl
cleaner label 2 as an example, the percentage of Uses responses following
other Uses responses (81.1 percent) is 1.32 times higher than the fraction
(61.5 percent) that would occur if responses were independent of each
other.

In table 5.3 the probabilities of remaining in the same category from one
response to another are shown by the diagonals. When these diagonal
elements are the largest elements in the rows, they indicate a high probability of remaining within a category rather than moving to any other category. Most of the diagonals in the unnormalized percentages are greater
than 50 percent, indicating quite reasonably that consumers tend to recall
successive responses within the same category than to move out of a category. All the normalized percentages in the diagonals of table 5.4 exceed
1.00, indicating that the likelihood of remaining in a category is higher
than would be predicted by using the overall percentages of responses in
each category. Again this result supports the finding that in recalling information from labels, consumers tend to search within categories of responses rather than searching randomly across all categories.

Two categories deserve special mention, however. The unnormalized
Uses responses in table 5.3 show the highest probabilities of remaining

Table 5.3   Transition matrices relating sequential responses (%)

Previous response	Subsequent response (given previous response)					
	Uses	Don'ts	Hurts	Do's	Antidotes	N
A. Toilet bowl cleaner						
Label 1: No risk information						
Uses	87.5	4.0	1.3	7.2	0	718
Don'ts	6.0	58.2	6.0	26.9	3.0	67
Hurts	28.6	9.5	28.6	19.0	14.3	21
Do's	20.5	26.9	7.7	42.3	2.6	78
Antidotes	0	25.0	0	25.0	50.0	4
Label 2: Risk information						
Uses	81.1	8.0	1.5	9.1	0.3	715
Don'ts	3.7	61.9	3.1	19.4	11.9	160
Hurts	19.0	19.1	28.6	33.3	0	21
Do's	22.7	35.3	6.7	30.3	5.0	119
Antidotes	7.3	14.3	2.4	9.8	65.9	41

Previous response	Subsequent response (given previous response)					
	Uses	Don'ts	Hurts	Do's	Antidotes	N
B. Insect Spray						
Label 1: No risk information						
Uses	75.0	8.6	0.4	16.0	0	268
Don'ts	20.0	45.4	7.3	27.3	0	55
Hurts	13.3	6.7	26.7	53.3	0	15
Do's	21.2	21.2	3.0	54.6	0	132
Antidotes	0	0	0	0	0	0
Label 2: Risk information						
Uses	64.3	10.2	3.7	20.4	1.4	216
Don'ts	7.1	49.0	1.9	31.0	11.0	155
Hurts	25.0	12.5	41.7	12.5	8.3	24
Do's	14.4	27.5	4.1	51.8	2.2	222
Antidotes	5.4	21.6	0	18.9	54.1	37
Lable 3: Risk information plus clutter						
Uses	64.9	16.7	4.8	13.1	0.6	168
Don'ts	2.6	52.2	4.5	38.0	12.7	157
Hurts	18.0	12.8	33.3	35.9	0	39
Do's	17.8	25.6	9.4	45.6	1.6	191
Antidotes	5.7	20.0	5.7	17.1	51.4	35

Table 5.4   Normalized transition matrices relating sequential responses

Initial response	Subsequent response (given previous response)				
	Uses	Don'ts	Hurts	Do's	Antidotes
A. Toilet bowl cleaner—label 2					
Uses	1.3[a]	0.5	0.6	0.6	0.1
Don'ts	0.1	3.7	1.2	1.3	2.8
Hurts	0.3	1.1	10.7	2.2	0
Do's	0.4	2.1	2.5	2.0	1.2
Antidotes	0.1	0.9	0.9	0.7	15.6
B. Insect spray—label 3					
Uses	2.5	0.6	0.6	0.4	0.1
Don'ts	0.1	2.0	0.6	0.8	2.3
Hurts	0.7	0.5	4.5	1.0	0
Do's	0.7	1.0	1.3	1.3	0.3
Antidotes	0.2	0.8	0.8	0.5	9.4

a. As an example, figure 1.3 measures the ratio of the percentage of Uses responses that follow directly after a Uses response (81.1 percent from table 5.3) divided by the percentage of Uses responses that would occur if all the responses were completely independent (61.5 percent from table 5.2).

within the category (81.1 percent for toilet bowl cleaner and 64.9 percent for insect spray), providing part of the explanation for the high prevalence of Uses responses recall (see table 5.2). In contrast, the unnormalized Hurts responses in table 5.3 indicate that among the five categories, Hurts are least likely to trigger recall of another response in the same category (28.6 percent for toilet bowl cleaner and 33.3 percent for insect spray), indicating that the Hurts responses cause consumers to remember other related, but nonrisk information. However, the normalized Hurts responses in table 5.4 show that recalling a Hurts response more than doubles the likelihood of recalling a Hurts responses in the next response. Together, these two results suggest that consumers tend to move from a Hurts response to either another Hurts response or a Do or Don't precaution related to the risk identified by the Hurt response. Thus in a cognitive sense Hurts are central, appearing to evoke other precautions that prevent the risks associated with the Hurts responses.

The degree to which one category evokes another is evidence of those categories being cognitively associated. For example, table 5.3 shows that Uses are unlikely to evoke any other category, but when the switching of categories occurs, the Hurts are most often followed by Do's (33.3 percent for toilet bowl cleaner and 35.9 percent for insect spray). Once a Do is evoked, however, it strongly evokes Don't responses and other Do's.

Don'ts then evoke more Don'ts as well as Do's (19.4 percent for toilet bowl cleaner and 28.0 percent for insect spray).

Two conclusions arise from this examination of the sequential patterns of responses. First, when consumers move out of the Uses category to recall other information on the label, they recall predominantly Do and Don't responses, which tend to generate mainly other Don't and Do responses. This switching pattern supports the hierarchical structure of recall presented earlier based on the timing of the recall. Second, it appears that certain categories are important in eliciting others. Don't and Do responses evoke more of each other, while Hurts elicit both types of precautionary responses. Thus, in recalling the information from labels on hazardous chemicals, consumers tend to first recall Uses, or Uses and Do's, followed by Do's and then by Don'ts, with the Do's and Don'ts evoking each other. Antidotes are more likely to be recalled near the end of the memory recall, with Hurts remembered throughout and playing a triggering role in recalling related Do's and Don'ts.

5.4   Impact of Labels on the Information Recall

We now assess the importance of several key attributes of labels in evoking recall of information. Comparisons of responses to different labels allow us to draw inferences about the impact on memory recall of systematic differences across labels. We contrast the responses to the labels using two approaches. First, table 5.5 displays the mean numbers of responses to each of the labels divided into the five response categories, as well as the combined group of the Don'ts, Do's, and Hurts responses. By comparing the mean numbers of responses across labels and consulting the t-statistics in table 5.6, we directly test the effects of the labels upon recall. Regression equations that add demographic and product usage variables to explain the variances across labels are not reported because the main effects of the labels were found to be unaffected by the addition of these covariates.[6]

The second approach examines the order of responses to the labels, contrasting the different labels, using the data in tables 5.1, 5.2, 5.3, and 5.4. While less informative than the mean numbers of responses in table 5.2, this information provides supporting evidence and helps explain the variations in the mean numbers of responses.

Effects of Precautionary Information on Labels
The first contrast of responses to labels tests whether the labels provided any new information about risks and precautions to consumers beyond

Table 5.5 Mean numbers of responses classified by response category and label

Response category	Overall	Label 1: No risk information	Label 2: Risk information
A. Toilet bowl cleaner			
Don'ts, Hurts, Do's	2.04 (0.06)	1.21 (0.10)	1.99 (0.11)
Don'ts	0.95 (0.04)	0.45 (0.06)	0.98 (0.09)
Hurts	0.21 (0.02)	0.12 (0.03)	0.16 (0.03)
Do's	0.88 (0.03)	0.65 (0.06)	0.86 (0.05)
Uses	3.53 (0.08)	3.81 (0.16)	3.54 (0.15)
Antidotes	0.18 (0.02)	0.04 (0.02)	0.24 (0.06)
Total	5.75	5.07	5.78

Response category	Overall	Label 1: No risk information	Label 2: Risk information	Label 3: Risk information plus clutter
B. Insect spray				
Don'ts, Hurts, Do's	2.74 (0.07)	1.94 (0.15)	2.98 (0.17)	2.94 (0.16)
Don'ts	1.04 (0.05)	0.53 (0.07)	1.06 (0.11)	1.14 (0.11)
Hurts	0.21 (0.02)	0.13 (0.04)	0.20 (0.04)	0.32 (0.05)
Do's	1.49 (0.04)	1.28 (0.10)	1.73 (0.10)	1.48 (0.10)
Uses	1.46 (0.06)	1.87 (0.15)	1.42 (0.12)	1.10 (0.12)
Antidotes	0.23 (0.03)	0.00 (0.00)	0.26 (0.06)	0.23 (0.06)
Total	4.43	3.81	4.67	4.27

Note: Standard errors of means in parentheses.

Table 5.6 Test statistics for differences in mean numbers of responses

Response category			Label 2–label 1
A. Toilet bowl cleaner			
Don'ts, Hurts, Do's			5.25
Don'ts			4.94
Hurts			0.92
Do's			2.66
Uses			−1.27
Antidotes			3.45

Response category	Label 2–label 1	Label 3–label 1	Label 3–label 2
B. Insect spray			
Don'ts, Hurts, Do's	4.55	4.57	−0.19
Don'ts	4.09	4.64	0.55
Hurts	1.19	3.09	1.88
Do's	3.23	1.50	−1.86
Uses	2.36	−4.14	−1.86
Antidotes	4.34	4.03	−0.35

what they already knew from using other products in the same product class. This contrast also reveals what new information they learned from the labels. Toilet bowl cleaner label 1 and insect spray label 1 both contain no risk and precautions information, but in all other respects they are identical to the labels on existing products (toilet bowl cleaner label 2 and insect spray label 3). The precautions recalled from the respondents who were shown labels without any risk and precautions information come predominantly from information stored in long-term memory before the experiment, and thus provide a baseline from which the marginal effects of precautions and risk information can be assessed.

As expected, the addition of precautions and risk information increased the recall of the combined Don'ts, Hurts, and Do's group by over 50 percent for both of the products, differences that were statistically highly significant. The individual Don't, Do, and Hurt category responses all increased for both products, with four of the six differences significant at the 95 percent confidence level.

For both products the Uses responses declined with the addition of risk and precaution information, although only the insect spray difference was statistically significant at the usual levels. Since the toilet bowl cleaner label had comparatively low informational content in all cases, it is likely that the informational demands on consumers' cognitive capabilities were more in line with their processing abilities.

Based on the insect spray results, which should be more meaningful, it appears that adding information to a complicated label decreases one's ability to recall other information on label. This important result suggests that there is an opportunity cost to any new item of information placed on a label. However, the total number of responses increased upon adding the precautions and risk information (see table 5.4), implying that the reduction in Uses responses is not a direct substitution of non-uses for Uses recall. Thus the bounds on consumers' cognitive limits are somewhat elastic, a finding that is replicated below in another context.

Examination of the order of responses also provides some insight into the changes in the mean responses. In table 5.5 the largest percentage increase in responses was in the Don't category, which more than doubled when the precautions and risk information were added to labels. This increase in Don't responses occurred because, with hazard warnings, consumers were more likely to repeat a Don't response or switch from another category of responses to the Don't category, especially from the central Hurts category. The probability of moving from a Hurts response to a Don't response increased from 9.5 percent to 19.1 percent for toilet bowl cleaner and from 6.7 to 12.8 percent for insect spray (see table 5.3).

The reduction in Uses responses caused by the addition of risks and precautions information to the labels appears to be caused by three effects: Consumers tended to start by recalling fewer Uses responses; they were less likely to repeat a Uses response; and once out of the Uses category they were less likely to return to a Uses responses. The fraction of Uses responses in the first two responses declined from 85.7 to 77.6 percent for toilet bowl cleaner and from 55.1 to 28.4 percent for insect spray (see table 5.4). Moreover the probability of remaining within the Uses category on successive responses declined from 87.5 to 81.1 percent for toilet bowl cleaner and from 75.0 to 64.9 percent for insect spray (see table 5.3). Finally, once out of the Uses category, the chances of switching to a Uses response declined from 73.6 to 58.7 percent for toilet bowl cleaner and from 51.5 to 26.4 percent for insect spray (calculated from, but not shown in table 5.3). All of these changes were statistically significant.

Effects of Clutter

The second contrast tested the effects of adding information to the label about how to use the product. Compared with insect spray label 2, the label 3 differs only in the additional usage information relating primarily to the ways the product should be applied. As is clear from an examination of the labels in figure 2.3, this new information makes the label more difficult to read. Indeed, the additional information made the regular usage statements so hard to read that the recall of usage information actually declined by a statistically significant amount (see tables 5.5 and 5.6). This manipulation provides an example where information overload results in less information retained by the consumer.

Although the number of responses in the combined category of Do's, Don'ts, and Hurts did not change significantly, the clutter did cause statistically significant changes in the recall of Hurts and Do's responses, augmenting the number of Hurts responses and decreasing the number of Do's responses (see tables 5.5 and 5.6). The Hurts responses tend to be general descriptions of the risks from using the product, while the Do's responses are much more specific instructions pertaining to insect spray and are more difficult to find on the label. This difference between the nature of the two categories of responses suggests that adding clutter to the label signals to the consumer that the product is hazardous and triggers the recall of ways in which it might hurt you, but the more product-specific Do's responses that avoid these problems were made more difficult to read and recall. Once again this illustrates the central role of the Hurts responses.

The process data in tables 5.2 and 5.2 help explain the effect of clutter on recall. The reduction in the recall of Uses information occurs primarily in the first half of the responses. The percentage of Uses in the first two responses declined from 37.7 to 28.4 percent due to clutter (see table 5.2, panel B, labels 2 and 3) and the percentages of Uses in the first-half responses decreased from 36.8 to 29.6 percent (see table 5.2, panel B, labels 2 and 3), with both declines being statistically significant. In contrast, the second-half responses in table 5.2 declined minimally from 23.0 to 21.1 percent. The increase in the Hurts responses occurred in both halves, but the decline in Do's responses was concentrated primarily in the last part of the recall.[7] Since the information recalled earliest tends to be given the most importance by consumers, these process effects suggest that the reduction in recall of Uses is particularly central to the consumers because the bulk of the reduction occurs early in their recall exercise. In contrast, the decline in recall of Do's information was concentrated at the end of the recall, which suggests that it may be less important to consumers.

We conclude from these findings that designers of product labels should be seriously concerned about the effects on recall of cluttering labels with additional information which, for many consumers, may be of subordinate importance. In our experiment the addition of more usage information caused a decline in the recall of the primary usage information, as well as decreased the recall of the specific Do's precautionary responses. Cluttered labels can be expected to be less effective where the goal of the label is to convey the same information to all consumers; however, they may be more effective where differing information needs require that different users recall different information from the label.

We caution that our laboratory results only suggest that in real purchase and use situations consumers will retain less information about products when the labels are cluttered with information of subsidiary importance. In some cases the information provided is redundant, and in others it has very little value with respect to likely consumer usage of the product, so the basic message of the label is obscured. Consumers could make up for the reduction in immediate recall of usage information by rereading the labels before using the products. Alternatively, before purchasing the products, they may choose to spend more time (than the two minutes we allotted them) in reading complex labels. Finally, they may overcome the immediate reduction in recall in their initial purchase experience by learning more about usage information through subsequent purchases.

5.5   Conclusions

We have developed and demonstrated a methodology for assessing the impact of different product labels on consumers' recall of the information on the labels. We found the unaided recall approach to discriminate well among the different labels in our study of consumer recall of information. To the extent that actual behavior in using the products and taking the recommended precautions corresponds to the memory recall from the labels, this approach allowed us to test the relative effectiveness of different product labels. We believe that similar methodologies can be designed to assess the effectiveness of other information programs beyond those relying upon product labeling, such as in-plant warning signs, safety training sessions, and public advertising programs.

An important advantage of the unaided recall approach is that it allows the researcher to track the order of responses and thereby assess the structure and priority of information in memory. For the two products we studied, this analysis revealed a natural hierarchy of the information recall by consumers, with Uses, or Uses and Do's, tending to be recalled first, and then Do and Don't responses. Hurts play a central role in leading to subsequent recall of the Do's and Don'ts associated with them, and Antidotes tend to be recalled last. The discovery of this hierarchy has important implications for the design of labels. Labels can be structured to reinforce this pattern of recall rather than compete with it.

Most consumers who use hazardous chemical products are already familiar with many of their risks and precautions. Nevertheless, the addition of risk and precautionary information on the product labels does lead to significantly more knowledge of specific risks and precautions. The cost of this increase is in the retention of risk and precautions information, for consumers then recall less information about product usage.

Additional information about product usage that cluttered the label created a complicated set of changes in the kind of information recalled by consumers. Individuals responded to the clutter by retaining less information about usage and the highly specific Do's precautions. At the same time they did recall more of the risk information (Hurts) on the label, perhaps because the clutter signaled to them that the product was more complicated and therefore more dangerous to use. These reactions to the addition of more usage information to the label indicate that adding more information to product labels does not necessarily lead to the recall of more information, and therefore to safer and more informed use of the products. Indeed, our results suggest that adding less important usage information can cause less recall of the most important information on the label.

Our findings support the view that there is an upper bound on individuals' abilities to process risk information and suggest that widely used chemical labels exceed consumers' information processing limits. The difficulty is not simply that individuals process only a small number of pieces of information on a product label and then stop. Rather, the type and quantity of information recalled may be affected by the amount of information presented, possibly in an adverse manner. These findings add to the mounting evidence that cognitive factors represent more than an intermediate black box that can be safely ignored by economists concerned with the rationality of risk-taking behavior. If better understood, the functioning and limitations of these cognitive factors might facilitate fuller assessments of the nature of market failures and the efficacy of informational remedies.

6

Effects of the Format of Labels on Consumer Responses to Labels

Chapter 5 analyzed the effects of adding risk and precautions information to labels for hazardous chemical products, holding constant the general character of the label design. There remain the questions of how these responses to label information are affected by the format used to present the information. This chapter addresses the issue of information formatting. This issue arises because the same types of cognitive factors that make label clutter and information overload matters of concern also will make other aspects of label design consequential.

Using the exact same wording on the labels, we analyze how consumers respond to the information when the format of the information is changed. First, we study whether improvements in the composition, or design, of the label induce more precaution taking. In this case the label is redesigned to group the uses, precautions, hazards, and antidotes and to clearly link the hazards to the precautions necessary to avoid them. The second format is a variation on this that increases the proportion of the label devoted to risk and precautions information. Finally, the third format deals with the effect of print size on consumer response to precautions noted on labels.

Although each of these three issues on information formatting must be addressed in the design of all labels, our goal is not to design the most effective label for hazardous chemical products. Rather, we wish to establish the importance of formatting on the effectiveness of a labeling program independent of the content of the information. To design the most effective label would require similar studies of the other characteristics of label effectiveness, such as color, symbols, and wording.

Section 6.1 first reviews some results from an earlier study of ours (Viscusi and Magat 1987) and then presents new evidence of information-formatting effects using a tighter label design based on the memory recall methodology described in the chapter 2. Section 6.2 analyzes consumer responses to labels in which the proportion devoted to risk and precautions information is varied, and section 6.3 studies the print size issue. Section 6.4 looks at multivariate results that support the conclusions reached in the earlier sections. The final section briefly discusses the implications of our results.

6.1   Composition of the Label

The received theory of consumer information processing (Bettman 1979; Bettman, Payne, and Staelin 1986) clearly establishes the link between the format of information programs and consumer responses to them. In general, consumers respond best to information that is presented in a way that is easiest for them to process, that is, information that is logically related to its usage and easily related to other information in memory that is also needed for making decisions. For example, labels that place risks and precautions in separate areas and that explicitly link the risks to the necessary precautions enable consumers to more easily identify the precautions they should take.

This section describes results from two experiments on formatting effects. The first experiment was initially reported in Viscusi and Magat (1987). In this earlier study we found strong evidence of label formatting affecting the effectiveness with which health risks were communicated. However, this experiment contained some possible problems in its design, and it covered only a limited number of precautions. The second experiment, which is the basis of our present study, is predicated on the open-ended recall methodology described in chapter 2; it uses a tighter design and covers all the major precautions intended to be communicated by the labels in this study.

Experiment 1

Using information-processing theory, Bettman, Payne, and Staelin (1986) identified nine rules for effective label design and then applied these rules to the design of two labels, one for a bleach product and another for a liquid drain-opener product. In Viscusi and Magat (1987) we compared the consumer responses to these two "Test" labels to the precaution-taking responses to labels patterned after best-selling brands of bleach (one label for Clorox and another label for Kroger Bright) and drain opener (a single label derived from those on Drano and Red Devil lye).

Although all the bleach and drain-opener labels identify a number of risks in using the products and recommend precautions for avoiding the risks, two risk/precautions pairs are particularly important for each product. Users of household bleach are urged both to store the product in a childproof location to avoid injuries from ingestion and not to mix the product with toilet bowl cleaners or other ammonia-based products to avoid chloramine gas poisoning. Drain openers also cause injury if ingested, so storage in a childproof location is suggested; they can cause skin injuries, mainly to the hands, and this can be avoided by wearing rubber gloves.

Our first experiment for testing the effects of the format changes on the test label was designed around consumers interviewed as part of the consumer study discussed in Viscusi and Magat (1987). Each consumer received one of the two products, a bleach or a drain opener. To induce the subjects to read the labels more carefully, rather than relying upon well-established patterns of behavior with the entire class of bleach products, we referred to the bleach product as a new cleaning agent with the fictitious product name "Vector" rather than calling it bleach. The drain opener was identified as a liquid drain opener and given the brand name "Unstop." Through a randomization procedure, a sample of 59 subjects received a cleaning agent product with the label patterned after the Clorox label, 42 subjects received a product label patterned after the Bright label, and 44 subjects received a Test label that differed from the other two labels primarily in the format of the information presented (but not in the information content). A random sample of 59 consumers received a drain opener with a label patterned after a combination of the Drano and Red Devil lye labels, and 50 subjects received a Test label, again differing primarily in the information format and not its content.

We informed subjects that they were participating in a marketing research study, rather than a study of risk avoidance behavior, and we mixed the risk-related questions with non-risk-related questions to keep them unaware of the true focus of the questionnaire. The responses to the primary risk-related questions in the questionnaire are described in tables 6.1 and 6.2.

For the bleach experiment, the Test label clearly outperformed the Clorox and the Bright labels in terms of the fraction of consumers who intend to take the required precautions. All differences between the Test label and the other two labels are statistically significant at the 95 percent

Table 6.1 Effects of labels on precautions for bleach

Precautions	Fraction taking precaution by label format		
	Clorox	Bright	Test
1. Do not mix with toilet bowl cleaner (if toilet is badly stained)	0.23	0.32	0.40
2. Do not add to ammonia-based cleaners (for particularly dirty jobs)	0.69	0.67	0.86
3. Store in childproof location	0.64	0.51	0.76

Table 6.2 Effects of labels on precautions for drain opener

Precautions	Fraction taking precaution by label format	
	Drano	Test
1. Wear rubber gloves	0.82	0.73
2. Store in childproof location	0.68	0.62

confidence level. Thus, in the case of the bleach experiment, the reformatting of the information on the store brands led to more precaution taking.

However, in the case of the drain-opener sample, the fractions of consumers taking the precautions listed in Table 6.2 indicate that the store label (which we call "Drano") induced more precaution taking than the Test label. This result seems to contradict the implications of the bleach experiment, and we suspect that this surprising effect may be due to a design variable that we did not control in these experiments, namely, the percentage of the label devoted to risk and precautions information.

The percentages in table 6.3 show that 69 percent of the Test label for bleach gave risk and precautions information, in contrast to only 31 percent for the Clorox label and 41 percent for the Bright label. However, for the drain-opener labels the Test label had 63 percent risk and precautions information as compared to 78 percent for the Drano label. Thus, if allocating a greater percentage of a product's label to risk and precautions information leads to more response to this information from consumers, then the different responses to the Test labels for bleach and drain opener (compared with store brands) might be explained by the risk/precautions percentage variable.

Experiment 2

To sort out the separate composition and the percentage effects, we designed another experiment that isolated each effect. The second experiment was based on the memory recall methodology of chapter 2. In this experiment we used the fictitious toilet bowl cleaner and garden insecticide. Labels 3 and 4 for the toilet bowl cleaner devoted 55 percent of their area to risk and precautions information, but label 3 was designed after a store brand; label 4 used the Test format described for the first experiment above. The differences in responses to labels 3 and 4 test the hypothesis that the improved composition of the Test format leads to a greater consumer response.

In contrast, toilet bowl cleaner labels 2 and 3 differ only in the percentage of the label devoted to risk and precautions information (37 percent

Table 6.3   Percentage of label containing risk and precautions information

Label	Percentage of risk and precautions information
Bleach	
Clorox	31
Bright	41
Test	69
Drain opener	
Drano	78
Test	63

versus 55 percent), thus providing an uncontaminated test of the percentage effect. In addition insect spray labels 4 and 5 differ primarily in their risk/precautions percentages (44 percent versus 66 percent), providing a second test of the percentage effect.

Table 6.4 shows that the reformatting in the Test label increased the mean number of the combined Don't, Hurt, and Do responses from 2.15 with label 3 to 2.68 with label 4, a difference that is statistically significant at 95 percent confidence level (see table 6.5). Although all three categories increased, only the Don't responses increased by a statistically significant amount.

Interestingly the increase in the recall of risk and precautions information appears to be created at the expense of less recall of the information about product usage, a phenomenon that was also observed in chapter 5 in the context of other label features that increased recall of risk and precautions information. The mean number of Uses responses recalled declined from 3.26 for label 3 to 2.85 for label 4, a statistically significant difference.

Table 6.6 provides more refined information about the differences in the responses to labels 3 and 4 by analyzing the 13 responses recalled by more than 10 percent of the sample. Note that 10 of these 13 responses were greater for label 4 than for label 3. However, due to the small number of these responses only four of the individual differences are statistically significant. For label 3, we reformatted the composition of label 4, and this caused users to be more cautious about skin contact or ingesting the product and also to be more aware of the toxic gas risk.

Taken together, the results in tables 6.4 and 6.6 corroborate the hypothesis that improvements in label design increase consumers' awareness of the risk and precautions information on the labels. By constructing a tighter design than that used in the Viscusi and Magat (1987) study, and by applying a new measurement approach that ties the product in with other

Table 6.4   Mean numbers of responses to different groups of possible responses to usage directions question

Response group	Label 2	Label 3	Label 4
A. Toilet bowl cleaner			
Don't, Hurt, Do	1.81	2.15	2.68
	(1.58)	(1.84)	(2.00)
Don't (200s)	0.88	1.02	1.37
	(1.21)	(1.25)	(1.59)
Hurt (300s)	0.12	0.22	0.28
	(0.40)	(0.65)	(0.74)
Do (400s)	0.81	0.91	1.03
	(0.82)	(0.86)	(0.98)
Uses (100s)	3.31	3.26	2.85
	(2.21)	(2.26)	(2.32)
Antidotes (500s)	0.19	0.22	0.16
	(0.71)	(0.70)	(0.59)

Response group	Label 4		Label 5
B. Insect spray			
Don't, Hurt, Do		2.60.	2.54
		(2.00)	(2.06)
Don't (200s)		1.10	0.93
		(1.45)	(1.31)
Hurt (300s)		0.20	0.15
		(0.68)	(0.63)
Do (400s)		1.30	1.46)
		(1.07)	(1.21)
Uses (100s)		1.41	1.22
		(1.52)	(1.49)
Antidotes (500s)		0.10	0.32
		(0.68)	(0.89)

Note: Standard errors in parentheses.

chemical products, we are able to conclude with more confidence that well-designed labels can produce significant gains in the awareness of precautionary information, and thus in the likely levels of precaution taking.

6.2   Proportion of Risk and Precautions Information on the Label

We have hypothesized that by devoting a larger portion of a label to risk and precautions information, consumer recall of this information can be increased. The larger warning area on the Drano label appeared to be an important factor in the excellent response to the hazards of using Drano. Contributing to this may also be the fact that the warning area itself may be a signal of product riskiness. Alternatively, the warnings prominence

Table 6.5   Normalized test statistics for differences across labels in mean numbers of responses to different groups of possible responses to usage directions question

Response group	Label 3–label 2	Label 4–label 3
A. Toilet bowl cleaner		
Don't Hurt, Do	1.6287	2.8856
Don't (200s)	0.9379	2.6966
Hurts (300s)	1.5099	0.9149
Do (400s)	0.9804	1.3827
Uses (100s)	−0.1844	−1.8396
Antidotes (500s)	0.3511	−0.8994

Response group	Label 4–label 2	Label 5–label 4
B. Insect spray		
Don't, Hurt, Do	−0.2830	−0.243
Don't (200s)	1.283	−1.0108
Hurt (300s)	0.2670	−0.7220
Do (400s)	−2.0912	1.1510
Uses (100s)	0.5240	−1.0372
Antidotes (500s)	−0.3270	2.5280

Note: Differences in numbers of responses are normalized to produce a test statistic distributed $N(0, 1)$.

may have caught the eye of the consumer who is likely to read risk information. The issue of label area devoted to warnings is explored using a toilet bowl cleaner label (label 2) in which 37 percent of its area has risk and precautions information, and then one (label 3) that expands that percentage to 55.5 percent (there are no other differences between these two labels).

Table 6.4 shows that label 3 led to more recall of the Don't, Do, and Hurt responses, both in the aggregate and when considered separately. The differences between the combined responses and the Hurt responses are statistically significant at the 90 percent confidence level, as shown in table 6.5. In addition 9 out of the 13 possible individual responses in table 6.6 were higher for label 3 than for label 2, although none of these individual differences was statistically significant (again because of the small number of times the response was recalled).

As with the design effect described in the last section, increasing the risk/precautions percentage improved the recall of risk and precautions information, and this was achieved at the expense of approximately 25 percent less recall of the usage information (see table 6.4). The difference here is easily significant at the 95 percent confidence level (see table 6.5).

Table 6.6 Proportions of subjects mentioning specific responses, by label and all labels combined

Response number[a]	Response	Combined	Label 1	Label 2	Label 3	Label 4
A. Toilet bowl cleaner						
201	Swallow/eat/drink	22.07	9.77	26.82	21.82	29.46
202	Breathe fumes	14.56	6.51	15.45	19.55	16.52
203	Get in eyes	23.55	13.02	23.64	27.73	29.46
206	Get on skin	21.39	11.16	18.64	23.64	31.70
300	Poisonous	33.67	24.65	37.73	37.27	34.82
301	Dangerous	40.39	29.30	43.64	45.45	42.86
302	Harmful if swallowed	24.12	9.77	25.00	27.27	33.93
303	Eye injuries	25.71	14.88	24.09	30.00	33.48
304	Skin damage	27.99	16.28	25.91	30.45	38.84
305	Toxic gas possible	21.96	7.91	21.82	24.55	33.04
401	Be careful in general	19.68	17.21	17.73	21.82	21.88
402	Keep in childproof location	38.00	24.65	42.27	40.91	43.75
403	Read label	20.25	18.60	19.09	19.09	24.11

Response number[a]	Response	Combined	Label 1	Label 2	Label 3	Label 4	Label 5
B. Insect spray							
201	Swallow/eat/drink	16.99	6.47	19.10	18.99	21.64	18.56
206	Breathe vapors or spray mist	13.41	8.82	14.04	11.73	15.79	16.77
207	Get in eyes	22.54	6.47	25.84	22.91	28.07	29.34
209	Get on skin/face	22.77	4.71	25.28	22.91	36.26	24.55
300	Poisonous/toxic	49.83	35.88	55.06	54.19	53.80	49.70
301	Dangerous	52.14	37.65	53.93	57.54	59.06	52.10
302	Harmful if swallowed	22.89	10.00	26.40	24.58	28.07	25.15
303	Damage to lungs, breathing	16.88	8.24	20.22	18.99	16.96	19.76
304	Eye injuries	28.32	10.59	32.02	31.28	32.16	35.33
305	Skin damage	31.68	13.53	32.58	34.08	41.52	36.53
307	Harmful to animals/fish	10.64	4.12	15.17	18.44	7.02	7.78
400	Be careful in general	34.34	21.76	41.57	41.90	31.58	34.13
401	Read label/follow directions	60.69	65.29	65.17	58.10	57.89	56.89
402	Keep in childproof location	22.77	19.41	24.16	22.35	23.39	24.55
410	Keep children/animals from treated areas	20.00	11.76	26.40	17.88	22.81	20.96

a. Restricted to responses mentioned by more than 10 percent of sample.

Thus we have more evidence of a trade-off between conveying risk and precautions information and information about product uses.

The risk and precautions percentage hypothesis is supported by the toilet bowl cleaner experiment; a second test using insect spray labels 4 and 5 did not yield the same result. As with the two toilet bowl cleaner labels, we increased the percentage of risk and precautions information on the insect spray label 4 by 50 percent, this time starting from a higher base of 44 percent and increasing the percentage to 66 percent for label 5. Because the risk and precautions information was to occupy a large fraction of label 5, we increased the print size to fill up this area. We will discuss a separate test on the effect of print size in the next section. Here we need only mention that the larger print size, the more likely the consumers will recall the information.

The statistics in tables 6.4 and 6.5 indicate that the increase in the percentage of the label devoted to risk and precautions information from 44 percent (label 4) to 66 percent (label 5) created no significant increase in the subjects' recall of precautions and risks. Neither the combined response group (Do, Don't, Hurt) nor the individual group differences in response rates were significant.

The responses to the two tests gave mixed results about the effects of increasing the proportion of the label devoted to risk and precautions information. For the toilet bowl cleaner, increasing the percentage from 37 to 55.5 percent induced a significant increase in the recall of risk and precautionary information. Yet increasing the percentage from 44 to 66 percent for the insect spray labels did not produce an increase in the recall of this information. There could be a threshold beyond which further increases in the attention given to this information causes no additional response; however, even if this were true, it is likely that the threshold differs across products as well as across users. While both experiments increased the percentage of risk and precautions information by 50 percent, the toilet bowl cleaner percentage started at 37 percent as compared with 44 percent for the insect spray label. Further research will be required to resolve the different outcomes of this risk/precautions percentage increase for the two product labels.

At this juncture the available results suggest a general principle, that increasing the fraction of the warning information has a beneficial but diminishing effect on the recall of risk information. At some point risk information recall gains drop to zero. One would expect that the optimal label area allocation will provide risk information that falls short of the point where there is no additional recall of warnings information because there is a trade-off in terms of total information recall. Usage information recall declines as risk information becomes more dominant.

6.3   Print Size

We compared the responses to labels 2 and 4 of the insect spray product to test the effect of increasing the print size on recall of information on the label, as these two labels differed only in that the print size was larger for label 4 than for label 2.

The results in tables 6.4 and 6.5 show mixed results for the effect of print size on precaution taking. The combined group of precautionary responses (Don't, Hurt, Do) were not significantly affected by increasing the print size compared to that used in label 2. However, the Don't response rates were augmented and the Do response rates were diminished. Table 6.6 indicates that subjects receiving label 4 responded significantly more to the "Don't get on skin" (209) precaution and were more aware of the "Skin damage" (305) hazard.

While increasing the print size may sometimes induce more recall of some types of information on labels, the results of this test are not decisive enough to indicate any clearcut effect of increasing print size.

This result is somewhat reminiscent of the label area findings for insecticide. The absence of any incremental influences of these format changes does not imply that such manipulations are never important. Clearly at some sufficiently small scale of print, the size of the label wording does matter. However, for the range of labels studied here, print size variations were not consequential. Once readability has been achieved, print size may not be a major concern.

6.4   Multivariate Results

Because of the randomization procedure used to assign subjects to the four label groups for the toilet bowl cleaner and the five subject groups for the insect spray, the differences in mean responses in table 6.4 should not have been affected by the variation in demographic and product usage characteristics across subjects. To ensure that the randomization procedure would not affect the results, we introduced dummy variables for the label groups into a set of regressions equations. These multivariate results, which are reported in appendix H, confirm all of the findings from univariate analysis about the effects of label format, the proportion of risk and precautions information, and print size.

6.5   Conclusions

This chapter was aimed at testing the importance of information formatting on the effectiveness of chemical product labels. That is, given the same information on a label, does the effectiveness of the label, as measured by information recall, depend upon how that information is presented on the label?

While there are many variations in label design that could affect its effectiveness, we chose to test three design variables: the design format of the label, the proportion of risk and precautions information on the label, and the size of the print. Of these variables only the design variable was shown to unambiguously influence recall. This result clearly demonstrates that information provision regulatory programs need to be carefully designed to induce the maximal response to the information conveyed by the program. Variations in print size and warning area may be less consequential once the label has achieved an adequate degree of readability.

7

The Correspondence between Actual and Experimental Behavior

We stressed in chapter 2 that the validity of the estimated directions of the effects of labels on precautionary responses requires only that the *relative* effects of different labels on actual precautionary responses to commercial products be directly related to the *differences* in recall of label information from our experiments. If one is only concerned with directions of influence and not with magnitudes, it is not necessary to establish the exact relationship between the *level* of memory recall of label information and the *level* of actual precaution taking when using the products.

Despite having made this weaker assumption, it is still informative to compare the characteristics of our sample and the subjects' recall responses to several other corroborating measures. This comparison will enable us to better assess whether the magnitudes of the differential effects of labels are also meaningful. Thus our concerns go beyond those of statistical hypothesis testing of the directions of effects. Although weaker assumptions are needed for assessing whether the differences that are observed are statistically significant, ideally we would also like to know *how much difference* changes in a label will make.

Analysis of actual precautionary behavior is also a useful check on the overall validity of the survey instrument. Although minor differences in precautionary intentions and precautionary outcomes are to be expected, a stark difference between experimental and actual behavior would be cause for alarm. Suppose, for example, that 95 percent of all respondents indicated that they would store toilet bowl cleaner in a childproof location, whereas in practice only 5 percent take such precautions. Such stark differences would call into question the validity of the survey instrument and the precautionary intentions that were elicited. Such contradictory results might, for example, be capturing reading comprehension and recall of label information rather than actual precautionary behavior. Thus, although an exact correspondence between the experimental results and actual behavior is not required, substantial differences would call into question the validity of our entire endeavor.

The level of actual precautionary behavior is also of independent interest in its own right. If all consumers currently take the required precautions, then attempts to ascertain whether there are desirable improvements in label content and structure are a needless exercise since current programs appear to be fully effective. At the opposite extreme, if consumers completely disregard the precautionary warnings now in place, one might question whether labeling is a viable regulatory alternative.

In this chapter we report on a new telephone survey that was designed to ascertain the present usage patterns of the product groups examined in our field survey. These reported precautions can then be compared with the stated intentions for the experimental test products with labels patterned after those now in use.

We make four comparisons between the experimental results and reported behavior. First, we compare the demographic characteristics of the experimental sample to another sample of users of the toilet bowl cleaner and insect spray products who were contacted by telephone. This comparison will suggest whether our sample does, in fact, reflect the likely consumer mix, or whether it is skewed toward people who may respond differently to warnings, such as people with young children or without a high school education. Using these same two groups, a second comparison relates characteristics of the subject associated with product usage, such as the amount and frequency of use. Since the products have multiple uses, such as spraying plants or elimininating household flea problems, one would like to establish comparability of the manner in which the product is used. The third comparison examines the responses of the same mall and telephone samples to a series of direct questions about several of the precautions suggested on the product labels. This comparison helps us assess how closely the precaution-taking intentions of the mall sample match the extent of precaution taking reported by the telephone sample of users of commercial brands of toilet bowl cleaner and insect spray. The survey data also enable us to asertain whether the extent of precaution taking is in an intermediate range or at an extreme value at which consumers ignore the warnings altogether or fully comply with the recommended actions on the warnings now in place. Finally, we make a *limited* attempt to correlate on an individual basis the mall sample's precautionary intentions responses from the last comparison with the same group's recall of the related precautionary information on the product labels.

The general character of the results is supportive of the validity of the experiment. The levels of the experimental effects are reasonably well correlated with the levels of precautionary behavior observed with the actual use of products. This correlation suggests that the magnitudes of the experimental effects are likely to be at least suggestive of the magnitudes of the likely effects to be observed in practice from changes in label design.

7.1   Demographic Characteristics

To establish a basis of comparison with the experimental subjects, we undertook a random telephone survey of 196 consumers who had used toilet bowl cleaner in the previous year and 198 different consumers who had used outdoor insect spray within the same period. Both the mall sample and the telephone sample were drawn from consumers in the Greensboro area. The telephone survey represented a new consumer group rather than follow-up calls to participants in the mall interviews. Thus their responses are not be biased by having participated in an earlier survey. Because the telephone interview subjects are representative of the population of product users in the Greensboro area, we can use them to assess how closely the behavior of the experimental sample matches that of the overall population of users.

Table 7.1 contrasts the demographic characteristics of the mall and hardware store intercept sample with the telephone sample. Despite a few statistically significant differences between the two samples, this comparison shows the mall subjects to be reasonably representative of the entire population of product users, with the possible exceptions of income in both products' samples and the proportion of males in the toilet bowl sample.

The income of the mall intercept sample averaged more than that of the telephone sample for both products, suggesting that shoppers at the mall where the subjects were recruited earned somewhat higher incomes than a typical user of either toilet bowl cleaner or outdoor insect spray. Of more concern, the proportion of males in the toilet bowl cleaner sample from the mall (14 percent) was much less than the proportion of males in the telephone survey of toilet bowl users (66 percent). We suspect that the true proportion of males in the population of regular toilet bowl cleaner users is between these two figures for the following reasons: Since the insect spray users were more difficult to recruit at the mall than toilet bowl cleaner users, subjects who regularly used *both* products tended to be assigned to the insect spray questionnaire. Since this latter group (of users of both products) probably contained a higher proportion of men than the remaining group of toilet bowl cleaner users (who did not use insect spray), the procedure resulted in a disproportionately small fraction of men in the mall sample. The telephone sample's proportion of males was probably inflated because most of the calls were made in the evenings when men tended to be home and available to answer the telephone.

Despite these two discrepancies in the demographic characteristics of the sample, we are confident that any oversampling of above-average in-

Table 7.1 Comparison of means of demographic characteristics of mall intercept subjects to telephone interview subjects

Characteristic	Mall	Telephone	Test statistic[a]
A. Insect spray subjects, mean responses			
FAMSIZE (# in family)	2.90 (0.47)	2.84 (0.83)	0.066
MARRY (% currently married)	79.26 (1.53)	79.70 (2.87)	−0.14
CHILD (% who are parents)	79.70 (1.53)	77.04 (3.01)	0.60
FIVE (# children 0–4 years)	0.17 (0.02)	0.67 (0.07)	−6.87
KIDS (# children 5–18 years)	0.49 (0.03)	0.33 (0.05)	6.84
AGE (years)	45.84 (0.55)	47.26 (1.12)	−1.14
EDUC (years of education)	13.30 (0.10)	13.42 (0.21)	−0.52
SPOUSE'S EDUC (years)	13.32 (0.08)	13.35 (0.24)	−0.08
WORK (% who work outside of home)	69.55 (1.73)	64.62 (3.43)	1.28
FARMER (% with commercial farmer in family)	6.37 (0.92)	5.67 (1.66)	0.37
USECHEM (% who use chemical labels at work)	28.65 (1.70)	17.98 (2.89)	3.18
TRAINED (% with training in using chemical labels)	21.14 (1.54)	11.79 (2.31)	3.37
INCOME (before-tax 1985$)	36.687 (718)	32.626 (1.632)	2.28
MALE (% male)	63.82 (1.81)	60.51 (3.51)	0.82
Sample size	893	198	
B. Toilet bowl cleaner subjects, mean responses			
FAMSIZE (#)	2.86 (0.06)	2.69 (0.10)	1.45
MARRY (%)	58.22 (2.15)	57.67 (3.60)	0.13
CHILD (%)	69.48 (1.99)	66.15 (3.40)	0.85
FIVE (#)	0.29 (0.22)	0.57 (0.08)	−3.40
KIDS (#)	0.56 (0.04)	0.12 (0.30)	8.80
AGE (years)	38.72 (0.63)	43.9 (1.20)	−3.82
EDUC (years)	13.43 (0.12)	13.05 (0.21)	1.57

Table 7.1 (continued)

Characteristic	Mall	Telephone	Test statistic[a]
SPOUSE'S EDUC (years)	13.41	13.39	0.068
	(0.09)	(0.28)	
WORK (%)	65.85	64.95	0.22
	(2.06)	(3.43)	
USECHEM (%)	28.76	20.00	2.39
	(1.98)	(3.08)	
TRAINED (%)	15.53	14.95	0.19
	(1.58)	(2.57)	
INCOME (1985 $)	36,293	25,728	6.08
	(308)	(1,711)	
MALE (%)	13.56	65.63	−13.82
	(1.49)	(3.44)	
Sample size	883	196	

Note: Standard errors of means in parentheses.
a. Normalized test statistics for differences in mall and telephone percentages.

come consumers and undersampling of male users of toilet bowl cleaner did not affect any of the conclusions we drew about the effects of the two labels. Both income and sex were used as explanatory variables in all the regression equations referred to in the last chapter, so that the demographic differences were explicitly taken into account. In addition it was differences across labels rather than differences in demographic background that drove most of the experimental results. The multivariate results supported the same conclusions as the simpler comparison of mean recall responses across different label groups.

7.2   Product Usage Comparisons

Table 7.2 compares the mean responses to the identical product usage questions asked of both the mall intercept subjects and the telephone survey sample. There are four possible primary uses of outdoor insect spray. Panel A of the table shows the distributions of these primary uses (PRIMUSE) to be quite close between the mall intercept and telephone samples of insect spray users. The product usage questions (YEARUSE, LASTUSE, and USENOW) show differences between the two samples. Although all three of these variables are probably difficult for consumers to recall, for the purpose of our survey YEARUSE is probably most important. The mall subjects' responses to the insect spray questions indicate somewhat more intensive use by them (YEARUSE) than by the subjects surveyed by telephone. However,

Table 7.2 Comparison of mall intercept responses to telephone responses about usage

Characteristic	Mall	Telephone	Test statistic[a]
A. Insect spray questions, mean responses			
YEARUSE (household usage in quarts/years)	11.66	3.87	1.08
	(7.08)	(1.07)	
LASTUSE (months since last use)	1.63	4.28	−6.89
	(0.06)	(0.38)	
USENOW (% with product currently	81.73	73.60	2.34
at home)	(1.46)	(3.15)	
PRIMUSE (% in each primary use)			
Ornamental trees	40.87	46.07	−0.65
	(1.91)	(7.78)	
Fruit trees	8.14	7.86	0.028
	(1.06)	(10.11)	
Vegetable plants	22.78	33.71	−1.24
	(1.63)	(8.63)	
Controlling fleas	28.21	12.36	1.57
	(1.75)	(9.92)	
BRAND			
Fertilome Malathion	1.62	0.70	1.082
Ortho Malathion	52.42	33.80	4.23
High Yield Malathion	0.88	0.00	2.46
Decon/Raid	5.29	18.31	−3.88
Other	39.79	47.18	−1.61
B. Toilet bowl cleaner questions, mean responses			
YEARUSE (quarts/year)	5.33	11.80	−4.056
	(0.22)	(1.58)	
LASTUSE (months)	1.04	1.33	−1.2
	(.10)	(0.22)	−1.2
BRAND			
Lysol	43.60	47.95	−0.92
Vanish	20.17	18.49	0.45
Saniflush	10.14	9.59	0.20
Cling	2.17	3.43	−0.76
Snowbowl	0.22	0.00	1.01
Swish	3.90	4.79	−0.45
Store brand	1.30	2.50	−0.58
Cleanser	18.22	0.00	10.13
Other	0.00	13.70	−4.81

Note: Standard deviations of means in parentheses.
a. Normalized test statistics for differences in mall and telephone percentages.

these differences may be explained by some large outliers in the mall responses. In contrast, the toilet bowl cleaner responses from the mall intercept sample show slightly less intensive use than by the telephone sample.

Given the difficulty that most consumers encounter in answering many of these product usage questions, such as their yearly usage rate, we are not surprised that the mean responses of the two samples are somewhat different. In view of the difficulties in accurately estimating usage patterns and the sensivity of mean calculations to large outliers, these data do not cause us any alarm about the extent to which our mall sample is representative of the populations of insect spray and toilet bowl cleaner users.

7.3   Responses to Direct Questions

Chapter 2 identified the problem of avoiding demand effects as the primary argument against asking consumers *direct* questions about which precautions they intend to take. Moreover, if a questionnaire began by asking direct questions about precaution-taking intentions, the responses to a subsequent memory recall task would be biased by the earlier questions. For these reasons we chose to use the memory recall approach rather than direct response questions to test the differential responses of consumers to chemical product labels. However, a limited number of direct response questions can provide a useful metric for studying whether the precautionary behavior that the mall intercept sample intended to take is consistent with the reported precaution-taking actions of actual product users. For direct questions to elicit meaningful responses, the questions must be carefully constructed to minimize demand effects and placed *after* the memory recall section of the questionnaire. Thus we included a few direct response questions in the mall intercept questionnaire after the memory recall section.

Table 7.3 compares the answers to a series of direct response questions posed to the mall intercept sample with the answers to the same questions asked of the telephone survey sample of commercial product users. To make the comparison as meaningful as possible, we restrict the mall intercept sample to those subjects who received a product label patterned after a popular commercial brand (Vanish for toilet bowl cleaner and Ortho Malathion for outdoor insect spray). Note that the last question in both panels A and B about storage in a childproof location was asked in the form, "Where would you store a product like this one?" without directly asking for whether the location was childproof.

Table 7.3   Comparison of mall intercept responses to telephone responses about precaution taking

Question	Mall—label 3	Telephone	Test statistic[b]
A. Insect spray precaution-taking responses, in percentages[a]			
1. Spray on pet's coat to kill fleas?[c]	3.33 (1.46)	21.80 (3.59)	−4.77
2. Take more or equal care than with general weed killer?[d]	85.08 (3.08)	87.50 (2.55)	−0.61
3. Take more or equal care than with any ant killer[d]	78.91 (3.61)	85.80 (2.74)	−1.52
4. Take more or equal care than with tree insect spray[d]	90.65 (2.81)	93.75 (2.14)	−0.88
5. Take more or equal care than with poison ivy spray?[d]	90.83 (2.76)	87.50 (2.92)	−0.77
6. Store in childproof location?[c]			
With small children	96.15 (3.77)	93.75 (4.35)	0.42
Without small children	83.87 (3.30)	70.55 (3.53)	2.76
B. Toilet bowl cleaner precaution-taking responses, in percentages[a]			
1. Mix with other cleaners?[c]	5.11	4.10	0.46
2. Take more or equal care than with window cleaner[d]	96.49 (1.40)	93.62 (3.56)	0.75
3. Take more or equal care than with bleach?[d]	89.47 (2.49)	80.00 (5.96)	1.47
4. Take more or equal care than with lye?[d]	58.27 (4.18)	51.61 (8.98)	0.67
5. Take more or equal care than with oven cleaner?[d]	79.05 (3.35)	78.72 (5.97)	0.048
6. Store in a childproof location?[c]			
With small children	94.00 (3.36)	70.00 (10.51)	2.18
Without small children	57.14 (4.41)	36.78 (3.67)	3.55

Note: Standard deviations of means in parentheses.
a. Respondents who answered "don't know" are deleted from the sample.
b. Normalized test statistics for differences in mall and telephone percentages.
c. Percentage responding "yes."
d. The percentage of respondents answering "less care" equals 1 minus the given percentage.

The last columns in panels A and B provide test statistics on the differences in the mall and telephone percentages. For both products only two of the seven test statistics indicate a statistically difference for the percentages, and there does not appear to be a clear pattern of over- or under-responding for the mall responses relative to the telephone responses, with the possible exception of the childproofing question. Thus, to the extent that the telephone respondents indicated their actual precaution-taking behavior, the intentions of the mall intercept sample appear to be reasonably representative of the extent of precautionary actions taken in the larger populations of toilet bowl cleaner and insect spray users.

The overall level of precautions taken in the telephone survey also suggests that precautionary behavior is sufficiently frequent that using labels to promote precautions may be a viable regulatory alternative. At the same time the frequency of precautions is not so great that there are no potential gains available from improved hazard communication systems. The one precaution for which we may be reaching a ceiling effect is that of storing insecticides outside the reach of children. The hazards of this product are well known, perhaps in part due to past labeling efforts, so almost all consumers take the recommended precaution.

We now turn to the final link in this effort to validate the differences in memory recall responses across labels as direct indicators of the differences in the levels of precaution taking induced by different labels, namely, the relationship between the recall of product label information about precautions and the consumer's intentions to take those precautions.

7.4   The Relationship between Recall and Precautionary Intentions Data

Although we have shown our unstructured recall approach to discriminate well among the responses to different product labels, the policy implications of our findings depend upon the experimental hypothesis that any *differences* in recall translate into *differences* in actual consumer behavior. As explained in chapter 2, measuring precaution-taking behavior in an unbiased manner is extremely difficult and expensive, but we can provide some evidence about the relationship between differences in *recall* of precautions across subjects and differences in their stated *intentions* to take those precautions. While establishing a positive relationship between recall of precautions and consumer intentions to follow them does not guarantee that they will carry out those intentions, the evidence from the direct questions reported in section 7.3 suggests that precaution-taking *intentions* are closely linked to *precautionary behavior*.

Table 7.4   Maximum likelihood estimates of relationship between recall of information and answers to related direct-response questions

Independent variables	Direct response questions	
	Would you use Conquer with other cleaners? (1 = yes, 0 = no)	Where would you store it? (1 = childproof location, 0 = non-childproof location
A. Toilet bowl cleaner		
Intercept	2.652 (0.142) [334.93]	0.352 (0.985) [17.05]
Recalled instruction *not* to mix with bleach or other household chemicals (1 = yes, 0 = no)	−0.875 (0.603) [2.10]	—
Recalled instruction to keep in a childproof location (1 = yes, 0 = no)	—	0.975 (0.163) [35.61]
−2 log likelihood	405.91	1,128.45
N	878	878

Independent variables	Direct response questions	
	Would you use Zinbryl for other tasks? (1 = yes, 0 = no)	Where would you store a product like this? (1 = childproof location, 0 = non-childproof location)
B. Insect spray		
Intercept	2.093 (0.110) [362.60]	1.646 (0.103) [256.65]
Recalled instruction *not* to use for other than intended use (1 = yes, 0 = no)	−0.740 (1.035) [0.51]	—
Recalled instruction to keep in a childproof location (1 = yes, 0 = no)	—	1.213 (0.358) [11.49]
−2 log likelihood	594.65	703.85
N	865	865

Note: Standard errors in parentheses, chi-square statistics in brackets.

As explained above, after asking the mall intercept subjects the open-ended recall questions, we asked them a few direct questions about precautions. Table 7.4 reports the results of four logit equations that relate the answers to these direct-response questions to two independent variables, a constant term and a dummy variable recording whether the subject recalled the associated precaution in the unstructured recall section of the interview. For example, equation (1) in panel A relates the dummy variable characterizing the answer to the question, "Would you use Conquer with other cleaners?" to two independent variables: a constant term and a dummy variable which equals one if the subject recalled the instruction on the label *not* to mix Conquer with bleach or anything else (and equals zero otherwise). Since the correct answer to the direct-response question is to *not* use Conquer with other cleaners, the coefficient on the instruction recall dummy variable should be negative. The correct answers to question 1 in panel B is also "no," whereas the correct answers to questions 2 in both panels is "store in a childproof location."

Of the four pairs of questions analyzed in table 7.4, the two most closely related pairs of direct-response questions and recall instructions are contained in question 2 in both panels. In these two pairs both the direct-response question and the recall instruction measure whether the subject knew (or, in the case of the direct-response question, whether the subject intended) to store the product in a childproof location. Note that the coefficients in both equations are positive, as hypothesized, and highly significant, indicating that subjects who recalled the instruction to store the products in a childproof location also intended to store them in such a place. The coefficients of the recall instruction variables in equation (1) in both panels are negative, as hypothesized, but not significant. The weakness of the relationship in equations (1) relative to equation (2) may be due, however, to the fact that the direct-response questions and recall instructions are much less closely related in equation (1) than in equation (2) of both panels.

While certainly *not* sufficient by themselves to establish the fact that consumers who recall precautionary information on labels also intend to take those precautions, these results are at least suggestive that the relationship is likely to hold.

7.5   Conclusions

The results of sections 7.1 and 7.2 indicate that, with a few exceptions, our mall intercept sample is fairly representative of the total population of toilet bowl cleaner and outdoor insect spray users, both in their demographic characteristics and in their usage of the two products. Thus we can be reasonably confident that the subjects in our recall study respond to labels in ways similar to the general populations of toilet bowl and insect spray users.

Furthermore, based on the results of sections 7.3 and 7.4, we cannot reject our fundamental experimental hypothesis that differences in the recall of information from labels translate into differences in their intentions to taking precautions when using the product, which themselves are closely related to actual precaution-taking behavior. While these results are not particularly strong ones, testing both the linkage between information recall and precautionary intentions and the linkage between intentions to take precautions and actual behavior is difficult to accomplish for the reasons explained in the chapter. After considering the results from our attempts to test these linkages and the considerable evidence in support of this maintained hypothesis from other fields, such as advertising research, we can find no reason to question its validity with respect to either the direction of effects or their magnitude.

IV

TWO STUDIES OF OTHER APPLICATIONS
OF INFORMATION REGULATION

8

Home Energy Audits

Information provision programs are based on the assumption that providing adequate information to consumers will lead them to make appropriate individual decisions.[1] Work in psychology and marketing, however, draws an important distinction between the *availability* of information and the *form* in which it is presented. The mere availability of information is not sufficient.[2] If consumers are to effectively comprehend and use information, it must be presented in a convenient, understandable form. The major implication of the distinction between "available" and "understandable form" is that the same available information can be formatted in ways that will increase or decrease its impact on decisions.

Continuing to apply this distinction to our first case study of hazardous chemical labeling, chapter 5 focused primarily on the effects of making information available, while chapter 6 analyzed issues arising from the form in which the information is presented. Chapter 9 will describe a second case study of proposition 65 in California which concerns food labeling of cancer risks, with one of the primary intentions of this law to make available adequate information about the health risks. Much of the chapter will analyze how failure to consider the second issue of the effect of the form of the information on the way consumers process that information is likely to result in poor consumer decisions regarding food choices.

This chapter analyzes a third example of an information provision regulatory policy, that of home energy audits provided by electric and gas utilities to their customers as a mechanism for identifying energy conservation investments. Again the distinction between making information available to consumers and presenting it in a form that induces them to make good decisions provides a useful framework for understanding the contribution of this chapter. Energy audits unquestionably provide information about the costs and energy-saving benefits of various energy conservation investments that is difficult, costly, and time-consuming for most homeowners to obtain through alternative channels. However, simply presenting the information from an energy audit to a homeowner does not mean that he will respond to the information in ways that are most beneficial to him. If he cannot easily process the information, he may ignore it, or select inefficient energy conservation investments.

The purpose of this case study is to apply what we learned from the chemical product labeling study to the design of an effective format for presenting energy audit results to homeowners. While both the chemical product labeling study and the cancer food labeling study addressed the question of what information to provide to consumers, this study focuses solely on the question of how to present the information so that consumers may process it in ways that lead them to make good decisions.

The issues considered in chapters 5 and 6 are closely related to this study. Chapter 5 explored how consumers process the information from chemical product labels, and chapter 6 used this knowledge about the information processing process to design and test labels that aid precaution-taking decisions. This study begins from an assumption about how consumers will process energy audit information, namely, that they will compare net benefits per dollar invested in different conservation measures. Based on this assumption, we design alternative formats for communicating the audit information to consumers and then test whether these conceptually superior formats do indeed improve the efficiency of their energy conservation investment choices.

If we are to be able to use information provision programs to as alternatives to more direct forms of regulation, it is important that they be designed in ways which induce significant changes in behavior, either by consumers, by workers, or by firms. Chapter 6 demonstrated that using an appropriate information format is a central to the success of this design task. However, chapter 6 applies to only one case study of a particular form of information mechanism, that of labels, applied to one class of desired behavior changes, that of consumer precaution taking to avoid health risks. This chapter provides a second case study of another method of conveying information, written reports produced from individual home audits, applied to another large and important class of behavior changes, non-risk-related financial investments made by consumers. We find that in this very different class of information provision program, format effects create surprisingly large changes in behavior, and we learn more about how to format financial information for it to be effective in changing consumer investment decisions.

Both studies use a methodology based on simulating consumer responses to the information program. In the chemical product labeling study we employed a survey approach to eliciting consumer responses to the information on the labels, but in this study we rely upon an experimental approach to infer the response of all residential energy users from the simulated decisions made by a representative sample of consumers.

Home energy audits are an important example of this second class of behaviorial changes, non-risk-related financial investment decisions which are potentially affectuated by information provision programs of regulation. Freiden and Baker (1983) trace the record of residential energy conservation since the early 1970s and conclude that most of the energy saved in this sector has occurred through curtailing the use of existing facilities rather than through investments to render the homes more energy efficient. Without an appreciation of the barriers to investment in household energy conservation, this finding may seem surprising. The residential sector of the United States economy utilizes over one-fifth of all energy consumed in the country, and studies indicate that one-third to one-half of this energy could be saved through cost-effective conservation.[3]

Freiden and Baker attribute this failure to capitalize on potential residential energy conservation to the lack of effectiveness of a national policy based primarily on raising the price of energy. Although price incentives may eventually induce more conservation investment, they work very slowly. The authors suggest that public policy should be directed toward increasing the availability of information about the benefits and costs of conservation investment. In addition evidence from field experiments by Winett and Kagel (1984) indicates that information format improvements yield energy use reductions as great or greater than relatively large energy price increases.

These studies suggest that policymakers should look to information programs to accelerate the process of investing in household energy conservation. Home energy audits are likely to be a central part of any effective information program; however, research that investigates how to make energy audits more effective is relatively meager.[4] In addition to the large energy savings potentially available from audits, the wide variation in success rates of different audit programs also emphasizes the need for research on the determinants of audit effectiveness. In one study, for example, the percentage of audits resulting in major investments was 3 percent for one utility and 60 percent for another.[5] Of particular importance is the fact that these figures mask the additional variation in success rates among segments of the customer base that differ by characteristics such as income, age, education, and family size.

The first energy crisis of the 1970s led to the passage of the 1978 National Energy Conservation Policy Act requiring most utilities to offer home energy audits to their customers. Congressional and utility support for this program waned during the early 1980s as energy prices fell; however, their interest has picked up considerably in the last four years. Congress enacted the Conservation Service Reform Act of 1986 to facilitate state efforts to improve residential energy conservation rates and in 1989 Representative Claudine Schneider (R-RI) introduced a bill requiring home energy audits as a condition for qualifying for all federally assisted home loans. Utilities such as Houston Lighting and Power Company and Nevada Power Company are responding to the 1986 Act with the introduction of improved, second-generation home energy audit programs.[6]

In a world of perfect information, low decision-making cost, and competitive energy markets, households would purchase only those conservation investments (such as storm windows, ceiling insulation, and weatherstripping) with a net present value greater than zero.[7] In our economy none of these three conditions hold. In particular, many consumers do not possess accurate estimates of the costs, and especially the benefits, of residential energy conservation measures such as clock thermostats and load control devices. Those consumers who do possess accurate information about the benefits and costs of alternative energy conservation measures may find the time and costs of processing the information, reaching a decision, monitoring the installation of (or installing) the chosen conservation measures, and evaluating the performance of these investments to be excessive. It is not surprising therefore to find the substantial forgone opportunities for cost-effective residential energy conservation as cited above.

To assess the impact of formatting on the effectiveness of information programs, we studied a typical utility home audit program, the Duke Power Company Residential Conservation Service (RCS) program as it was operated in the 1981-82 period.[8] The Duke Power audits required a two to three hour home visit and cost the customer ten dollars.[9] The audit reports provide customers with information on the costs, benefits, and paybacks of various conservation measures that are applicable to their homes, creating a difficult information-processing task for them.

This chapter explores ways to simplify the difficult information-processing task of households. This is done by evaluating several formatting strategies that economics, psychology, and marketing suggest should render the processing task easier and more effective. Section 8.1 describes the experimental method, the subjects, the five different formats used to present the audit information, and our experimental procedures. Section 8.2 presents the results of our statistical analysis of homeowner responses to the experimental audits, using both regression analysis and a logit model formulation. Finally, section 8.3 discusses our research findings and their policy conclusions.

8.1   The Experiment

Method

Format efficiency was examined through the use of a laboratory experiment. A dominant premise of any laboratory experiment is that those ideas that work best in simple laboratory contexts also produce the best response from consumers in more complex real world environments.[10] It is important to recognize that the key issue in most experiments is not the absolute levels of behavior but how changes in tasks affect relative levels of behavior. In these terms numerous laboratory experimental findings have replicated themselves in field studies.[11]

Applying this premise to our experimental study implies that the formats that show the most response in terms of choice efficiency or energy savings are also likely to yield the largest responses when used by utilities in their audit programs. While the magnitudes of actual responses may also reflect those found in the experiment, the study was not designed to make population estimates of the levels of consumer responses to different audit programs.

Subjects

The subjects were 122 residents of the Durham area who were recruited in 1982.[12] They ranged from 20 to 79 years old, with a mean age of 41. The sample consisted of 82 percent whites and 47 percent males. The educational levels ranged from 10 to 22 years of schooling, with a mean of 16.8 years. Seventy-five percent owned their own houses. The subjects expected to stay in their current residence for an average of 11 years, with the expected stay ranging from 1 to 20 years. Income ranged from below $4,000 to above $50,000, with an average of $29,885. Each subject was paid four dollars for participation and became eligible for lottery prizes to be awarded at the end of the project. Our consistency checks showed that this incentive structure provided adequate incentives for the subjects to provide meaningful responses to the simulated audits.

Stimuli

We presented each subject with one of five home energy analysis reports that contained essentially the same information but differed in format, as described below.[13] The energy analysis reports were prepared from an actual audit of a house that was representative of homes in the Research Triangle area of North Carolina. By providing consumers with audit information on the same house, we held constant one factor (housing characteristics) that affects conservation decisions, and thus were able to identify more precisely which variations in the audit formats cause significant impacts on conservation behavior and which classes of customers react most favorably to home energy audits.

Format 1: The Duke Power Format   A control group of subjects received an audit analysis report arranged in the format used by the Duke Power Company during 1981–82 (see appendix J, figure J.1). Three other formats were considered based on theoretical arguments for their improved effectiveness, and a fifth format was studied for the practical reason that it was under consideration by the participating utility.

Format 2: Ordering by Payback   Format 2 alters the control format by listing the conservation measures in order of increasing payback years (see appendix J, figure J.2). If a consumer uses payback as his primary criterion in making investment choices, this format change greatly simplifies the information processing problem. Specifically, it enables consumers to easily move down the list of measures to identify all those measures that pay back their initial investment faster than their longest acceptable cutoff period. We hypothesized that by focusing the consumers' attention on the payback ordering, they would select more efficient conservation measures (e.g., those with higher savings/investment ratios).

Format 3: Savings Column Switch   Format 3 differs from the control format by switching the estimated first-year energy savings column with the installation cost column on the energy analysis report (see appendix J, figure J.3). We hypothesized that by switching columns on the form, consumers learn the benefit (i.e., energy savings) of each measure before learning the installation cost, making them focus more on the benefits and less on the costs than with the control format.[15] This rearrangement of attention should lead them to select measures resulting in greater energy savings. Further, if under the control format, consumers overemphasize installation cost in comparison to energy savings in making their choices (because installation cost appears first on the report), then moving energy savings to the first column should lead to more efficient choices.

Format 4: Reference Point Change   This format makes several changes in the control format that are designed to change the reference point used by households to make conservation decisions (see appendix J, figure J.4).[16] Under the control format consumers use the first-year energy savings for each measure to evaluate the benefits of individual conservation investments. They use an annual energy savings level of zero savings as a frame of reference for evaluating these benefits. Format 4 provides an alternative reference point for evaluating the benefits. This format presents the benefits made possible by the installation of each individual measure as reductions in estimated energy costs below a reference point, where that reference point is given by the annual energy costs for the house *without* any conservation investments. The second column in this format lists the estimated annual energy costs for the household with the installation of each individual measure, which consumers can then compare with the baseline estimated annual energy costs (with no investment) listed at the top of the page. In addition to this reference point change, the information on reductions in annual energy costs is placed in the first column, immediately after the description of measures column with the purpose of focusing more attention on this column.

The research by Kahneman and Tversky (1978) suggests that consumer decisions are more sensitive to information which is presented as a reduction in an undesirable effect (in our case, the reduction in annual energy costs) rather than when it is presented as an increase in a desirable effect (in our case, the increase in energy savings above the zero savings reference-level). Thus, we hypothesized that both (1) changing the consumer's reference point from an annual energy savings level of zero to the level of the household's estimated annual energy costs without conservation,[17] and (2) presenting the energy savings information as a reduction in an undesirable effect rather than as an increase in a desirable effect, would induce households to invest and save more from conservation investments relative to format 3 (which also switched the position of the savings information column, but did not make the two reference point changes).

Format 5: Highlighting the RC Rate   This final format differs from the control format only by highlighting the five measures necessary to qualify for Duke Power Company's lower RC electric rate on the energy analysis report (see appendix J, figure J.5). A homeowner installing the five measures (ceiling insulation, attic ventilation, R-19 floor insulation, storm/insulated windows, and duct insulation) benefits through reduced energy usage and an approximately 5 percent lower electric rate, while the utility benefits from the reduced load. This format change was examined because many electric utilities offer a conservation rate, and their auditors often highlight the qualifying measures in order to focus attention on them.

Procedure

The subjects were first given a verbal description of the task, followed by a photographic, written, and verbal description of the audited home, and finally the audit itself was administered.[18] Energy audit information was presented using one of the five formats and the order of formats across individuals was randomized to ensure that subject characteristics were uncorrelated with the format treatments. The auditor verbally described the information on the energy analysis report to the subjects and provided them with a packet containing information relevant to the task of selecting the conservation measures they would invest in for the audited home described.[19] The auditor then asked the subjects to fill out the conservation measures questionnaire (see appendix L), assuming that they were the owner of the house.[20] The entire experiment required slightly less than one hour for most subjects.

8.2   Results of the Experiment

Statistical Approach

The primary interest of this study is determining the effects of format changes on the efficiency of consumer choices and on the level of total investment and total energy savings achieved by an audit. To examine this, we use two statistical approaches.

First, regression analysis is used to analyze the impact of the format effects on four aggregate variables. These aggregate variables, TOTINV, TOTSAV, SAVINV and EFLOSS, which will be defined in the next section, describe, for each subject, the total savings and investment level and the cost-effectiveness of the conservation measures chosen. Table 8.1 contains the mean values of TOTINV, TOTSAV, SAVINV, and EFLOSS for the entire sample as well as for each of the five formats.

Second, logit analysis is used to analyze the impact of the formats on the probabilities of selecting each of the measures. Table 8.2 summarizes the data on measure selection by listing the percentage of subjects that choose each of the thirteen conservation measures listed on the home energy analysis report for the entire sample and for each of the five formats. Using the logit analysis, the impact of the formats on the probability of selecting the measures is analyzed in two ways. First, we estimate a logit

Table 8.1   Mean values for the dependent variables

	Number of Subjects	TOTINV ($)	TOTSAV ($)	SAVINV[a]	EFLOSS (%)[b]
Entire sample	122	1,876.35	275.27	0.1680	0.92
Format 1 (control format)	31	1,875.90	252.10	0.1572	1.33
Format 2 (ordering by payback)	23	1,582.09	258.96	0.1835	0.95
Format 3 (column switch)	23	1,718.39	268.35	0.1770	0.85
Format 4 (reference point change)	22	2,269.64	320.82	0.1688	0.61
Format 5 (highlighting RC measures)	23	1,953.00	286.26	0.1573	0.73

a. SAVINV is the mean of TOTSAV/TOTINV computed for each subject; it does not equal the sample mean of TOTSAV divided by the sample mean of TOTINV.
b. EFLOSS measures the absolute value of the difference between the savings/investment ratio for the bundle of conservation measures that the subject actually chose and the maximum savings/investment ratio possible for the same total investment in energy conservation, measured as a percentage of the actual savings/investment radio. Thus the value of 1.33 for format 1 indicates that, on average, subjects that received the control format could have achieved 133 percentage more energy savings for the same expenditure on energy conservation.

equation for each of the measures individually.[21] Second, the impact of the formats on the probability of selecting the measures is estimated collectively. This greatly increases the number of observations in the estimated equations, and hence the explanatory power as each subject's choice about selecting a measure represents an observation.[22] Since the regression analysis is more straightforward and easier to understand, it is described first.

Regression Results

Table 8.3 reports six ordinary least squares (OLS) regression equations using dependent variables that summarize the behavioral effects of interest.[23] TOTINV measures the total investment cost of all measures selected by households, and TOTSAV measures the total first-year energy savings from those measures. SAVINV and EFLOSS provide alternative measures of the efficiency of the consumer's conservation investment choices.

SAVINV is the ratio of savings to investment and measures the absolute amount of savings achieved per dollar invested by the household. EFLOSS is the percentage efficiency loss relative to the most cost-effective expenditure of the total amount invested and is a measure of the relative efficiency of actual household choices compared to the most cost-effective investment choices (given the same budget.)[24] EFLOSS is formally defined as

Table 8.2 Percentage of subjects who chose each measure

Conservation measure	Total sample	Format 1 (control format)	Format 2 (payback)	Format 3 (column switch)	Format3 (reference point)	Format5 (highlighting)
1. Ceiling insulation	56.6	67.7	60.9	43.5	40.9	65.2
2. Attic ventilation	32.8	45.2	34.8	13.0	27.3	39.1
3. Floor insulation R-11	41.0	45.2	30.4	26.1	50.0	52.2
4. Floor insulation R-19	27.0	12.9	26.1	47.8	27.3	26.1
5. Storm/insulated windows	49.2	48.4	34.8	43.5	68.2	52.2
6. Shading sun-exposed glass	4.9	9.7	4.3	0.0	9.1	0.0
7. Caulking doors/windows, etc.	77.0	71.0	69.6	87.0	86.4	73.9
8. Weatherstrip doors/windows	34.4	35.5	34.8	30.4	27.3	43.5
9. Water heater insulation wrap	68.9	67.7	78.3	73.9	63.6	60.9
10. Clock thermostat	38.5	32.3	52.2	30.4	50.0	30.4
11. Duct insulation	51.6	38.7	60.9	47.8	45.5	69.6
12. Replacement oil burner	27.9	25.8	8.7	30.4	50.0	26.1
13. Replacement central air conditioner	2.5	3.2	0.0	0.0	9.1	0.0

Table 8.3 Regression results

Explanatory variables	Dependent variables					
	(1) TOTINV[a]	(2) TOTSAV[a]	(3) SAVINV[a]	(4) EFLOSS	(5) SAVINV[a]	(6) EFLOSS
INTERCEPT	2.23 (1.52)	2.98 (2.11)	0.75 (0.72)	0.64 (0.71)	1.40 (1.44)	0.58 (0.70)
FORMAT2[b]	−0.33 (−2.20)	−0.095 (−0.65)	0.24 (2.19)	−0.22 (−0.77)	0.14 (1.39)	−0.41 (−1.58)
FORMAT3[b]	−0.32 (−2.20)	−0.042 (−0.30)	0.28 (2.68)	−0.49 (−1.81)	0.19 (1.90)	−0.65 (−2.55)
FORMAT4[b]	−0.075 (−0.49)	0.099 (0.67)	0.17 (1.60)	−0.49 (−1.73)	0.15 (1.52)	−0.42 (−1.59)
FORMAT5[b]	−0.21 (−1.34)	0.026 (0.18)	0.23 (2.12)	−0.47 (−1.67)	0.17 (1.70)	−0.61 (−2.29)
TOTINV					−0.29 (−4.67)	-4.3×10^{-4} (4.47)
AGE	0.53 (2.73)	0.11 (0.59)	−0.42 (−3.03)	0.0070 (0.93)	−0.27 (−2.02)	0.016 (2.21)
INCOME	0.34 (3.46)	0.25 (2.73)	−0.081 (−1.16)	-4.6×10^{-6} (−0.67)	0.018 (0.26)	-4.9×10^{-7} (−0.08)
EDUC	−0.057 (−0.14)	−0.13 (−0.35)	−0.075 (−0.27)	0.0050 (0.11)	−0.092 (−0.36)	0.024 (0.57)
YRTILMOV[c]	0.26 (0.37)	0.01 (0.21)	−0.012 (−0.24)	−0.011 (0.69)	−0.0044 (0.10)	−0.0038 (−0.26)
SEX[b]	−0.084 (0.86)	−0.19 (2.01)	−0.27 (−3.91)	0.55 (3.00)	−0.25 (−3.87)	0.63 (3.67)
RACE[b]	−0.030 (−0.20)	−0.42 (2.98)	−0.39 (−3.73)	1.03 (3.81)	−0.40 (−4.15)	1.11 (4.47)
Adjusted R^2	0.27	0.19	0.35	0.21	0.46	0.33

Note: All equations were estimated with the full sample of 122 subjects. The numbers in parentheses are the t-statistics.
a. Equations 1, 2, 3, and 5 are estimated using a logarithmic specification. Hence both the dependent variables and the continuous explanatory variables are expressed in logs.
b. These explanatory variables are indicators (1 = yes, 0 = no). Sex = 1 if the subject is female. Race = 1 if the subject is nonwhite.
c. Measures the number of years before the subject expects to move.

$$\text{EFLOSS} = \left[\left. \frac{\text{TOTSAV}}{\text{TOTINV}} \right|_{\text{max}} - \left. \frac{\text{TOTSAV}}{\text{TOTINV}} \right|_{\text{actual}} \right] \div \left. \frac{\text{TOTSAV}}{\text{TOTINV}} \right|_{\text{actual}}.$$

In calculating the most efficient savings/investment ratio (i.e., ($\text{TOTSAV}/$ $\text{TOTINV}|_{\text{max}}$) for each level of investment chosen by a household, we used an integer programming routine to compute the maximum savings possible with that household's investment budget.

Differences in the effects of the five formats on investment, savings, and efficiency are captured through the use of four indicator, or dummy, variables (FORMAT2, FORMAT3, FORMAT4, and FORMAT5). These variables equal one if the subject received formats 2, 3, 4, or 5, respectively, and otherwise equal zero. Six demographic variables (age, income, education, YRTILMOV [years until household moves from house], sex, and race) are used to measure the effects of subject-specific differences.

Based on the comparison of adjusted R^2 values and the significance of individual coefficients, the logarithmic form was judged to fit the TOTINV, TOTSAV, and SAVINV equations better than the linear form and thus we report the logarithmic results in table 8.3.[25] The two EFLOSS equations are estimated in the linear form.

One further technical issue needs to be resolved. As equation (1) shows, formats 2, 3, and 5, and possibly 4, tend to result in conservation choices with less total investment. Since only thirteen conservation measures were available to each audited customer, any choice process resulting in more efficient decisions than with a random strategy would tend to exhaust the measures with higher savings/investment ratios first. Thus the existence of a fixed, rather than an unlimited, number of conservation measures results in an inverse relationship between the level of investment and the average savings/investment ratio of those measures selected.

As a result of this inverse relationship, some portion of the format effects on SAVINV and EFLOSS in equations (3) and (4) are "caused" by the reduced investment levels, rather than by improvements in consumers' information processing abilities due to format changes. To separate the investment level effect from the effect of improved information processing, we reestimated the SAVINV and EFLOSS equations using TOTINV as an explanatory variable; see equations (5) and (6). The format coefficients in these equations allow the isolation and analysis of the directions and magnitudes of the effects of the four format changes on the consumer's ability to process the audit information, independent of the investment level effect.

Logit Results

Logit models are useful for inferring behavior when the dependant variable is qualitative in nature.[26] The logit model can be thought of as describing the following situation: Assume that we are trying to determine whether an individual i will choose to invest in a specific conservation measure, say, ceiling insulation. Define E as the event that ceiling insulation is purchased. Individual i will choose event E if the utility associated with that event is high enough. Let $I_i = x_i\beta_i$ be an unobservable index that is linear in β and represents an estimate of the individual's utility function. X_i is a vector of characteristics of the measure and of individual i (i.e., a vector of independent variables affecting the choice of the measure) and β_i is a vector of coefficients, or weights, on the elements of X_i that describe individual i's tastes. The conditional logit model assumes that (1) the larger the value of the linear utility function I_i, the greater will be the probability that the event E will occur, (2) the taste parameters β_i do not vary across subjects (i.e., $\beta_i = \beta$ for all i), and (3) the random disturbances ε_i on the utility function $U_i = X_i\beta + \varepsilon_i$ possess the logistic conditional distribution function.

We used two different formulations of the logit model. The individual logit analysis in the next subsection analyzes each of the most frequently selected conservation measures independently, while the stacked logit analysis in the following subsection combines the choices of the different conservation measures into one estimation equation.

Individual Logit Analysis   We use a logit model to relate the two sets of explanatory variables (i.e., format indicator variables and demographic variables) to the probabilities of selecting each of the measures. Then the entire group of equations is used to examine patterns of influence by the explanatory variables.[27]

Consider the subjects' choices for *each* of the ten frequently selected conservation measures.[28] We applied the logit model to estimate the parameters of (1) a set of four dummy variables characterizing the five format variables and (2) a set of six demographic variables that explain the log odds, $\log(p_j/1 - p_j)$, of selecting each measure j, where p_j is the probability of choosing measure j.

Table 8.4 presents the results of the logit analysis of each of the ten measures. Because the dependent variable (the odds of selecting measure j) takes the logarithmic form, each coefficient of a dummy variable (FORMAT2, FORMAT3, FORMAT4, SEX, and RACE) measures the percentage change in the odds of selecting a measure corresponding to a change in the dummy vari-

Table 8.4 Individual logit results

Explanatory variables	Conservation measure equations				
	Clock thermostat	Water heater insulation wrap	Duct insulation	Replacement oil burner	R-11 floor insulation
INTERCEPT	0.11 (2.20)	5.29 (2.41)	-1.40 (2.08)	-1.24 (2.17)	0.081 (2.03)
FORMAT2	0.75 (0.64)	0.68 (0.76)	1.04 (0.64)	-1.56* (0.88)	-0.64 (0.62)
FORMAT3	-0.24 (0.66)	0.98 (0.76)	0.42 (0.63)	0.19 (0.63)	-0.93 (0.64)
FORMAT4	0.35 (0.64)	-0.14 (0.70)	0.12 (0.63)	0.82 (0.62)	0.13 (0.61)
FORMAT4	-0.21 (0.69)	-0.16 (0.70)	1.50* (0.67)	-0.21 (0.68)	0.45 (0.61)
AGE	-0.0040 (0.018)	-0.043* (0.019)	0.0095 (0.017)	-0.0067 (0.018)	-0.0011 (0.017)
INCOME	2.4×10^{-5} (1.6×10^{-5})	-1.5×10^{-5} (1.8×10^{-5})	-6.4×10^{-6} (1.6×10^{-5})	8.8×10^{-6} (1.6×10^{-5})	-7.4×10^{-6} (1.5×10^{-5})
EDUC	-0.019 (0.11)	-0.13 (0.12)	0.097 (0.11)	0.017 (0.11)	0.040 (0.10)
YRTILMOV[b]	-0.021 (0.037)	0.037 (0.043)	-0.014 (0.036)	0.024 (0.039)	0.019 (0.036)
SEX[c]	-1.08* (0.43)	-0.028 (0.47)	-1.03* (0.42)	-0.47 (0.45)	-1.07* (0.41)
RACE[d]	-1.44* (0.78)	-2.79 (0.70)	-1.47* (0.67)	0.086 (0.63)	0.30 (0.60)
D statistic[e]	0.172	0.217	0.184	0.103	0.119
Model chi-square[f]	23.06	30.82	24.97	12.72	14.94
% correctly predicted	65.6	79.5	69.7	73.8	68.9
Predictive accuracy coefficient[g]	0.175	0.287	0.148	0.222	0.112
Payback[h]	1	2	3	4	5
Installment cost[h]	2	1	3	5	8
Energy savings[h]	8	1	6	5	10

Conservation measure equations

Explanatory variables	Caulking doors/windows	R-19 floor insulation[a]	Ceiling insulation[a]	Storm/insulated windows	Weatherstrip doors/windows
INTERCEPT	-3.00 (2.41)	-1.27 (2.35)	-2.14 (2.02)	-1.34 (2.08)	-5.13* (2.19)
FORMAT2	0.37 (0.71)	0.54 (0.77)	-0.69 (0.63)	-0.81 (0.66)	-0.31 (0.68)
FORMAT3	1.15 (0.79)	1.81* (0.73)	-1.43 (0.63)	0.19 (0.63)	-0.77 (0.70)
FORMAT4	1.40* (0.81)	0.40 (0.78)	-1.72* (0.65)	0.89 (0.69)	-0.77 (0.71)
FORMAT5	0.79 (0.74)	0.47 (0.78)	-0.62 (0.65)	-0.70 (0.67)	-0.36 (0.60)
AGE	-0.022 (0.022)	-0.0046 (0.019)	0.021 (0.017)	0.045* (0.018)	0.044* (0.018)
INCOME	2.8×10^{-5} (1.9×10^{-5})	4.7×10^{-5} (1.8×10^{-5})	2.9×10^{-5}* (1.6×10^{-5})	-1.4×10^{-6} (1.7×10^{-5})	1.7×10^{-5} (1.7×10^{-5})
EDUC	0.24** (0.12)	0.10 (0.12)	0.086 (0.10)	-0.076 (0.11)	0.073 (0.11)
YRTILMOV[b]	-0.047 (0.044)	-0.0049 (0.040)	0.0070 (0.35)	0.053 (0.037)	0.043 (0.038)
SEX[c]	0.63 (0.51)	0.45 (0.48)	-0.11 (0.41)	0.82* (0.44)	1.02* (0.46)
RACE[d]	-0.98 (0.67)	-1.01 (0.76)	0.28 (0.60)	0.0028 (0.64)	0.61 (0.61)
D statistic[e]	0.157	0.165	0.136	0.225	0.198
Model chi-square[f]	20.75	21.95	17.44	32.20	27.43
% correctly predicted	82.0	77.9	68.9	73.0	74.5
Predictive accuracy coefficient[g]	0.346	0.288	0.116	0.191	0.233
Payback[h]	6	7	8	9	10
Installment cost[h]	4	9	7	10	6
Energy savings[h]	8	1	6	5	10

Table 8.4 (continued)

Note: Asterisks denote statistical significance at two-tailed 90 percent confidence level. Numbers in parentheses are standard errors.

a. Measure required to qualify for Duke Power Company's lower RC rate for electricity.

b. Measures the number of years before the subject expects to move.

c. Sex $= 1$ if subject is female.

d. Race $= 1$ if subject is nonwhite.

e. The D statistic is a measure of the goodness of fit of the model. The statistic ranges from 0 to 1 with higher value implying better fit. See Harrell (1980).

f. Degrees of freedom $=$ equals 10.

g. This coefficient measures how close the predicted probabilities are to the observed outcomes. A predictive accuracy of 1 means perfect prediction, whereas 0 means that the model predicts no better than a random choice model. See Harrell (1980).

h. A rank of 1 indicates the best value on that factor (i.e., shortest payback, cheapest installation cost, and greatest energy savings), whereas a 10 indicates the worst value.

able from 0 to 1. For example, the 0.75 coefficient of FORMAT2 in the clock thermostat equation implies that all else being equal, individuals who receive the audit results in format 3 possess 75 percent higher odds of selecting a clock thermostat than if they are given the control format. Similarly each coefficient of a continuous variable (AGE, INCOME, EDUC, YRTILMOV) measures the percentage change in the odds of selecting a measure with a one unit increase in that variable. As an example, the 0.045 coefficient of AGE in the storm/insulated windows equation means that all else being equal, one homeowner 10 years older than another has 4.5 percent higher odds of investing in storm/insulated windows. At the bottom of table 8.4 we report the D-statistic, model chi-square, percent correctly predicted, and predictive accuracy coefficient, which are all measures of the goodness of fit of the model.

Stacked Logit Analysis   The second logit model approach used to analyze consumer responses directly examines how the log odds of conservation investment choices, $\log(p/(1 - p))$, are affected by three classes of variables. These classes are (1) characteristics of individual measures, such as their cost, first-year energy savings, and payback; (2) format effects as captured by the four format dummy variables; and (3) subject-specific demographic characteristics.

In addition this approach allows us to examine interaction effects between format change and payback. By crossing (multiplying) the format dummy variables with the payback variable, we are able to analyze how variations in format influence the direction and magnitude of the effect of a measure's payback on the probability of choosing that measure. For example, we hypothesize that the coefficient on $FORMAT2 \times PAYBACK$ should be negative, reflecting the greater salience of the payback information when measures are ordered by payback.

We first stacked each of the 122 subject's decisions about whether to invest in each of twelve conservation measures, yielding 1,464 binary choice observations.[29] The conditional logit model then was used to analyze the stacked data. This model has an advantage over the individual logit approach because the stacked logit model succinctly summarizes the individual measure equations; in addition it possesses greater statistical power. It does have one disadvantage, however, which is the possible violation of the logit model's assumption of independence of irrelevant alternatives.[30] We were forced to use the binary logit model despite this possible violation because other formulations of the logit model, such as multinomial logit and fixed effects, were not feasible.[31] The twelve decisions made by each subject about the twelve conservation measures may not have been independent, as the model assumes. However, the results are consistent with the regression results, implying that this assumption was probably not violated seriously enough to create a significant bias in the results.[32]

Table 8.5 presents the results of the logit analyses of the effects of formats 2, 3, 4, and 5 in comparison to the control format used by Duke Power Company. Equation (1) combines the responses to formats 2, 3, and 4 and compares them to the responses to format 1.[33] Equation (2) contrasts the responses to format 2 only with those from format 1, with equations (3), (4), and (5)[34] measuring, respectively, the effects of format 3 alone, format 4 alone, and format 5 alone.[35] The large values of the model chi-square statistics for all the equations indicate that they are all significant.

Overall Effects of the New Formats

The regression results in table 8.3 and the logit results in tables 8.4 and 8.5 vividly demonstrate that the new format changes markedly alter consumer choice behavior from the control format. Our findings strongly demonstrate just how sensitive the effectiveness of an information provision regulatory program is to relatively minor format changes. They also show the importance of considering program design when comparing the effectiveness of information programs to other regulatory alternatives.

Consider first the regression results in table 8.3. The three new information formats show reductions (relative to format 1) in the total amount invested in energy conservation as the consequences of an audit, with the effects of formats 2 and 3 being both significant and large (a one-third reduction in the amount spent on home energy conservation). None of the new formats appears to have had much effect upon the total amount of energy saved, implying that the conservation choices must have become more efficient. Indeed, this is the case. All of the coefficients of the three indicator variables for formats 2, 3, and 4 in the efficiency equations have consistent signs, and most of them are significant at traditional confidence levels.

The logit results in table 8.4 support the conclusion that formats 2, 3, and 4 improve the efficiency of measure choice. Collectively the three formats increase the purchase probabilities of the three measures with the fastest paybacks seven out of nine times. For the three measures with the slowest payback, the three formats decreased the purchase probabilities nine out of ten times.

Logit equation (1) in table 8.5 also supports the above conclusion about efficiency enhancement. As expected, the negative (and significant) coefficient of PAYBACK indicates that the odds of investing in a measure are inversely related to the length of its payback. Relative to the control format, formats 2, 3, and 4, as a group, twist the relationship between the log odds of investing in a measure and its payback. The result of this twist is that the line becomes more steeply sloped, and its vertical intercept is raised. Although this increase in the intercept is not statistically significant, the increase in slope is significant. This shift implies that measures with fast paybacks (i.e., efficient choices) are more likely to be selected under the new formats, and measures with slow paybacks (i.e., inefficient ones)[36] are less likely to be chosen. Thus the total bundle of measures chosen is likely to yield more savings per dollar under the new formats than under the control format.[37]

An explanation is necessary as to why the coefficient of first-year energy savings (SAVINGS) is negative and highly significant in equations (1) through (4). We estimated the same equations adding investment cost and found cost and savings to be highly collinear. For example, substituting cost for savings in equation (1) yields a significant negative coefficient for cost. Thus in equation (1) SAVINGS also measures the scale of the investment, and its negative sign indicates the expected result that larger-scale, more expensive measures are less likely to be chosen. Essentially SAVINGS plays the same normalization role as TOTINV does in the regression equations (5) and (6) in table 8.3, equations that measure the efficiency effects of format changes.[38]

Having shown that when analyzed as a group, the new formats 2, 3, and 4 markedly alter consumer responses to energy audits, we now consider the effects of each of the format changes.

Format 2: Ordering by Payback   The regression and logit results support our hypothesis that reordering the conservation measures in order of payback years induces households to make more efficient conservation decisions. As shown in table 8.3, the savings/investment ratio increased 24 percent and the efficiency loss declined 22 percent, although only the first of these two measures is statistically significant at the 95 percent confidence level. Adjusting for the decline in investment gave similar results. Table 8.4 demonstrates that the purchase probabilities of the three measures with the fastest paybacks increased, while the purchase odds declined for all three measures with the longest paybacks.[39]

Table 8.5 Stacked logit results

Explanatory variables	Equation number				
	1	2	3	4	5[a]
INTERCEPT	0.223 (0.718)	2.035** (1.151)	1.506* (1.002)	0.670 (1.027)	1.391 (1.729)
FORMATS234	0.215 (0.217)				
FORMAT2		0.170 (0.295)			
FORMAT3			0.199 (0.284)		
FORMAT4				0.249 (0.283)	
FORMAT5					1.220** (0.735)
PAYBACK × FORMATS234	−0.0368** (0.0220)				
PAYBACK × FORMAT2		−0.0478* (0.0301)			
PAYBACK × FORMAT3			−0.500** (0.0302)		
PAYBACK × FORMAT4				−0.0210 (0.0274)	
PAYBACK × FORMAT5					−0.161** (0.088)
PAYBACK	−0.115** (0.0184)	−0.125 (0.0193)	−0.121** (0.019)	−0.110** (0.019)	0.142** (0.057)
SAVINGS	−0.0150** (0.00213)	−0.0184** (0.0030)	−0.0167** (0.0030)	−0.0130** (0.0028)	−0.0281** (0.0058)

AGE	0.0124**	0.0110*	0.0101	-0.00277
	(0.0057)	(0.0076)	(0.0010)	(0.01370)
INCOME	4.49×10^{-4}**	1.52×10^{-5}**	9.98×10^{-6}**	2.965×10^{-5}**
	(4.93×10^{-6})	(6.87×10^{-6})	(7.24×10^{-6})	(1.56×10^{5})
EDUC	0.0379	-0.0244	-0.00339	-0.107
	(0.0340)	(0.0475)	(0.0483)	(0.090)
YRTILMOV[b]	0.00492	-0.00452	-0.000654	0.0314
	(0.01122)	(0.01828)	(0.0183)	(0.0330)
SEX[c]	-0.141	-0.390**	-0.0490	0.374
	(0.139)	(0.206)	(0.202)	(0.327)
RACE[d]	-0.517**	-0.642**	-0.0769	-0.645*
	(0.203)	(0.270)	(0.280)	(0.497)
Number of observations	1188	648	636	216
Model chi-square[e]	202.78	123.18	81.68	21.35

Note: The single asterisk denotes statistical significance at the 90 percent confidence level, one-tailed test. The double asterisk denotes statistical significance at the 95 percent confidence level, one-tailed test. Numbers in parentheses are standard errors.

a. Restricted to those measures that Duke Power Company highlights.

b. Measures the number of years before the subject expects to move.

c. Sex = 1 if subject is female.

d. Race = 1 if subject is nonwhite.

e. Degrees of freedom = 10.

Logit equation (2) in table 8.5 also supports the conclusion that ordering by payback increases choice efficiency. Relative to the control format, format 2 shifts the relationship between payback and the log odds of investments, making it significantly more steeply sloped and starting at an insignificantly higher vertical intercept. This implies that more efficient measures are more likely to be chosen under format 2 than under format 1.[40]

Note from table 8.3 that the efficiency gains from ordering by payback were achieved through reducing investment by a statistically significant level of 33 percent, with a much smaller (and statistically insignificant) 9.5 percent decline in savings. Conversely, households do not select perfectly efficient investments, even with the conservation measures ordered by payback. Despite the fact that the efficiency loss with format 2 was significantly less than the efficiency loss with the control format, the mean efficiency loss with format 2 was a surprisingly high 95 percent (see table 8.1). This large loss implies that even with format 2 an average consumers' energy cost savings are only half of the maximum savings possible, given their total level of conservation investments.[41]

Format 3: Savings Column Switch   The results suggest that switching the first-year energy savings column from the far right to the left of the audit report increases the efficiency of household conservation decisions. All four efficiency measures showed statistically significant efficiency gains in the regression equations: a 28 percent increase in the savings/investment ratio (19 percent holding investment constant) and a 49 percent decline in the efficiency loss (65 percent holding investment constant). The logit results in table 8.4 show that the purchase probabilities of two out of the three measures with the fastest paybacks were raised, while the odds of purchasing each of the three measures with the slowest paybacks declined. Similarly logit equation (3) in table 8.5 demonstrates a shift in the relationship between the payback period and the log odds of investment in conservation measures. Relative to the control format, format 3 twists the line, making it significantly more steeply sloped and raising the intercept, although the difference in intercepts is statistically insignificant. This change implies that the odds of selecting less efficient measures fall and the odds of choosing efficient measures rise, which means that the bundle of conservation measures selected will be more efficient.[42]

These results suggest that the savings column switch raises the salience of the savings information, but consumers do not then ignore the cost information. They appear to use the savings data in conjunction with the cost data to make more efficient decisions.[43]

Format 4: Reference Point Change   We find only weak support from the regression results for the two hypotheses that the reference point change induces households to both invest and save more from conservation investments, relative to format 3, although both formats 3 and 4 incorporate the column switch. Switching from the control format to format 4 induces only a 7.5 percent decline in investment, compared to a 32 percent drop with format 3; however, this difference is significant only at an 85 percent confidence level. Although savings actually increase 9.9 percent by changing from the control format to format 4, in comparison to a savings decline of 4.2 percent under format 3, this difference is statistically insignificant.

Like format 3, the regression equations show that the savings information column switch made in format 4 increases the efficiency of consumer decisions relative to the control format. The savings/investment ratio increases 17 percent (15 percent holding investment constant) and the efficiency loss declines 49 percent (42 percent holding investment constant), with significance levels ranging from 90 to 95 percent. The logit equation (4) in table 8.5 provides weaker support for this hypothesis than the regression results. Although relative to the control format, format 4 has a steeper line relating payback and the log odds of investment and the line has a higher intercept, neither the slope nor the intercept differences are significant at traditional levels.

Format 5: Highlighting the RC Rate   The results reported in logit equation (5) of table 8.5 show that highlighting does not increase the likelihood of purchasing all conservation measures that are highlighted, contrary to what Duke Power Company had hypothesized in highlighting specific measures on its Home Energy Analysis Report. Both the coefficient of FORMAT5 (1.220) and the coefficient of PAYBACK × FORMAT5 (−0.161) are statistically significant in an equation which explains the log odds of investing in highlighted measures.[44] Because the intercept increase is 7.5 times the slope decrease, for all measures with paybacks greater than 7.5 years the coefficients imply that the odds of selecting measures with paybacks faster than 7.5 years are increased by highlighting. Thus highlighting increased the probabilities of investing in duct insulation and R-19 floor insulation (with paybacks faster than 7.5 years) and decreased the likelihood of investing in either ceiling insulation or storm/insulated windows (with paybacks longer than 7.5 years).[45]

The logit analyses of the individual measure choice probabilities reveals that the greater attention value of highlighting is not sufficient to induce more investment in measures with slow paybacks. Of the four RC measures analyzed, the two with the fastest paybacks (duct insulation and R-19 floor insulation) show positive signs, suggesting a higher probability of investment under format 5, while the two with the longest paybacks (ceiling insulation and storm/insulated windows) show negative signs, indicating a reduced probability of purchase. All four coefficients are relatively large in absolute magnitude (greater than a 45 percent increase in the odds of purchase), although only the duct insulation coefficient, the measure with the fastest payback of the four, is statistically significant at the 90 percent level.[46] The nonhighlighted measures' purchase probabilities tended to decline and total investment decreased.

Taken together, the logit and regression results suggest two conclusions. First, highlighting probably causes consumers to substitute highlighted for nonhighlighted measures. Second, highlighting is likely to increase purchase probabilities only if the targeted measure possesses a relatively attractive payback. In addition the regression results that analyze all possible conservation measures, not just those highlighted on the form, indicate that highlighting, as practiced by Duke Power Company, decreases total investment and increases choice efficiency, with statistical significance levels of 90 and 95 percent, respectively.

Demographic Results
Although the main purpose of our study is to assess the effects of format changes on household conservation decisions, the analysis also reveals interesting results about the effects of six demographic variables (AGE, INCOME, EDUC, YRTILMOV, SEX, and RACE) on these decisions. These results help explain some of the variation seen in household behavior in response to having their house audited, independent of the format in which audit information is presented.

Age
Tables 8.3, 8.4, and 8.5 show that conservation choices vary systematically with age. Age primarily affects the investment level and the efficiency with which the measures are selected. All else being equal, a homeowner who is 10 percent older than another homeowner invests 5.3 percent more in energy conservation, a result significant at the 95 percent confidence level. This age difference also results in a statistically insignificant 1.1 percent increase in energy savings. Adjusting for the investment effect, this 10 per-

cent age difference implies that less efficient decisions are made by older homeowners. The resulting savings–investment ratio falls 2.7 percent, and the efficiency loss increases by 16 percent (both significant at 95 percent).[47]

The age effect on the investment level is shown by the logit results in table 8.5. These results show that the purchase probability increases with age in three out of five equations. The age effect on choice efficiency is also demonstrated by the logit results. Table 8.4 shows that the purchase probability of four out of the five measures with the fastest paybacks declines, while the odds increase for four out of the five measures with the lowest paybacks. These results are consistent with Redinger and Staelin's (1980) study of energy efficiency decisions in appliance choices in which they found that older consumers have longer implicit payback periods. These consumers are willing to invest in energy efficiency features of appliances that have longer paybacks than would be acceptable to younger buyers.

Income

As was expected, income was found to be significantly related to both investment and first-year savings, with a 10 percent increase in income estimated to result in a 3.4 percent rise in investment and a 2.5 percent increase in savings. These results are generally confirmed by the logit results. The two efficiency measures were both insignificantly related to income, again agreely with Redinger and Staelin's (1980) result that higher income does not affect consumers' implicit payback periods.[48] However, we should note that Hausman's (1979) results show a strong positive relationship between payback and income.

The positive correlation between income and energy savings suggest that affordability is an important factor in program effectiveness. All five of the logit equations in table 8.5 show a significant positive relationship between the level of family income and the probability of investing in energy conservation, while regression equation (1) in table 8.3 shows an income elasticity of energy savings of 0.25. Additional light will be shed on this issue in the next section.

Education

We found no statistically significant education results and the individual coefficients on EDUC are all of small magnitude. For example, 1 percent more education is estimated to cause only a 0.057 percent decrease in conservation investment. Higher education levels do not appear to significantly influence residential energy conservation decisions. The lack of any significant effect of education on choice efficiency is inconsistent with Redinger and Staelin's (1980) results that less educated consumers tend to have longer implicit paybacks. We can offer only one possible explanation for the lack of any education effects on energy conservation behavior: the strong correlation between EDUC and INTERCEPT in all our data, plus the somewhat weaker correlation between EDUC and INCOME in equations (1), (2), (3), and (5).[49]

Expected Stay in Current House
We hypothesized that a household expecting to remain in the same location for many years would invest more in energy conservation that a household who plans to move within a few years. The results show no significant effect of the years until moving (YRTILMOV) variable on investment, first-year savings, or efficiency. Either households do not consider this factor in making conservation decisions, perhaps because they expect their investment to raise the resale values of their homes, or the subjects in our sample did not internalize well the instructions to make conservations decisions for the model based on how many years they expected to live in their *own* residences.

Sex and Race
Both and logit and regression results show that men tend to make more efficient energy conservation decisions than women. The logit equations in table 8.4 show that men possess higher purchase probabilities for all five of the measures with fastest paybacks and lower purchase probabilities for four out of five measures with the longest paybacks. Adjusting for the investment level effect, the regression equations (5) and (6) indicate that men save 25 percent more per dollar invested and their efficiency loss is 63 percent lower than for women. Men achieve these efficiency gains by saving 19 percent (significant at 95 percent), while investing (an insignificant) 8.4 percent less.

The analysis shows similar results for race differences, with whites saving more than nonwhites and making approximately the same level of investment, implying more efficient conservation decisions. The SEX and RACE dummy variables were not significantly correlated with any of the other demographic variables or with each other, so we cannot attribute these results to any statistical correlation problems. More study is needed to understand whether these results are idiosyncratic to our particular sample of 122 households or whether some other reason is causative, such as cultural differences that effect the energy conservation knowledge acquired and preferences developed by these groups.

8.3 Research Findings and Policy Conclusions

Although this chapter has focused primarily on the determinants of the effectiveness of home energy audits, the findings allow us to make several conclusions about the entire class of information provision regulatory programs. To be effective, information programs must be designed to be useful to consumers, which requires that the underlying consumer decision processes be well understood. Knowing what pieces of information are used in reaching decisions and how they are combined determines both what information is most important and how it should be conveyed to consumers. Moreover, the provision of new information, possibly in a different order or format, can affect the choices consumers make with that information.

The results of this chapter support the results of chapter 6. They demonstrate the importance of information format influences on program effectiveness for two different classes of information provision programs, one using labels to change precautionary behavior toward health risks and another relying upon written reports to change non-risk-related financial investment decisions. Both chapters go beyond a demonstration of formating's importance to explore how to most effectively present information to consumers.

Consumer responses to the existing home energy audit program indicate considerable inefficiency in consumer conservation investment choices. Under the control format used by Duke Power Company, consumers selected combinations of conservation measures with average savings/investment ratios of *less than half* that of the most efficient combination of measures.[50] This finding implies that given the same level of investment in energy conservation, consumers, on average, could have achieved more than twice as much energy cost savings by selecting the most cost-effective set of conservation measures.

Three simple format changes (formats 2, 3, and 4) improved the efficiency of household conservation choices. It appears that households respond to each of the format changes primarily by lowering the amount they invest in conservation, without significantly altering the total energy savings form the measures they select. For example, the mean household in our sample could achieve its same annual savings of $252 while spending $230 to $300 less.[51]

When energy audits imply that consumers should make significant financial expenditures to achieve efficiency, information alone, no matter how well presented and understood, may not be able to overcome the barriers presented by lack of income or cash flow. In such cases additional features, such as loans and subsidies, then need to be added to the program to make it effective.[52] Indeed, many utilities have added these features to their audit programs in recent years. This suggests the need for further research on the influence on the effectiveness of information provision programs of other types of government programs directed at the same behavioral changes. In the case of energy audits, loans and subsidies may greatly enhance the effectiveness of the program, especially for low-income homeowners and for renters. For labels aimed at reducing health risks, school-based educational programs and television advertisements may turn out to be critical factors in the success of the labeling programs.

Predicting the Effects of Food Cancer Risk Warnings on Consumers

California residents initiated a potentially sweeping expansion of the scope of labeling policies through their endorsement of a statewide referendum known as Proposition 65. This statute, entitled the Safe Drinking Water and Toxic Enforcement Act of 1986, was passed by California voters on November 4, 1986.[1] Among the many requirements of this act is the stipulation that all products containing significant amounts of chemicals known to cause cancer or that are reproductive toxicants must have these effects made known to consumers through a hazard warning program.[2] Although the act had not yet been fully implemented by 1991 because of court battles over the scope of the statute's coverage, the ultimate impact of this measure may be the most dramatic expansion of consumer product labeling in the last decade. Other states, including Illinois, Ohio, New York, Oregon, and Massachusetts, are contemplating similar measures.

This chapter will address the implications of Proposition 65, as well as specific aspects of the interpretive regulations that have been issued by the state of California to enable firms to assess how they should comply with these new statutory requirements. Our emphasis will be twofold. First, one can assess the desirability of this labeling effort using the insight developed in the two case studies discussed in the previous chapters. In particular, we will find that by focusing only on what information is to be made available to consumers without considering the forms in which it is presented, consumer food purchase and consumption decisions may be changed in ways that were not intended by the California state legislature. Second, the new character of the proposed labeling provides an instructive target for analysis since the nature of consumer responses to this warning furthers our understanding of how warnings regulation will affect consumer behavior. Food labeling to reduce cancer risks offers a second case study in the class of labeling programs for health risks that adds further insights to our first case study of household chemical product labeling.

The precise requirements of the implementing regulations were finalized in 1988,[3] and the final arbiter will be the courts since enforcement of the statute will be handled through judicial action. Thus the regulatory guidelines are only intended to provide general indications of the actions by manufacturers that will be sufficient to achieve compliance status.

Even if the precise details of the compliance requirements change after judicial review, examination of the approaches already undertaken under this proposition is instructive both from the standpoint of determining what effect such a labeling system will have on consumers as well as its likely effect on other labeling efforts in the future. In all likelihood there will eventually be federal regulation of carcinogenic food substances. The food industry advocates federal preemption because of the cost that will be imposed by having a wide variety of state warning requirements that will have to be met.[4] In addition, if there is to be a warning system in the United States, there are strong policy rationales for federal involvement, including the advantage of establishing a sound scientific basis for a warning system and the desirability of having a uniform and generally understood system to be applied by all states. As of 1991 firms had an exemption for products regulated by the FDA (e.g., pharmaceuticals), but consumer groups have challenged this exemption in court. The scope of the regulation hinges on how the court rules on this issue.

By February 27, 1988, firms marketing products in the state of California that either cause significant risks of cancer or reproductive toxicity were required to provide warnings to consumers.[5] Most food products were temporarily exempted from this requirement since the cancer risk criteria were still being developed. Products that were not exempted and that require warnings include alcoholic beverages, tobacco products (e.g., pipe tobacco), and a diverse group of hundreds of consumer products ranging from shoe polish to spices. The focus of this chapter's analysis will be on the cancer warning component of the Proposition 65 approach.

9.1   What Do We Know about the Effect of Labels?

A major concern for manufacturers is how the warning program that is mandated by Proposition 65 will influence consumer purchases. Before attempting to assess this outcome as it relates to the warnings that will be used under Proposition 65, it is helpful to apply some of the earlier results about the effectiveness of labeling to this policy situation.

As the findings presented in chapters 5 and 6 indicate, labels generally influence behavior in the intended way, though there will be some consumers who will not undertake the recommended precautions. If the precautions require some effort, everyone may not choose to undertake the precaution. For example, people without children do not need to store a product in a childproof location. Similarly people who find wearing rubber gloves burdensome may not take this precaution and may rationally choose to incur the small risks by failing to do so. The additional number of the people who choose not to take precautions no doubt reflects in part the consumer population for whom labels do not serve as an effective risk communication device. Not every consumer will read the label carefully and make sound decisions based upon it, but the absence of a labeling program that induces 100 percent compliance does not imply that right-to-know policies cannot serve a constructive role.

The carcinogenic food substances labeling policy will, however, be of a different nature than the standard risk warning label that instructs the consumer to undertake protective actions such as wearing rubber gloves. The principal intent of the cancer risk labeling risk policy is to convey information that will alter individual decisions about exposure to carcinogens.[6] To be effective, the warning must either alter the decision to purchase or the decision to consume the product after it is purchased. Thus the issue is what effect, if any, will hazard labels have on decisions to engage in potentially hazardous activities such as ingesting risky products?

The potentially powerful response to changes in product risk perceptions was borne out in the results of Chapter 3. Consumers exhibited an alarmist response to risk increases, as their current "reference risk" level played a pivotal role. Thus policies that warn consumers about small risk levels that are greater than those believed to be present are particularly likely to induce extreme responses.

These aspects of behavior will define an essential element of the behavioral context in which any cancer risk labeling program will operate. In particular, when individuals are informed of small cancer risks, there is a tendency for them to overreact to the information and to treat the risk as being greater than it actually is. It is very difficult to convey information to people in a meaningful fashion about very low probability risks. The major danger from any risk communication effort is that instead of informing people, these programs may serve to unduly alarm them and cause an overreaction to the risk information. Recognition of this behavioral phenomenon is essential to structuring a sound risk policy and will be a central element of this review of California's Proposition 65.

9.2   The Requirements of California's Proposition 65

Under Proposition 65 manufacturers are required to communicate to consumers any "significant" risks associated with their products.[7] In addition this communication must be in a clear and reasonable fashion.[8]

The significant-risk threshold is an interesting concept that has been interpreted in a singular fashion by the state of California.[9] What risk is significant is essentially a policy question that depends on how people will respond to this risk. Thus scientists cannot state whether a lifetime risk of cancer of 1 in 10,000 or 1 in 100,000 is significant. The question of where to establish a significant-risk threshold depends on what kinds of risks a society is willing to face and not how many zeros are in the significant-risk statistic.

The state of California is currently interpreting significant risk in terms of a lifetime cancer risk of 1 in 100,000.[10] Even if this were the actual policy threshold, it would be at too low a risk level to pose truly substantial risks for individual decisions. If individuals with typical attitudes toward risk–dollar trade-offs fully understood the risks involved and could act on them, then to avoid this risk, they would be willing to pay less than a penny more for a product that they purchased weekly and that posed a lifetime risk of 1 chance in 100,000.[11] Thus a risk of 1 in 100,000 might well be viewed as the *de minimus* risk level rather than a significant-risk threshold. Nevertheless, this threshold is more reasonable than the 1 in 1,000,000 threshold that dominated policy discussions prior to the issuance of the final regulations.

In establishing its risk assessments, California has adopted a variety of risk assessment assumptions that are intended to be conservative, such as the use of a linear dose–response relationship, reliance on studies of the most sensitive animals, and use of the upper 95 percent confidence limit.[12] Use of the animal studies that display the most sensitivity to a chemical exposure will overstate the average animal response and may be a mis-leading guide to the likely human response. A more serious bias may result from reliance on the upper end of the 95 percent confidence limit for the risk level. To provide accurate risk information, the significant risk level should be based on the mean risk assessment—the average risk implied by the evidence—not the upper bound of what this risk conceivably could be. The current procedure leads to greatly overstated risk levels in situations where scientific evidence is most uncertain. This risk assessment procedure is not a minor statistical quirk but is a pivotal feature of the policy.

The net effect of these biases may distort the true level of risk by several orders of magnitude.[13] Thus consumers will need to be warned about some risks that actually may pose an actual lifetime chance of cancer of 1 in 100,000,000. The reliance on a fundamentally dishonest scientific basis for an informational policy jeopardizes the program and its credibility. More-over it may mislead consumers and distort their risk-averting decisions.

9.3   Content of the Warning Message

Rather than attempt to adjust the hazard communication policy to account for biases in the scientific basis, it is both simpler and more honest to address the scientific issues in a statistically unbiased manner. Suppose that the true risks of the foods under consideration involve a lifetime risk of cancer of at least 1 in 100,000. How then should the hazard communication effort be structured? The two issues that must be resolved are the content of the warning and the placement of the warning.

The first entry in table 9.1 summarizes the wording of the draft of the warning that California's regulations indicate is acceptable. In the case of food products, the warning begins with the human hazard signal word

Table 9.1   Warning content summaries

Subject	Warning message
Proposition 65: food	"WARNING: This product contains a chemical known to the state of California to cause cancer."
Proposition 65: restaurants	"WARNING: Chemicals known to the state of California to cause cancer or birth defects or other reproductive harm may be present in foods or beverages sold or served here."[b]
Proposition 65: occupational or environmental	"WARNING: This area contains a chemical known to the state of California to cause cancer."[c]
Saccharin	"USE OF THIS PRODUCT MAY BE HAZARDOUS TO YOUR HEALTH. THIS PRODUCT CONTAINS SACCHARIN WHICH AS BEEN DETERMINED TO CAUSE CANCER IN LABORATORY ANIMALS."[d]
Cigarette warning, 1965	"Caution. Cigarette Smoking May Be Hazardous to Your Health."[e]
Cigarette warning, 1969	"Warning: The Surgeon General Has Determined That Cigarette Smoking Is Dangerous to Your Health."[e]
Cigarette warning, 1984	1. "SURGEON GENERAL'S WARNING: Smoking Causes Lung Cancer, Heart Disease, Emphysema, and May Complicate Pregnancy."[e] 2. "SURGEON GENERAL'S WARNING: Quitting Smoking Now Greatly Reduces Serious Risks to Your Health."[e] 3. "SURGEON GENERAL'S WARNING: Smoking by Pregnant Women May Result in Fetal Injury, Premature Birth, and Low Birth Weight."[e] 4. "SURGEON GENERAL'S WARNING: Cigarette Smoke Contains Carbon Monoxide."[e]

a. Emergency Regulations, art. 6, 12601(b)(4)(A), to be codified at Cal. Admin. Code tit. 22, 12601(b)(4)(A).
b. *Id.* art. 6, 12601(b)(4)(C), to be codified at Cal. Admin. Code tit. 22 12601(b)(4)(C).
c. *Id.* art. 6, 12601(c)(3)(A), to be codified at Cal. Admin. Code tit. 22 12601(c)(3)(A).
d. Saccharin Study and Labeling Act (Nov. 1977).
e. 15 U.S.C. 1331–1341 (1982)

"warning," which is followed by a succinct fourteen-word statement that indicates that the product includes a chemical known to cause cancer. By almost any standard this is a strong warning. Before discussing its appropriateness, it is helpful to address what criteria would be used to assess the effectiveness of the warning message.

The basic standard we apply is that a warning will be successful if it conveys to consumers risk information in an accurate and effective manner. We want individuals to read the information, process it, and form accurate assessments of the risk. These risk assessments in turn will affect consumers' purchase decisions.

Perhaps the most important factor in assessing the effectiveness of warnings is the criterion that it should provide information that is as accurate as possible. The objective is not to formulate warnings that alarm the public. If the objective were to stop consumers from purchasing the product altogether, these products should be banned. Indeed, there are a variety of federal regulatory efforts that eliminate food products that pose substantial health risks. Thus the policy question is whether the content of the warning is appropriate for the level of risk that is involved.

The food cancer risk information that has been suggested under Proposition 65 appears inappropriate for the modest levels of risk involved. It is instructive to bear in mind that even with unbiased risk assessment procedures, the California risk-warning threshold requires that consumers be warned of risks that might alter their willingness to pay for particular products by as little as a penny. Thus the warning program is required to apply to what are essentially chemical residues that may pose only a minimal risk of cancer. Ideally the content of the warnings on these products should reflect the low level of risk involved.

Instead, the legislation requires a warning that begins with a very strong human hazard signal word: "Warning." In terms of the hierarchy of human hazard signal words, "danger" is the most severe, "warning" is the second most severe, and "caution" represents the next tier of the hierarchy.[14] For lesser risks one might wish to forgo use of a human hazard signal word altogether. The use of the "warning" terminology conveys the impression of a high level of risk, which is certainly not the case given the risk assessment threshold that has been set for the California hazard communication system.

The verbal description of the risk following the signal word is also quite strong. Essentially, the claim is that the product contains a substance known to cause cancer. The use of the word "cancer" evokes a strong response among people to the risk said to be present. In addition the warning does not indicate that the knowledge of the risk may be highly uncertain or that the level of risk may be very low. The uncertainties involved in extrapolating results from animal experiments and applying them to humans are not taken into account. In addition there is absolutely no indication given that the risk level might be as small as 1 chance in 100,000. Rather, the risks are portrayed as being entirely nonstochastic. "This product causes cancer" is the essential message, not that there is 1 chance in 100,000 that a lifetime of consumption of this product will cause cancer.

The substantive content of the warning will inevitably lead to consumer overreaction. Even if individuals were given accurate information about the risk, which is difficult to do because it is hard to convey technical information, there will be a systematic tendency to overreact to the information. For products posing small risks near the "significant-risk" threshold, not only will consumers overreact to what might have been accurate information, but this tendency toward overreaction will be augmented by the use of a human hazard signal word that is totally inappropriate and by a formulation of a warning message that is appropriate only if the risks are much greater than they actually are.

It is possible to err in either direction with respect to the terms of the unreasonableness of the warning. On the one hand, a warning could be worded in such an innocuous fashion that consumers ignore it altogether; it is this chance of underwarning that seems to have been the primary concern of supporters of Proposition 65. With respect to the policy outcome, California is erring in the opposite direction in terms of reasonableness. Products with minimal risks are required to bear a warning that conveys to consumers that the risks are very substantial. Such warnings will be required unless one can show that a lifetime consumption of a product containing a listed carcinogen poses no significant risk.[15] It is no more reasonable to distort consumers' perceptions in an overalarmist fashion than to lull them into complacency.

9.4   Proposition 65 Food Warnings versus Other Warnings

It is instructive to compare the proposed warnings for food in California with the warnings for other sources of carcinogens. In the case of food products sold in California, the warning must be an on-product label, some other product-specific warning such as shelf labeling, or a system of information (e.g., signs, advertisements, or toll-free numbers) that provides clear and reasonable warnings.[16] Companies initially adopted an 800 number approach that was overturned by the courts. The ultimate mode of compliance with the regulation is still in flux and may continue to be subject to future changes since the regulations do not mandate a single mechanism for conveying the risk. The warnings that have been proposed for restaurants and occupational exposures are much more broadly based. The second warning appearing in table 9.1 is for restaurants, whereby restaurants simply must post a sign that states that they use some substances that cause cancer. A broadly based warning sign such as this would be of no assistance in enabling consumers to use a restaurant menu to avoid cancer risks. Should they avoid the corned beef sandwich, or was the risk at the restaurant only from the apple juice that was served?

Similarly for occupational and environmental contaminants firms need only to post a sign noting that the general area contains chemicals that cause cancer.[17] Once again the warning is broadly based and does not need to be focused on any particular exposure. This case is particularly striking since the more severe chemical exposures that are likely to be encountered are environmental and occupational, and not risks from food. It is the more modest risks in the spectrum of hazards that have been targeted for detailed product-specific warnings. Sellers of consumer products cannot post a general sign warning shoppers that the store sells products that may cause cancer but must adopt a system that leads to "identification of the product at the retail outlet in a manner that provides a warning."[18] Consumers will encounter a hazard communication system that conveys a series of such warnings for each product or class of products that poses such risks. The overall character of the warning system for food products is more severe than for other classes of products, even though the risks posed by foods sold in the grocery store are considerably less than those posed by other classes of regulated hazardous products. The emphasis of California's warning program is unbalanced, with the direction of the emphasis being the opposite of what it should be given the risk levels that are involved.

As a final reference point, compare the Proposition 65 warnings to the other food product warnings that already exist. Table 9.1 includes the text of the saccharin warning that appears on all food products that include this low-calorie sugar substitute. The same kinds of risk assessment procedures that will be used to determine whether a food product has a risk of 1 chance in 100,000 or more yielded the results that saccharin exposures posed an individual lifetime risk of cancer of 1 in 2,500.[19] Thus saccharin products pose a risk that is believed to be 40 times greater than the risk threshold for the California hazard communication system.

Despite the possibility of this substantial difference in the severity of the two risks, the warning that has been used for saccharin is much milder than the warning used for food products sold in California. The content of the warning (which appears in the fourth group in table 9.1) has two distinct differences from the Proposition 65 food warnings. First, no human hazard signal word, such as "warning," has been used for the saccharin warning. The absence of such a signal word implies that the risk is of lesser consequence. In addition the clearcut conclusiveness of the risk warning, as in the case of Proposition 65's labeling requirements for food products, is absent in the case of saccharin warnings. Rather, the warning includes appropriate caveats such as the product "may be hazardous to your health," with the implication being that it will not necessarily be hazardous to your health. Thus an attempt is made to convey that this is a probabilistic relationship, not a certain link. Also the fact that it is not known that saccharin necessarily causes cancer in humans is indicated at least implicitly as the warning notes that this product has been found "to cause cancer in laboratory animals."

Although the saccharin warning is weaker, it is not necessarily inappropriate. With the advent of the warning and the attendant publicity concerning the saccharin test results, there was a substantial drop in the sale of saccharin products.[20] One would not expect there to be a complete disappearance of a market for saccharin since this was a valuable consumer product for dieters, particularly before the entrance of Nutra-Sweet into the market.

When consumers attempt to interpret the Proposition 65 food warning, they will do so in terms of other similar classes of warnings they have been given. The warning does not tell them a precise probability but gives a general impression about the riskiness that will only be useful in enabling consumers to classify products in terms of differing degrees of hazard. The California system will lead consumers will place all food products bearing the warning in a category that represents a more severe risk than saccharin, even though for many products such a conclusion is entirely inappropriate.

Perhaps the most dramatic comparison to be made is with cigarettes. Cigarettes have long been cited as one of the main voluntary consumer risks; the potential hazards of cigarette smoking have been known by consumers for decades.[21] In addition for over two decades there has been an annual assault on cigarettes in the media following the issuance of the Surgeon General's reports. The widespread media discussion of the health aspects of smoking have been accompanied by selective bans on cigarette advertising and a series of policy initiatives to restrict smoking in public places. Although the scientific studies underlying the cigarette smoking risks are subject to the same kinds of biases discussed before, it is noteworthy that these risk are believed by some scientists to be of a different order of magnitude.[22]

In that regard, let us compare the content of the Proposition 65 food warning with the various cigarette warnings. Certainly the Proposition 65 warning is stronger than the 1965 cigarette warning label (listed in table 9.1). The food warning includes the human hazard signal word "warning," whereas the cigarette warning includes the milder cautionary word "caution." In addition, whereas the food cancer warning indicates that the product is known to cause cancer, the cigarette warning only indicates that the product "may be hazardous to your health." The cigarette warning notes appropriately what is essentially a probabilistic linkage, whereas the food warning abstracts from the probabilistic aspect. If a consumer's reference point were the 1965 cigarette warning, he might believe that eating a salad with mushrooms from the grocery store salad bar would be riskier than smoking two packs of high tar cigarettes.

The second warning that was imposed on cigarettes beginning in 1969 (see table 9.1) is more comparable to the California food warning. In each case the hazard signal "warning" is used; however, the California warning is in capital letters, whereas the cigarette warning only involves capitalization of the first letter and is consequently a milder form of warning. In addition, the cigarette warning that the product is "dangerous to your health" is a milder form of warning than the California warning that states that the product will "cause cancer," since the word "cancer" has a strong impact in hazard warnings. Consequently the food product warning is similar in spirit, and yet stronger, than the cigarette warnings that were used from 1969 through 1983.

Only for some of the cigarette warnings that were instituted as part of the warning rotation strategy of 1984 is there a stronger warning given for cigarettes (see bottom of table 9.1). In this case the human hazard signal "warning" is in uppercase letters for both the Proposition 65 and the cigarette warnings. The cigarette warning also includes information that the warning is from the Surgeon General, which adds to its specificity but may not necessarily increase its authoritativeness any more than the indication that the food warning in California comes from "the state of California." The first cigarette warning is closer in spirit to the California warning in terms of the causal linkage to disease. The main difference between the two warnings is that the cigarette warning includes a more diverse set of ailments that may arise and leads consumers to believe that cigarette smoking is more hazardous than foods bearing the California warning. The other three labels for cigarettes are less stringent in terms of the risk information being conveyed.

The third warning deals with reproductive risks; the California legislation addresses this risk with a reproductive toxicity warning that is distinct from the cancer warning.[23] The fourth warning for cigarettes, which states the product contains carbon monoxide, may be of dubious relevance to consumers who do not know the health implications of carbon monoxide inhalation. The warning also appears to be weaker than the food warning that has been proposed.

In the absence of field experiments, it is not possible to ascertain with great precision the types of cigarette warning that would be viewed as being more severe than the food cancer risk warnings. However, in some cases it is apparent that the wording of the Proposition 65 cancer warning will be more stringent than some of the cigarette warnings that have been used. At the very least, this warning puts food cancer risks in the same general class as cigarette risks.

Such labeling of products represents one of the pitfalls of any hazard-warning initiative. For a warning program to be credible, it must provide accurate information to consumers about the risk. To take a very broad view that includes minor risks and then designates all risks as being of substantial consequence would be ineffective. Either consumers will dismiss the warnings as being nonsensical or take them too seriously by over-reacting to the information that is given.

It would not be surprising if Proposition 65 fails, for already many critics have faulted the right-to-know movement's educational campaigns to persuade people to change their behavior.[24] Excessive detailing on labels can undermine what could be a very effective and viable regulatory medium.

The task of labeling cancer risks is in some ways not different from the problem a store has in grading eggs. If a store grades all eggs as jumbo, irrespective of their size, then the grading system will be tantamount to having no grading system at all. Similarly, if all risks that consumers are exposed to are stamped as being consequential, with no distinctions being made about the severity of the risk, then there will be little or no informational content to the warning program, and it will have no beneficial effect on consumer choice.

9.5   Evidence Regarding the Message Conveyed by the Warning

In addition to applying the lessons from the hazard warning literature to assess the implications of California's approach, it is also possible to undertake a direct consumer test. In particular, we showed a group of consumers alternative warnings and obtained information regarding product riskiness implied by Proposition 65. This type of test is particularly useful in ascertaining whether the warning message distorts the true risk.

To obtain this assessment, one of the authors distributed a questionnaire to 99 participants in a Northwestern University's continuing education program in the fall of 1987. The survey included three different tests of the informational content of Proposition 65 warnings.

The first test involved a series of pairwise comparisons of labels that might appear on a product such as breakfast cereal. Respondents were asked to select the risk warning that conveyed the lower risk or to indicate a tie when appropriate. The Proposition 65 format that was used was the following:

WARNING: This product contains a chemical known to the state of Illinois to cause cancer.

Illinois was substituted for California in the wording because of the difference in the respondents' state of residence, but otherwise the warning is the same as under Proposition 65.

The results of the three comparisons involving this Proposition 65 label are reported in table 9.2. The first warning, which had wording that is identical to that used on products containing saccharin, was viewed as less risky than the Proposition 65 warning by 56 percent of the sample. Only 26 percent of the sample viewed the Proposition 65 warning as being less risky

Table 9.2   Comparison of Proposition 65 warning with other hazard warnings

Hazard Warning	Fraction who regard as less risky than Prop. 65	Fraction who regard as more risky than Prop. 65	Fraction who regard as equally risky than Prop. 65
1. "Use of this product may be hazardous to your health. This product contains a chemical that has been determined to cause cancer in laboratory animals."	0.56	0.26	0.18
2. "Warning: The state of Illinois has determined that this product is dangerous to your health."	0.36	0.16	0.48
3. "Caution: Use of this product may be hazardous to your health."	0.14	0.17	0.69

than the saccharin warning even though the 1 in 100,000 lifetime risk threshold for Proposition 65 warnings is about 40 times safer than the assessed lifetime risk of saccharin.[25]

The second warning comparison was made with a variant of the 1969 cigarette warning, with a statement by the Surgeon General being replaced by the state of Illinois. Even in this case 36 percent of the sample viewed the cigarette warning as implying lower risk than the Proposition 65 warning, and 48 percent of the sample viewed the warning as implying a risk equal to that suggested by the Proposition 65 warning.

The third warning comparison was made with a warning that is identical to the 1965 cigarette warning. Since there was no change in wording, this warning may evoke general risk perceptions for cigarettes rather than attributes contained only in the warning. It appears that this warning was stronger than the 1969 variant (i.e., cigarette warning number 2 in table 9.1) for which there was some wording change. Sixty-nine percent of all consumers viewed the Proposition 65 warning as comparable to the 1964 cigarette warning, with the remainder being roughly evenly divided. Overall the results in table 9.2 imply that consumers view the Proposition 65 warning as stronger than the saccharin warning and at least as strong or stronger than the early cigarette warnings.

In the second test of the informational content of Proposition 65 warnings, consumers were given the Illinois variant of the Proposition 65 warning and then asked to pick one of the three risk ranges shown in the first column of table 9.3 and asked where the risk of the product fell within that range. About one-fifth of the consumers viewed the risk as below that of a can of saccharin cola, 44 percent viewed the risk as being between that of a can of saccharin cola and a pack of cigarettes, and 35 percent of the sample viewed the risk as being between that of one and five packs of cigarettes.

For the risk range each consumer selected, he or she indicated where within that interval the risk fell, using a ten-point scale. These responses appear in the final column of table 9.3. Consumers tended to average around the midpoints of the intervals, except in the final case.

Even if we treat the risk perception of individuals in the first risk range as being essentially zero, on average consumers view a product bearing the Proposition 65 warning as posing the same risk as 0.58 packs of cigarettes. This risk level is much different than the risk threshold used for the California warning system.

A third test of the risk implied by the Proposition 65 warning was a question that asked respondents how many of the 11 million Illinois residents would develop cancer from daily, lifetime consumption of a product

Table 9.3   Risk assessment for Proposition 65 warning

Risk range	Fraction who put product in range	Score within range on a 10-point scale[a]
1. Zero risk–one 12 oz. Saccharin cola	0.21	4.86
2. One 12 oz. Saccharin cola– 1 pack of cigarettes	0.44	4.27
3. One pack of cigarettes– five packs of cigarettes	0.35	2.25

a. A score of 0 indicates the bottom of the range, and a score of 10 indicates the top (of highest risk) of the range.

bearing the Illinois variant of the Proposition 65 warning. The average response was 1,316,729 deaths, or a lifetime risk of 0.12.

This risk assessment dwarfs the 1 in 100,000 risk threshold for warning. Moreover, in conjunction with the earlier results on cigarette equivalents, consumers viewed the lifetime risk of a daily pack of cigarettes as being 0.21.[26] Even in the case of cigarettes, consumers overestimate the risk, which is consistent with psychological studies of risk perception.[27]

Although all of the tests suggest that the Proposition 65 warning is excessive, predicting the actual consumer response is more complex. In response to a survey question regarding whether they would purchase a $2.59 box of cereal bearing such a warning, 34 percent said they would not do so at any price, and the remaining 61 percent wanted an average price discount of $1.60. These are substantial responses, indeed, for a warning intended to convey low risk of carcinogenicity.

After administering the survey, the survey participants discussed the merits of this labeling policy. They had two major reactions. First, if the products really are risky enough to warrant these labels, the government should have banned them. Second, if such labeling will affect a wide class of products, many will dismiss it as an ill-founded regulation.

The thrust of these results is that the content of the Proposition 65 warning greatly exaggerates the actual risks, creating the twin dangers of excessive alarm and possible dismissal of the warning program.

9.6   Placement of the Warning

Ideally a warning should be provided in a manner that will provide information to consumers that can be integrated into purchasing decisions. The prominence of the warning in terms of its physical display also will influence the level of risk associated with the product. A very prominent point-of-purchase display that boldly indicates the nature of the warning will have a more dramatic effect than a printed on-product warning that is not given a prominent place on the package. Similarly a reference book at a supermarket that lists all of the potentially carcinogenic substances being sold at the market or an 800 number that consumers can call would have a weaker impact than either the label or the point-of-purchase display.

In the case of the warning message, the placement objective should not be to have the strongest impact possible but to have an impact that is most commensurate with the risk level that is posed by the product. A more prominent warning program is more appropriate for severe risks than it is for trace risks of carcinogenic chemicals.

California has recommended the following manner of implementation.[28] In the case of beer and wine, which some experts believe pose more substantial risks of cancer than the typical food product,[29] stores will be able to achieve compliance through a general point-of-purchase display that will be apparent to consumers at the point of sale or at the point of product display.[30] A liquor store must post a single warning sign upon entry rather than post individual product displays. This broad coverage will not, however, enable consumers to distinguish different degrees of riskiness of individual products within the alcoholic beverage class

In the case of food products, one can provide the warning using the following methods, either individually or in combination: (1) a product label; (2) identification of the carcinogen through shelf display, signs, or menus; or (3) public ads, toll-free numbers, or any other system that provides a clear and reasonable warning.[31] The warnings must be product specific, however, and with the possible exception of the last mode of regulatory compliance, they must be more compelling in their prominence than the liquor warnings. The basic problem is not that the beer and wine warning is too lenient. Indeed, it too may be excessive, but California's overall warning system makes no attempt to differentiate different degrees of risk and their treatment.

The most traditional form of product warning is the application of on-product labels. If these labels are to be of assistance to consumers in making their purchase decisions, they should be prominently displayed on the package, presumably on the front of the box or in some other location likely to be examined by the shopper.

Having an on-product label simply serves to reinforce the image created by the wording of the warning. In particular, use of an on-product label reinforces the consumer's belief that the product poses a greater risk than saccharin and harbors a risk comparable to the estimated risks of cigarette smoking. For many food products this is clearly unreasonable, given the minimal risk threshold that has been established for the warning requirement.

The importance of having an on-product label is exemplified by the following example: In presenting our warning research at seminars ranging from a Harvard Law School class to a faculty seminar at the National Bureau of Economic Research, we have polled audiences on their perceptions of riskiness of different products. One label that we tested on these groups was for sodium bicarbonate, which included instructions such as "keep in a dry place" and "sweep up spills" when used in a workplace context. No risks were mentioned on the label. The majority of the respondents regarded working with this substance as an above-average risk job in the chemical industry. After calling their attention to the fact that sodium bicarbonate is simply household baking soda, their defense to their overreaction was that the product should not have had a formal label if it wasn't risky. The very fact that a product bears a label has strong informational content.

Firms also face an important practical problem of complying with state-specific regulations in labeling nationally marketed products. Quite simply it can be very expensive to manufacture products with state-specific packaging for hazard warning labels. For example, frozen pizzas may be marketed in both California and Nevada, and it may be very costly for the pizza manufacturer to have separate packaging operations for shipments that are targeted for different states. Moreover, if this product can be purchased at a discount out of state, the manufacturer has no control over its ultimate distribution. As the warning efforts proliferate in different states and different warning requirements are imposed, compliance costs will increase with the most substantial burdens being placed on large firms that market on a national basis. These concerns suggest that warning options other than on-product labels will be far less costly as these labeling policies proliferate.

The second policy option of in-store displays and shelf labeling creates potential burdens for grocery operators, interferes with effective marketing of products, and clutters the appearance of a store. From a consumer information standpoint, such an approach could be effective if the number of hazardous products were small.

A final regulatory option is to adopt a combination of advertisements and a toll-free 800 number that consumers can call to obtain product risk information. This option imposes fewer disruption costs on firms since the marketing of products and their production does not need to be altered.

The more restrained nature of this mode of intervention also is in keeping with the low level of risks involved. The 800 number was widely adopted by consumer product companies in 1989 so that consumers could call a toll-free number to obtain information on the status of a product. Did the product include a listed chemical, and if so, what is the pertinent warning?

The 800 number was not upheld by the courts, however. Their reasoning was that the necessity of calling a number to obtain the warning creates a barrier to becoming informed. The result has been that Proposition 65 has remained a nonevent. The mandated wording is strong, but there is still no generally accepted mode of risk communication.

One policy alternative that offers considerable promise would be the provision of a reference book listing products with carcinogenic substances at stores that sell them. This is a viable option since the regulations state that firms can adopt "any other system that provides clear and reasonable warnings."[32] Consumers then would be notified on entering a store that sells potentially carcinogenic products that they can refer to this book for risk information. This approach of course decreases the prominence with which the risk warning is given. Another alternative would be for the Grocery Manufacturers of America or some other industry group association to publish listings of carcinogenic products. Consumers groups such as the Consumers Union might undertake the effort as well. This list would be widely accessible and the subject of substantial media coverage.

The use of reference materials for risks is not unprecedented. The principal analogue is the material safety data sheets for workplace risks which are used in compliance with the Occupational Safety and Health Administration's (OSHA) hazard communication standards.[33] Exposure to carcinogens in the workplace may be many times larger than that ingested in a product bought in a food store.

9.7 Can We Do Better?

The labeling provisions of Proposition 65 do not appear sufficiently desirable to serve as a model for a national labeling system, but it seems that ultimately there will be some federal regulation. If California's approach is not the ideal solution, how can it be improved?

The idea of labeling carcinogenic food substances is appealing since it provides useful information for consumers who have serious concerns about certain food products. There is clearly a need for an effective food cancer warning system if it could be devised. To be effective, a warning system should have the following components: First, the scientific basis for the regulation should be determined from unbiased assessments of the risk. A risk assessment should not be distorted in an effort to be "conservative"; rather, it should operate on the basis of true risk relationships. If consumers then choose to be conservative in their consumption decisions or if more conservative regulatory policies are desired, that can be done once the scientific findings are understood. With an unbiased scientific assessment of a risk, society can decide on the most logical course of action to protect itself from that risk.

Second, when more than one risk must be mentioned on a label, the risks should be differentiated with a risk-warning system rather than lumped into a single warning. Risk levels that are present in food are simply too diverse to be captured by a single food cancer warning. To lump into the same category products that pose many thousands of times lower risks than other products is too deceptive a risk-warning scheme.

A simple way to differentiate among risks would be to use a two-tiered warning system in which relatively low levels of risk would be in the first tier and higher levels of risk would be treated in a second tier of warnings. With this approach the risk threshold could be set at a lifetime cancer risk level, such as 1 chance in 100,000, which is the risk level that should affect purchase decisions. For products meeting the minimal risk threshold, consumers could be apprised of the nature of the risk through a labeling system appropriate for the low level of the risk involved. Consumers could consult a reference binder at stores like the material safety data sheets used under OSHA hazard communication regulations. For products with low levels of cancer risk, the mode of communication chosen should avoid stigmatizing the products with on-product labels which by their very nature imply a higher-risk level.

The second tier of the warning system would consist of a more visible warning such as on-product labeling or a point-of-purchase display. The warning for this class of products could be ascertained after a better assessment of the distribution of risks across food products was obtained. As in the case of grading eggs, we cannot decide which eggs should be classified as jumbo or which eggs should be classified as extra large until the eggs in a population are sorted by size. Similarly, before more substantial risks can be assessed, more information needs to be known about different risk levels. California has proposed a warning system before ascertaining the level and distribution of risks that are present.

The exact wording of a warning for either low- or high-level risks cannot be determined in the abstract. Although enough is known about the effects of labels to enable a government agency to decide on the appropriateness of a warning message, more precise knowledge is needed on what effect the label's wording will have on consumers. Experiments should be carried out to determine the effect of labels on consumer groups in much the same way as we have been done in our labeling experiments earlier in this book. It is irresponsible for any government agency to mandate a specific warning without tests or an experimental foundation to assess the likely consumer responses. Consumer surveys can provide the means for policymakers to refine their knowledge of the effect of a major food cancer risk policy.

9.8   Conclusion

Proposition 65 may not have established a sound basis for food cancer risk labeling, but it does raise the question of a national food cancer risk warning program. Examination of the warning requirements of Proposition 65 in comparison with other warning labels, and evidence of how people respond to warning programs, suggest that the wording of warnings may convey too high a risk level and may not achieve the objective of informing consumers.

Ideally informational policies, such as a food cancer warning effort, can play an instructive role in better informing consumers about hazardous products and enabling them to make better decisions. If nothing else, Proposition 65 has put this policy at the top of the food safety agenda. Any national policy that emerges from this initiative could be based on greater recognition of the principles for hazard communication. But sound policies can evolve only if policymakers recognize that the task of designing and implementing a successful warnings system consists of much more than duplicating cigarette warnings in other contexts. As the findings of this chapter and the rest of the book indicate, warning information must be accurate and provided in a way that it can be processed reliably and acted upon in a rational manner.

10

Implications for Information Provision Policies

Because of the novelty of informational alternatives to regulation, there is no direct policy experience that can be used to project the effects that informational policies will have. Complicating matters further, it is difficult to make inferences about adaptations of effective policies in other contexts. Well-known examples of cigarette and saccharin warnings included substantial advance publicity about health risks that led to the introduction of the hazard warnings, making it difficult to disentangle the specific effects of warnings. Nevertheless, for the most part the warnings for these products appear on a single communication channel, such as the product label. The implications that different types of warnings would have in other contexts remain unclear. The choice of the optimal form of the information program cannot be resolved using data on available market experiments.

As a result we adopted our strategy of creating simulated markets in which individuals are presented with different information and their responses to it are assessed. Our goal was to explore the influences of different information provision programs on consumer behavior, including decisions on products posing serious health risks and decisions involving many complex non-risk-related choices with differing financial consequences. The major case study focused on labeling of pesticide and chemical risks regulated by EPA, with two additional case studies addressing the labeling of food cancer risks and information on energy audit reports related to financial savings achieved by improving the energy efficiency of one's house.

For this methodology to be useful, there should be a close correspondence between likely market behavior and the behavior implied by the experimental design. No general conclusions are possible about the generalizability of experimental results because much will depend on the character of the experiment being run. If there are important demand effects or if the experiment does not create a realistic market context in which participants can give meaningful responses, then the experiment will not elicit results that can be used to provide a reliable guide to expected behavior.

In addition to providing an extended discussion of the substantial care that was devoted to developing a sound experimental design for all three of our case studies, we also provided an internal check on the validity of the experimental design for eliciting precaution-taking intentions from the chemical product labeling study. In particular, the results in chapter 7 indicated that there is a reasonably close correspondence between the results implied by our experimental labels and the comparable hazard warnings available on currently marketed products. These results suggest that the precautionary behavior elicited in the survey would be similar to consumers' response to the same informational treatments in actual purchase and use contexts. Since both the field study and the telephone survey pertained to precautionary intentions rather than actual behavior, this comparability does not completely guarantee that all of the survey results are indicative of actual behavior. They do, however, add to the confidence we can place in the survey results. In addition in our earlier study (Viscusi and Magat 1987) we report on a reliability test of the risk valuation methodology that was also used on this study. In that case as well, the market and survey responses were similar. Thus both the informational and the valuation segments of the study have been subjected to validation procedures.

Before embarking on any government regulation, including information policies, government agencies generally should ascertain that these policies are in society's best interests. More specifically, the task is to ensure that the benefits of these programs to society exceed the costs that they impose. In the case of policies that are truly informational and that involve few costs of providing the information, much of this calculation is done on a decentralized basis. Once consumers are apprised of the true risks associated with an activity, they will be able to undertake the precautions whose benefits exceed the costs. It is this decentralized feature that makes informational policies so attractive. Unfortunately, in many cases the informational program is not designed so much to inform individuals as to exhort them to undertake particular kinds of behavior. Thus the programs may be more dictatorial than informational in nature as, for example, they may urge individuals to wear rubber gloves while using drain opener. In these instances it is especially important to ascertain whether the benefits of the prescribed behavior exceed the costs that we impose both in term of the costs of the precautions as well as the costs of information transfer.

Perhaps the most important component of such a benefit calculation undertaken by government agencies such as EPA is the value of the risk reduction to society. In particular, how much is it worth to prevent a child's poisoning or a skin burn? These magnitudes are difficult to ascertain because they do not represent economic commodities traded in markets. Rather, they are nontransferable health attributes for which there are no explicit market prices.

The approach we have taken here is to measure the implicit price that consumers are willing to pay to obtain a reduction in these risks, thus establishing the risk–dollar trade-offs that can be used in establishing the value that a government agency can place on the benefits achieved through the informational program. The results in chapter 3 indicated that the benefit values to the individual of preventing the various kinds of injuries studied in the insecticide and toilet bowl cleaner study were on the order of several thousand dollars. Although such estimates by no means pinpoint the precise benefit values, they do present a reasonable order of magnitude for the likely health improvement benefits. Moreover these estimates are consistent with other research findings on other adverse health effects.

Perhaps the most noteworthy feature of the valuation results in chapters 3 and 4 is that they indicated that the manner in which individuals respond to risk is quite complex and is strongly influenced by cognitive factors. Three findings of this type were particularly striking.

First, consumers were willing to pay an additional premium for risk reductions that completely eliminated the risks that they faced, rather than simply reducing then by a particular amount. Thus any risk reduction of a particular magnitude will be regarded as more valuable by consumers if that risk reduction leads to complete certainty that no residual risk will remain. Such a result cannot be traced to standard economic reasoning on individual risk valuation, but it may reflect two other effects that loom quite large in this context. The assurance of complete certainty may have a benefit in terms of anxiety reduction or the elimination of the cost of worrying about the potential risks and how to address them. In addition the premium attached to certain safety is quite consistent with the research findings indicating that individuals tend to overestimate low probability events. Thus a reduction in a small risk to zero will tend to be overvalued if individuals correctly perceive a zero risk but overestimate the magnitudes of small nonzero risks.

A second finding pertains to the rather dramatic role of what we term "reference risk" effects. In particular, when consumers were faced with the prospect of purchasing products for which the risk has increased, there was a substantial willingness to bear this risk at any price. This alarmist response to increases in the risk above the customary risk level greatly exceeded any possible effect that could be justified based on the risk–dollar trade-offs that the respondents exhibited to risk reductions. This phenomenon may explain, in part, the strong public reactions to new risks for established products, since perceived tinkering with the status quo may give rise to a misperception of the subsequent risks that are being imposed.

A final and potentially important aspect of the benefit valuation process that we explored pertains to the role of altruism. Individuals' stated altruistic valuations for insecticide-related injuries greatly exceeded their private valuations. Even though the willingness-to-pay amounts were small for individuals, when aggregated over the entire society the total benefits become quite large. What these findings suggest is that policymakers perhaps should devote more attention to the potential role of altruism, particularly since this component best reflects the special status accorded to individual health in our society—a phenomenon that is often cited as being an important omitted component of benefit analyses.

Two caveats should be emphasized before one embarks on such altruistic benefits assessments, however. First, because of the broad coverage of the individuals for whom altruistic motives are being ascribed, individual willingness to pay of only a few cents to prevent a particular health outcome may be a quite impressive total when summed across the entire country. When individuals' benefit valuations are being multiplied by scale factors in the millions, one must be particularly careful in establishing that the original benefit valuations per person are estimated precisely. Second, the exact extent of altruism and the strength of these motivations should be subjected to more refined empirical tests. The results presented here should be regarded as exploratory in nature. What we found in our study of altruism in chapter 4 is that there was no deep pocket for altruism, as individuals' altruistic intentions greatly diminished once we moved from preventing poisonings within one's state to preventing poisonings nationwide. Individuals in survey contexts may tend to overstate their willingness to contribute to such charitable causes, particularly when confronted with only one charitable cause. If they had to face the full range of charitable causes for which society must make decisions, the amount they may be willing to allocate to a particular cause, such as poisoning prevention, may be much less than what these single-cause results indicate.

A strong focus of our study was on the role of cognitive processes in using information. The difficulties of making decisions under uncertainty have long been established. Cognitive processes are a particularly salient consideration in communicating information about risks. Equally important is the framing of information in contexts in which risk is not involved, as our study of home energy audits in chapter 8 indicated.

In general, one cannot equate informational programs with transmittal of all of the information about a product or activity. In the extreme case it would be foolish to refer individuals to a pile of complex scientific articles so that they can infer the dose-response relationships relevant to their hazard exposures. Indeed, it would require educating consumers on how they should think about probabilistic information and act on it for specific quantitative information to be of value.

These difficulties serve as a reminder of the pitfalls that can be encountered when implementing an informational program. The preliminary work on California Proposition 65 perhaps best exemplifies how a well-intentioned informational program can fall short. It was apparently believed that one could establish an effective informational program by simply copying the approach taken in other contexts. The result of patterning warnings after that of cigarettes is likely to be that individuals will overestimate the risks and thus overreact.

A successful informational policy must take into account the specific context in which it is operating. In wording, format, and general approach the objective of informational policies should not be to have as strong an impact on behavior as possible but rather to foster informed decisions. The objective should be sound decisions, not altered decisions. It may be that when we are communicating risks that are quite minor, the subsequent behavioral response should in fact be modest.

The three case studies presented in this book are based on a methodology in which the informational program is tailored to the context in which it is used and is then evaluated with respect to the degree to which it fosters improved decision making. The first set of results from chapters 5 and 6 demonstrated that there may be substantial trade-offs in the information that can be conveyed. As we provide more risk information, individuals tend to process and recall less information about other aspects of the product, such as its proper use. Even if the concern is with the risk posed by the product, it may be better to avoid excessive risk information as this might lead to product misuse. In fact many government officials believe excessive risk information to be a major source of the risks that arise from products.

Problems of label clutter and information overload occur both within products and across products. Thus we may be sacrificing the informational value of labels by providing excessive information. This trade-off arises due to the cognitive limitations that individuals have with respect to their ability to process such information. From a broader societal standpoint we run the risk of overloading consumers with warning information if we are cavalier about the use of informational regulations. If all products have warnings associated with them, then effectively no distinctions are being made. Society should reserve warnings to situations where they are truly warranted and likely to be effective, recognizing that there is a dilution effect from overuse of this regulatory policy tool.

A second set of guidelines that emerged from these studies pertains to the format in which we provide the information. For risk information as well as the energy audit information, the design of the label mattered as much as its wording. Making information available to consumers is insufficient to guarantee that they will respond to it. It is essential to organize information in a manner in which it can be understood and processed reliably, and then acted on. The most telling examples of our research were the reorganizations of the risk information on the chemical product labels and the financial information on the energy audit reports. Much less effective were the examples that pertained to the percentage of the chemical product's label devoted to risk information and print size.

The extent to which these variations in label design are important depends in large part on the starting point one is analyzing. Once a label has achieved a satisfactory degree of readability, additional warning area or larger print size adds little to the efficacy of the label. But before this threshold is established there may be additional gains to be reaped through more prominent messages.

A recurring theme of our research on information and warnings policies is that format effects are important. Consumers must have a standardized basis from which they can make judgments about products from label information. Since the wording of warnings on labels is often established in a decentralized way by different agents, ranging from government agencies to private firms, there has not been sufficient standardization. What is needed is a national warnings vocabulary that will facilitate consumers' comprehension of such information.

The broader purpose of this study is to develop principles for formulating and evaluating regulatory policies. Most important is that one must ascertain whether the benefits of these policies merit the costs incurred both through the direct regulatory costs as well as the costs of the precautions. The fundamental concern in this area is not so much a question of individuals' rights, or a question of whether people have a right to know. Rather, we should provide information that enables people to make more informed and better decisions with respect to the risks they face.

This information may affect whether one chooses to use a product, or it may affect the precautions one takes with it. Nevertheless, an economic analysis of the merits of the decisions promoted through the informational effort is an essential component of the policy design and evaluation process. The second set of results derived in our study pertains to analyzing the structure of the informational effort that should be adopted. It is large-ly because of consumers' cognitive limitations and lack of knowledge re-garding the benefits or costs of a product that the regulatory effort can play a productive role.

Informational regulations are attractive in situations where we cannot monitor the behavior, yet we know that people will continue to engage in it, and so we want to provide the information needed for that activity to be conducted safely. We do not, for instance, ban the use of knives but we do apprise our children of the risk of being cut by them. Risks have prolifer-ated with increasing frequency; it is infeasible to regulate all of them direct-ly. The principal motivation for OSHA's regulation of chemical hazard warnings was that the enormous number of chemical hazards swamped its ability to formulate command and control regulations to deal with all of them. Hazard-warning regulations were viewed as a stop-gap measure to ensure the safe handling of chemicals as the agency contemplated which chemicals should be addressed more directly. There may be other situa-tions in which society may choose to adopt informational regulations as such a stop-gap measure.

In addition we are frequently faced with risks that are sufficiently severe that we should make note of them but not so severe that we should ban them. Consumers must be given correct information in order to act on this information in a reliable and sensible manner. Hazard-warning efforts have an obvious role in fostering informed risk-averting actions. Some individuals will choose to use food products, notwithstanding the warning of a possible cancer risk. This does not necessarily mean that they are irrational in doing so. Rather, they may be making a trade-off between the net benefits, as in the case of saccharin, and the risks and other costs posed by other forms of higher calorie consumption. A matter that should be continually scrutinized with these efforts is whether the decisions that re-sult from the warnings are sound. The gaps in how individuals process information and the impediments to sound decisions suggest that a study of the efficacy of a warnings effort should be undertaken on a broader basis for other hazard-warning programs.

Informational regulations can be successful in addressing the market failures that stem from informational shortcomings. It is clear that these remedies are far from a trivial matter to design. There is often a reason why markets may fail. It may be that the needed information may be difficult to process or may involve subtle behavioral changes that are difficult to make. Decisions involving health risks and uncertainty are hard for some people to handle, as are decisions involving complex financial investment options. Many of these informational efforts are addressing issues that are at the boundary of individual rationality. The design and implementation of informational regulations in a manner that will ensure their success will continue to be the object of regulatory policy research.

Toilet Bowl Cleaner

Stage 2: Examination of the Toilet Bowl Cleaner
(Show the subject the toilet bowl cleaner.)

Please examine this *new* toilet bowl cleaner, Conquer, as if you are about to use it in your home *for the first time*. I will give you a few minutes to look at this product. Please take as much time as you would take if you were going to use Conquer in your home for the first time.

Once you have examined the Conquer bottle, I will ask you some questions about it. There are *no* right or wrong answers to any of the questions—just answer them as well as you can.

(Give the subject at least two minutes to read the label without interruption. Do *not* allow him/her to refer back to the product label once he/she has finished reading it.)

Stage 4: Precaution Questions
Now I'm going to ask you questions about how you would use Conquer.

4.1 Suppose you had extremely dirty toilets. Would you mix Conquer with other cleaners to make it more effective?

_____ Yes _____ No

4.2 Would you use Conquer for any cleaning tasks other than cleaning toilets?

_____ Yes _____ No

(If yes) Please explain.

(Acceptable probe: Would you use the product to clean a stained kitchen sink?)

(List other tasks: _____)

4.3 Please tell me whether you would take more or less care with Conquer than with window cleaner?

_____ More _____ Less _____ Equal _____ Don't know

4.4 What about with Conquer compared with bleach?

_____ More _____ Less _____ Equal _____ Don't know

4.5 What about with Conquer compared with lye?

_____ More _____ Less _____ Equal _____ Don't know

4.6   What about with Conquer compared with oven cleaner?

_____ More   _____ Less   _____ Equal   _____ Don't know

4.7   Where in your home would you store a product like Conquer?

(Do not read. Probe if necessary.
In a childproof location?   _____ Yes   _____ No)

(Acceptable probes are:

Is that location above or below the counter? How easy is it to reach the product in that location? If in a low cabinet, is that cabinet locked?)

Stage 5: Frequency of Use Questions

5.1   Do you use liquid or crystal toilet bowl cleaner? (Check all that apply.)

_____ Liquid or foam   _____ Crystal   _____ Cleanser

5.2   When was the last time you used a toilet bowl cleaner? (A cleanser is not counted as a toilet bowl cleaner for this question.)

_____

5.3   Approximately how many bottles or containers of toilet bowl cleaner the same size as the one I showed you does your household use in a given year?

(Ask by month if necessary.

Bottles per year = _____

Bottles per month = _____

Indicate either.)

5.4   I am going to show you a card with some common toilet bowl cleaner brands. Please indicate which brands you use?

_____

(Show Toilet Bowl Cleaner card.)

Stage 6: Injury Valuation Questions

A toilet bowl cleaner can cause injuries if it is misused. According to a recent newspaper article two serious injuries using the product are (1) chlorine gas poisoning and (2) eye burn injuries. (Read Chlorine Gas Poisoning card, and hand it to the subject.)

6.0a   Have you heard of this *injury*?

_____ Yes   _____ No

6.0b   (If yes) How?

_____ Personal experience (know person injured)

6.0c   Cue if necessary.

_____ Heard about it/common knowledge

6.0d   Check all that apply.

_____ News articles/magazine/television

6.0e

_____ Other _____

(Read Eye Burn Injury card, and hand it to the subject.)

6.0f   Have you heard of this *injury*?

_____ Yes   _____ No

6.0g   (If yes) How?

_____ Personal experience (know person injured)

6.0h   Cue if necessary.

_____ Heard about it/common knowledge

6.0i   Check all that apply.

_____ News articles/magazine/television

6.0j

_____ Other _____

6.0k

_____ Read on label

Suppose that you currently use a toilet bowl cleaner that costs you $2.00, and it results in 15 chlorine gas poisonings and 15 eye burn injuries for every 10,000 containers of toilet bowl cleaner that are used. (Show Current Toilet Bowl Cleaner card, and point to numbers on the card.)

6.1   I want you to think about a new formulation of toilet bowl cleaner, which a manufacturer might develop, that cleans as well as your current product but eliminates all chance of gas poisonings. The number of eye burn injuries caused by the product remains the same. (Show last card. Point to card but cover the number of gas poisonings with finger.) Would you be willing to pay more than what you currently pay to reduce this risk of injury to your household?

_____ Yes   _____ No (put $0 in 6.2a and go to 6.3)

6.2a   What is the most over the current price that you would be willing to pay to avoid this risk of chlorine gas poisoning?

$_____ more per container to reduce the risk of chlorine gas poisoning to zero

(If necessary cue with: Would you pay $2, $1, 50 cents, 25 cents, 10 cents, 5 cents, 1 penny?
Mark here if cue was used. _____)

In asking this question, I didn't intend for you to assume that fewer gas poisonings would occur to other households if you purchased the new toilet bowl cleaner. Did you assume other households were affected? (If yes, record ____ and ask 6.2b; if no, record ____ and skip to question 6.3.)

6.2b   Now consider the value of the safer new cleaner to your household, recognizing that your response and purchase decision have *no effect* on the number of injuries incurred by other households.

What is the most that you would be willing to pay above your current costs for the new toilet bowl cleaner that avoids the risk of chlorine gas poisonings for just your household?

$____ more per container to reduce chlorine gas poisoning risk to zero

(If necessary cue with: Would you pay $2, $1, 50 cents, 25 cents, 10 cents, 5 cents, 1 penny? Mark here if cue was used. ____)

6.3   Suppose that the manufacturer was able to develop another formulation of the product that could to reduce the risk of eye burn injuries from 15 injuries to zero for every 10,000 containers used, but the risk of chlorine poisoning remained at the original level of 15. You indicated you would pay $____ more a container (take from 6.2) for a toilet bowl cleaner that totally avoids chlorine poisonings. (Show Current Toilet Bowl Cleaner card. Point to card but cover the number of eye burn injuries.) What is the most above current costs that you would be willing to pay for the product that completely avoids eye burn injuries?

$____ more per container to reduce the risk of eye burn injuries to zero

(Cue with: Would you pay $2, $1, 50 cents, 25 cents, 10 cents, 5 cents, 1 penny?
Mark here if cue was used. ____)

6.4   Now suppose that a company could offer a product that reduces *both* risks of eye burn injuries and chlorine gas poisoning to zero. You said you were willing to pay $____ more a container (take from 6.2) to avoid the chlorine gas risk, and $____ more a container (take from 6.3) to avoid the risk of eye burn injuries. What is the most above the current cost of toilet cleaner that you would be willing to pay for a product that reduced the risk of *both* injuries to zero? (Show card. Cover the number of eye burn injuries and gas poisonings with finger.)

$____ more per container to reduce both risks to zero

(Cue with: Would you pay $2, $1, 50 cents, 25 cents, 10 cents, 5 cents, 1 penny?
Mark here if cue was used. ____)

(If 0 in 6.2, 6.3, and 6.4, then go to 6.7.)

6.5   Unfortunately, it is not always possible to develop a product that reduces the risks of all injuries to zero. You indicated that you would be willing to

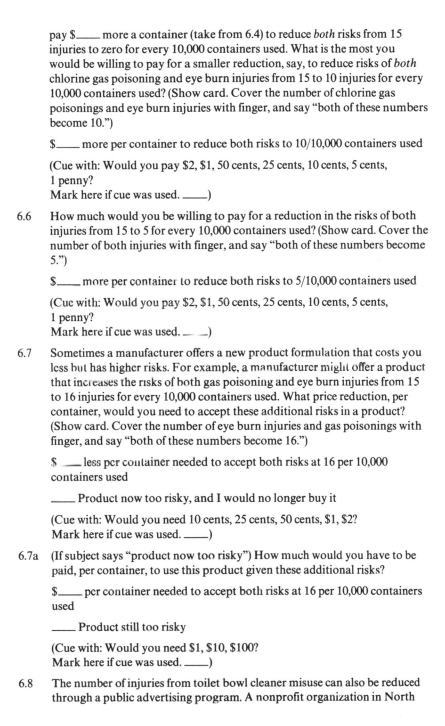

pay $____ more a container (take from 6.4) to reduce *both* risks from 15 injuries to zero for every 10,000 containers used. What is the most you would be willing to pay for a smaller reduction, say, to reduce risks of *both* chlorine gas poisoning and eye burn injuries from 15 to 10 injuries for every 10,000 containers used? (Show card. Cover the number of chlorine gas poisonings and eye burn injuries with finger, and say "both of these numbers become 10.")

$____ more per container to reduce both risks to 10/10,000 containers used

(Cue with: Would you pay $2, $1, 50 cents, 25 cents, 10 cents, 5 cents, 1 penny?
Mark here if cue was used. ____)

6.6   How much would you be willing to pay for a reduction in the risks of both injuries from 15 to 5 for every 10,000 containers used? (Show card. Cover the number of both injuries with finger, and say "both of these numbers become 5.")

$____ more per container to reduce both risks to 5/10,000 containers used

(Cue with: Would you pay $2, $1, 50 cents, 25 cents, 10 cents, 5 cents, 1 penny?
Mark here if cue was used. ____)

6.7   Sometimes a manufacturer offers a new product formulation that costs you less but has higher risks. For example, a manufacturer might offer a product that increases the risks of both gas poisoning and eye burn injuries from 15 to 16 injuries for every 10,000 containers used. What price reduction, per container, would you need to accept these additional risks in a product? (Show card. Cover the number of eye burn injuries and gas poisonings with finger, and say "both of these numbers become 16.")

$ ____ less per container needed to accept both risks at 16 per 10,000 containers used

____ Product now too risky, and I would no longer buy it

(Cue with: Would you need 10 cents, 25 cents, 50 cents, $1, $2?
Mark here if cue was used. ____)

6.7a   (If subject says "product now too risky") How much would you have to be paid, per container, to use this product given these additional risks?

$____ per container needed to accept both risks at 16 per 10,000 containers used

____ Product still too risky

(Cue with: Would you need $1, $10, $100?
Mark here if cue was used. ____)

6.8   The number of injuries from toilet bowl cleaner misuse can also be reduced through a public advertising program. A nonprofit organization in North

Carolina is considering running such a public advertising program about toilet bowl cleaner safety. To be effective, the program needs to be administered once a year. The advertising campaign will reduce the risks of both gas poisonings and eye burn injuries from 15 to 10 injuries for every 10,000 containers used. This means the number of both types of injuries for the 10 million containers used in North Carolina would drop from 1,500 to 1,000. Suppose that the sponsoring organization asked *you* and others in the state to contribute to this advertising program. Although in this interview I will *not* ask you for money, would you contribute to the program?

____ Yes   ____ No

(If yes, continue. If no, proceed to 6.10.)

6.9   What is the *very most* you would contribute this year to support this public advertising program?

$____ per year contribution to the North Carolina advertising campaign

(Cue with: Would you contribute $50, $25, $10, $5, $2, $1?
Mark here if cue was used. ____)

6.10   Suppose that the advertising campaign included all of the United States. Would you contribute anything (more)?

____ Yes   ____ No

6.11   How much *more* would you contribute?

$____ more per year contribution to U.S. advertising campaign

(Cue with: Would you contribute $50, $25, $10, $5, $2, $1?
Mark here if cue was used. ____)

Stage 7: Demographic Questions
(Where answer is obvious, do not ask.)

Now I want to ask you some questions to help us group your responses with the responses of others.

7.1   How many people live in your household?

____

7.2   Are you now married?

____ Yes   ____ No

7.3   Have you ever had children?

____ Yes   ____ No

(If children were adopted, check yes.)

7.4   How many people in your household are between 5 and 18 years old? ____

7.5   How often do children under 5 years old, other than your own, visit your home?

_____ Every day

_____ 2–3 times a week

_____ Once a week

_____ Once or twice a month

_____ Once a year

_____ Never

7.6   What is your age? _____ years old

7.7   What was the last grade of regular school that you completed?

_____ Grade school or less (0–8)

_____ Some high school (9–11)

_____ High school graduate (12)

_____ Some college or junior college

_____ College graduate (4- or 5-year degree)

_____ Post graduate work or degree

7.8   (Ask if married) What was the last grade of regular school that your (*husband, wife*) completed?

_____ Grade school or less (0–8)

_____ Some high school (9–11)

_____ High school graduate (12)

_____ Some college or junior college

_____ College graduate (4- or 5-year degree)

_____ Post graduate work or degree

7.9   Do you work outside the home?

_____ Yes   _____ No

7.10   Are you (or your family) a commercial farmer?

_____ Yes   _____ No

7.11   Does your job require you to use chemicals that contain hazard warnings on their labels?

_____ Yes   _____ No

7.12   Do you have any formal professional training in the use and interpretation of warning labels on hazardous chemical products.

_____ Yes   _____ No

(If yes, ask what training:

_____)

7.13   Please tell me which category best describes the total income that you (and your household) earned *DURING 1984 BEFORE TAXES*. This information is completely confidential and *will not* be traced to you in any way. (Show Income Before Taxes card, and circle response below.)

A   B   C   D   E   F   G   H   I   NA

7.14   Is subject

_____ female or _____ male?

7.15   Is subject

_____ black, _____ white, or _____ other?

Sometimes, later on, we may need to clarify a response you've given. Would you mind giving me your name and telephone number?

Name _____

Phone _____

Thank you for helping with our project!

Insecticide

Stage 1: Potential Uses of the Insect Spray

1.1 There are many uses for outdoor insect spray. Do you use insect spray to control insect problems on ornamental plants such as roses, camellias, azaleas, and chrysanthemums?

_____ Yes   _____ No

1.2 How about to control insects on fruit trees such as apples, pears, peaches, and cherries, or fruit plants such as grapes and strawberries?

_____ Yes   _____ No

1.3 Do you use insect spray on vegetable plants such as broccoli, beans, tomatoes, squash and lettuce?

_____ Yes   _____ No

1.4 Do you apply it to kennels, pens, yards, and/or lawns to control fleas on dogs and cats?

_____ Yes   _____ No

1.5 (Ask only if the subject checked more than one use above.) Which one of these four uses of the inspect spray is your most likely one? (Hand subject Uses of Insect Spray card. Check off the response below.)

_____ Ornamental plants

_____ Fruit trees

_____ Vegetable plants

_____ Controlling fleas

Stage 2: Examination of the Insect Spray
(Show the subject the insect spray.)

Please examine this _new_ insect spray, Zinbryl, as if you are about to use it _for the first time_ _____ (fill in subject's primary use from card above). I will give you a few minutes to look at this product. Please take as much time as you would take if you were going to use it for the first time _____ (fill in subject's primary use from card above).

Once you have examined the Zinbryl bottle, I will ask you some questions about it. There are _no_ right or wrong answers to any of the questions—just answer them as well as you can.

(Give the subject at least two minutes to read the label without interruption. Do *not* allow him/her to refer back to the product label once she/he has finished reading it.)

Stage 4: Precaution Questions

Now I'm going to ask you questions about how *you* would use Zinbryl.

4.1   Would you use this product for any tasks other than the four uses specified above?

_____ Yes   _____ No

(Acceptable probe: Would you use the insect spray in your house for any reason?

List other uses: _____)

4.2   Would you apply the insect spray to your pet's coat in order to kill fleas?

_____ Yes   _____ No

4.3   Please tell me whether you would take more or less care with Zinbryl than with a general weed killer such as Roundup?

_____ More   _____ Less   _____ Equal   _____ Don't know

4.4   What about with Zinbryl compared with ant killer, such as chlordane?

_____ More   _____ Less   _____ Equal   _____ Don't know

4.5   What about with Zinbryl compared with tree insect spray, such as Lindane?

_____ More   _____ Less   _____ Equal   _____ Don't know

4.6   What about with Zinbryl compared with poison ivy spray, such as 2-4-D?

_____ More   _____ Less   _____ Equal   _____ Don't know

4.7   Where would you store a product like this one?

(Do not read. Probe if necessary.

In a childproof location?   _____ Yes   _____ No

Acceptable probes are:

Is that location above or below the counter?
How easy is it to reach the product in that location?
Is the location in a storage shed?)

Stage 5: Frequency of Use Questions

5.1   Do you currently have any bottles of outdoor insect spray at your home?

_____ Yes   _____ No

5.2   When was the last time you used an outdoor insect spray like Zinbryl?

_____

5.3   Approximately how many bottles of insect spray equivalent to the one I showed you does your household use in a given year?

(Ask by month if necessary

Quart bottles per year = _____
Quart bottles per month = _____
Gallons per year = _____
Gallons per month = _____

Indicate the applicable quantity.)

5.4   I am going to show you a card with some common outdoor insect spray brands. Please indicate which brands you use?

_____

(Show Insect Spray card.)

Stage 6: Injury Valuation Questions

Insect spray can cause injuries if it is misused. According to a recent newspaper article, two serious injuries using the product are (1) inhalation poisoning and (2) skin poisoning. (Read Inhalation Poisoning card, and hand it to the subject).

6.0a   Have you heard of this *injury*?

_____ Yes   _____ No

6.0b   (If yes) How?

_____ Personal experience (know person injured)

6.0c   Cue if necessary.

_____ Heard about it/common knowledge

6.0d   Check all that apply.

_____ News articles/magazine/television

6.0e

_____ Other _____

(Read Skin Poisoning Injury card, and hand it to the subject.)

6.0f   Have you heard of this *injury*?

_____ Yes   _____ No

6.0g   (If yes) How?

_____ Personal experience (know person injured)

6.0h   Cue if necessary.

_____ Heard about it/common knowledge

6.0i   Check all that apply.

_____ News articles/magazine/television

6.0j

_____ Other _____

6.0k

_____ Read on label

Suppose that you currently use an insect spray that costs you $10.00 per bottle and it results in 15 inhalation poisonings and 15 skin poisonings for every 10,000 bottles of insect spray that are used. (Show Current Insect Spray card, and point to numbers on the card.)

6.1   I want you to think about a new formulation of insect spray, which a manufacturer might develop, that is as effective as your current product but eliminates all chance of inhalation poisonings. The number of skin poisonings caused by the product remains the same. (Show last card. Point to card but cover the number of inhalation poisonings with finger.) Would you be willing to pay more than what you currently pay to reduce this risk of injury to your household?

_____ Yes   _____ No (put $0 in 6.2a and go to 6.3)

6.2a   What is the most over current costs that you would be willing to pay to avoid this risk of inhalation poisoning?

$_____ more per bottle to reduce the risk of inhalation poisoning to zero

(If necessary cue with: Would you pay $10, $5, $2, $1, 50 cents, 25 cents, 10 cents, 5 cents, 1 penny?
Mark here if cue was used. _____)

In asking this question, I didn't intend for you to assume that fewer inhalation poisonings would occur to other households if you purchased the new insect spray? Did you assume other households would be affected? (If yes, record _____ and ask 6.2b; if no, record _____ and skip to question 6.3.)

6.2b   Now consider the value of the safer new insect spray to your household, recognizing that your response and purchase decision have *no effect* on the number of injuries incurred by other households.

What is the most that you would be willing to pay above your current costs for the new insect spray that avoids the risk of inhalation poisonings?

$_____ more per bottle to reduce inhalation poisoning risk to zero

(If necessary cue with: Would you pay $10, $5, $2, $1, 50 cents, 25 cents, 10 cents, 5 cents, 1 penny?
Mark here if cue was used. _____)

6.3   Suppose that the manufacturer was able to develop another formulation of the product that could reduce the risk of skin poisonings from 15 injuries to zero for every 10,000 bottles used but the risk of inhalation poisoning remained at the original level of 15. You indicated you would pay $_____

more a bottle (take from 6.2) for a insect spray that totally avoids inhalation poisonings. (Show Current Insect Spray card. Point to card but cover the number of skin poisonings.) What is the most above current costs you would be willing to pay for the product that completely avoids skin poisonings?

$____ more per bottle to reduce skin poisoning risk to zero

(Cue with: Would you pay $10, $5, $2, $1, 50 cents, 25 cents, 10 cents, 5 cents, 1 penny?
Mark here if cue was used. ____)

6.4   Now suppose that a company could offer a product that reduced both risks of inhalation and skin poisonings to zero. You said you were willing to pay $____ more a bottle (take from 6.2) to avoid the risk of inhalation poisonings, and $____ more a bottle (take from 6.3) to avoid the risk of skin poisonings. What is the most above the current cost of insect spray that you would be willing to pay for a product that reduces the risks of *both* injuries to zero? (Show card. Cover the number of inhalation poisonings and skin poisonings with finger.)

$____ more per bottle to reduce both risks to zero

(Cue with: Would you pay $10, $5, $2, $1, 50 cents, 25 cents, 10 cents, 5 cents, 1 penny?
Mark here if cue was used. ____)

(If 0 in 6.2, 6.3 and 6.4, then go to 6.7.)

6.5   Unfortunately, it is not always possible to develop a product that reduces the risk of all injuries to zero. You indicated that you would be willing to pay $____ more a bottle (take from 6.4) to reduce *both* risks from 15 injuries to zero for every 10,000 bottles used. What is the most you would be willing to pay for a smaller reduction, say, to reduce risks of *both* inhalation poisoning and skin poisoning from 15 to 10 injuries for every 10,000 bottles used? (Show card. Cover the number of inhalation poisonings and skin poisonings with finger, and say "both of these numbers become 10.")

$____ more per bottle to reduce both risks to 10/10,000 bottles used

(Cue with: Would you pay $10, $5, $2, $1, 50 cents, 25 cents, 10 cents, 5 cents, 1 penny?
Mark here if cue was used. ____)

6.6   How much would you be willing to pay for a reduction in the risks of both injuries from 15 to 5 for every 10,000 bottles used? (Show card. Cover the number of both injuries with finger, and say "both of these numbers become 5.")

$____ more per bottle to reduce both risks to 5/10,000 bottles used

(Cue with: Would you pay $10, $5, $2, $1, 50 cents, 25 cents, 10 cents, 5 cents, 1 penny?
Mark here if cue was used. ____)

6.7   Sometimes a manufacturer offers a new product formulation that costs you less but has higher risks. For example, a manufacturer might offer a product that increases both inhalation poisoning and skin poisoning risks from 15 to 16 injuries for every 10,000 bottles used. What price reduction, per bottle, would you need to accept these additional risks in a product? (Show card. Cover the number of inhalation poisonings and skin poisonings with finger, and say "both of these numbers become 16.")

$_____ less per bottle needed to accept both risks at 16 per 10,000 bottles used

_____ Product now too risky, and I would no longer buy it

(Cue with: Would you need 10 cents, 25 cents, 50 cents, $1, $2, $5, $10? Mark here if cue used. _____)

6.7a   (If subject said "product now too risk") How much would you have to be paid, per bottle, to use this product given the additional risks?

$_____ per bottle needed to accept both risks at 16 per 10,000 bottles used

_____ Product still too risky

(Cue with: Would you need $1, $10, $100? Mark here if cue was used. _____)

6.8   The number of injuries from insect spray misuse can also be reduced through a public advertising program. A nonprofit organization in North Carolina is considering running such a public advertising program about insect spray safety. To be effective, the program needs to be administered once a year. The advertising campaign will reduce the risks of both inhalation poisonings and skin poisonings from 15 to 10 injuries for every 10,000 bottles of insect spray used. This means that the number of both types of injuries for the 2 million household bottles used in North Carolina would drop from 3,000 to 2,000. Suppose that the sponsoring organization asked *you* and others in the state to contribute to this advertising program. Although in this interview I will *not* ask you for money, would you contribute to the program?

_____ Yes   _____ No

(If yes, continue. If no, proceed to 6.10.)

6.9   What is the *very most* you would contribute this year to support this public advertising program?

$_____ per year contribution to the North Carolina advertising campaign

(Cue with: Would you contribute $50, $25, $10, $5, $2, $1? Mark here if cue was used. _____)

6.10   Suppose the advertising campaign included the rest of the United States. Would you contribute anything (more)?

_____ Yes   _____ No

6.11   How much *more* would you contribute?

$____ more per year contribution to U.S. advertising campaign

(Cue with: Would you contribute $50, $25, $10, $5, $2, $1?
Mark here if cue was used. ____)

Stage 7: Demographic Questions
(Where answer is obvious, do not ask.)

Now I want to ask you some questions to help us group your responses with the responses of others.

7.1   How many people live in your household?

____

7.2   Are you married?

____ Yes   ____ No

7.3   Have you ever had children?

____ Yes   ____ No

(If children were adopted, check yes.)

7.4   How many people in your household are between 5 and 18 years old?

____

7.5   How often do children under 5 years old, other than your own, visit your home?

____ Every day
____ 2–3 times a week
____ Once a week
____ Once or twice a month
____ Once a year
____ Never

7.6   What is your age?

____ years old

7.7   What was the last grade of regular school that you completed?

____ Grade school or less (0–8)
____ Some high school (9–11)
____ High school graduate (12)
____ Some college or junior college
____ College graduate (4- or 5-year degree)
____ Post graduate work or degree

7.8   (Ask if married) What was the last grade of regular school that your (*husband, wife*) completed?

___ Grade school or less (0–8)

___ Some high school (9–11)

___ High school graduate (12)

___ Some college or junior college

___ College graduate (4- or 5- year degree)

___ Post graduate work or degree

7.9   Do you work outside the home?

___ Yes   ___ No

7.10   Are you (or your family) a commercial farmer?

___ Yes   ___ No

7.11   Does your job require you to use chemicals that contain hazard warnings on their labels?

___ Yes   ___ No

7.12   Do you have any formal professional training in the use and interpretation of warning labels on hazardous chemical products.

___ Yes   ___ No

(If yes, ask what training:

_____

7.13   Please tell me which category best describes the total income that you (and your household) earned *DURING 1984 BEFORE TAXES*. This information is completely confidential and *will not* be traced to you in any way. (Show Income Before Taxes card, and circle response below.)

A   B   C   D   E   F   G   H   I   NA

7.14   Is subject

___ female or ___ male?

7.15   Is subject

___ black, ___ white, or ___ other?

Sometimes, later on, we may need to clarify a response you've given. Would you mind giving me your name and telephone number?

Name _____

Phone _____

Appendix C
Narrative Description of Mall Intercept Questionnaire

First Stage

In the first stage the interviewer introduces the questionnaire and requests the assistance of the subject in a Duke University project. If the subject agrees to participate, the subject is screened to determine which of the two products he or she used in the last year, if either, and whether children under the age of five live in the household. Depending on the subject's responses to these preliminary questions, the subject is either thanked and dismissed or asked to respond to further questions from the appropriate questionnaire (e.g., see appendixes A and B).

Since there are four major uses of the outdoor insect spray and only one use for toilet bowl cleaner, stage 1 of the insect spray questionnaire also determines which of the four uses of the product apply to the subject and which of these uses is his or her most likely one.

Second Stage

In stage 2 the subject is shown a product and asked to examine it as if he or she were using it for the first time. The fictitious toilet bowl cleaner was named Conquer, and the outdoor insect spray was named Zinbryl. The labels on the bottles were professionally printed in color so that they would appear to be commercially sold products.

Subjects were given two minutes to read the labels before the interviewer proceeded with the questions; the subjects were not allowed to refer back to labels after their initial inspection.

Third Stage

In stage 3 the subject is asked a series of open-ended questions about how he or she would use the product. The interviewer starts with a general statement: "Suppose a friend of yours has *never* used this kind of product before. Explain to me the directions you would give to your friend about the proper use of Conquer (or Zinbryl, given your primary use)." The interviewer can use only general probes, such as "Is there anything else you would say?" The responses are recorded on a coding sheet supplied with the questionnaire (see figures C.1 and C.2). Each response is given a number that indicates the order in which the response was given.

To facilitate analysis, all possible usage responses are grouped into five categories: Use, Don't, Do, Hurt, and Antidote. The possible directions for product use ("Use") are numbered 100, 101, 102, etc. The precautionary actions are divided into those things that the user should not do ("Don't") and numbered 200, 210, 202, etc.

QUESTIONS ABOUT THE TOILET BOWL CLEANER USAGE

SUPPOSE A FRIEND OF YOURS HAS *NEVER* USED THIS KIND OF PRODUCT BEFORE, EXPLAIN TO ME THE DIRECTIONS YOU WOULD GIVE TO YOUR FRIEND ABOUT THE PROPER USE OF CONQUER.

DIRECTIONS FOR USE

PART 1 PROBE: ARE THERE ANY OTHER INSTRUCTIONS YOU'D GIVE YOUR FRIEND?

____ LIFT SEAT (A)	____ BRUSH (A)	____ USE REGULARLY (A)
____ SQUIRT (A)	____ FLUSH (A)	____ CLEANS AND DISINFECTS (A)
____ 15 SECONDS (A)	____ REPEAT IF NECESSARY (A)	____ SAFE FOR PLUMBING (A)
____ 4 OZ. (A)		
____ LET STAND (A)	____ RINSE BRUSH (A)	____ OTHERS (A)
____ 10 MINUTES (A)	____ DEODORIZES (A)	
____ LONGER IF STAINED (A)		_____

DON'T	HOW IT CAN HURT YOU	DO
(PART 2 PROBE: "WHY?")	(PART 2 PROBE: "IS THERE ANY OTHER THING YOU WOULD SAY SO YOUR FRIEND WOULD AVOID THIS PROBLEM?")	(PART 2 PROBE: "WHY?")
		____ WASH HANDS AFTER USE (MM)
____ USE IT AT ALL (B)	____ POISONOUS (O)	____ BE CAREFUL IN GENERAL (W)
____ SWALLOW/EAT/DRINK (C)	____ DANGEROUS (KK)	____ KEEP IN CHILD-PROOF LOCATION (X)
____ BREATHE FUMES (D)		____ READ LABEL (LL)
____ GET IN EYES (E)	____ HARMFUL IF SWALLOWED (P)	____ KEEP IN LABELED BOTTLED (Y)
____ SPLASH WHEN USING (F)	____ EYE INJURIES (Q)	____ USE SAFETY CAP (AA)
____ GET ON FACE (G)		____ WEAR GLASSES (BB)
____ GET ON SKIN (H)	____ SKIN DAMAGE (R)	____ STAND AWAY FROM BOWL (CC)

Figure C.1 Coding sheet for toilet bowl cleaner responses

DON'T	HOW IT CAN HURT YOU	DO
(PART 2 PROBE: "WHY?")	(PART 2 PROBE: "IS THERE ANY OTHER THING YOU WOULD SAY SO YOUR FRIEND WOULD AVOID THIS PROBLEM?")	(PART 2 PROBE: "WHY?)

____ GET ON CLOTHES (I)		____ WEAR GLOVES (DD)
____ TOUCH AT ALL (J)	____ TOXIC GAS POSSIBLE (S)	____ USE BRUSH (EE)
____ MIX WITH BLEACH (K)		____ WEAR SMOCK (FF)
____ MIX WITH ANYTHING (L)	____ FLAMMABLE (T)	____ USE IN WELL VEN-TILATED AREA (GG)
____ GET ON COUNTER (M)		____ CLOSE DOOR (HH)
____ OTHER (SPECIFY) (N)	____ CORROSIVE (U)	____ USE ONLY FOR TOILET BOWLS (II)
_____		
_____	____ OTHER (SPECIFY) (V)	____ OTHER (SPECIFY) (JJ)
_____	_____ _____	_____
	_____	_____

ANTIDOTES:

____ DRINK MILK OR WATER (Z)	____ FLUSH EYES (Z)	____ CALL PHYSICIAN (Z)
____ RINSE MOUTH (Z)	____ 15-30 MINUTES (Z)	____ OTHER (Z)
____ FLUSH SKIN (Z)	____ INDUCE VOMITING (Z)	_____
____ 15-30 MINUTES (Z)	____ DO NOT INDUCE VOMITING (Z)	_____

Figure C.1 (continued)

Actions that should be done ("Do") are numbered 400, 410, 402, ect. The risks from improper usage ("Hurt") are numbered 300, 301, 302, etc. Finally, the possible antidotes ("Antidote") are numbered 500, 501, 502, etc.

After all the unprompted responses are recorded, the interviewer probes for responses in each of the Don't, Hurt, and Do categories. The interviewer continues to record all the prompted answers using letters to indicate the unprompted response from which they were elicited. We found that prompting did elicit the recall of more information from the label for most subjects, but a separate analysis of the prompted responses indicated them to be much less sensitive to differences in label content and design than the unprompted responses. Since the unprompted responses provided more discriminating evidence of the effectiveness of labels and were more likely to be recalled in actual use situations, we focused our analysis on them.

SUPPOSE A FRIEND OF YOURS HAS *NEVER* USED THIS KIND OF PRODUCT BEFORE. EXPLAIN TO ME THE DIRECTIONS YOU WOULD GIVE YOUR FRIEND ABOUT THE PROPER USE OF ZINBRYL (for primary use given above.)

DIRECTIONS FOR USE

PART 1 PROBE: "ARE THERE ANY OTHER INSTRUCTIONS YOU WOULD GIVE TO YOUR FRIEND?"

____ USE 2-3 TEASPOONFULS (A)   ____ USE FOR VEGETABLES (A)   ____ DILUTE/MIX WITH WATER (A)

____ USE FOR FLEAS/ANTS (A)   ____ USE FOR FRUIT TREES (A)   ____ REPEAT AS NECESSARY (A)

____ USE LARGER DOSE FOR FLEAS   ____ SPRAY ALL PLANT SURFACES/SPRAY EVENLY (A)   ____ USE BEFORE HARVEST (A)

____ USE MOST INSECTS (A)   ____ USE SPRAYER (A)   ____ DON'T USE BEFORE HARVEST (A)

____ USE FOR ORNAMENTALS (A)   ____ OTHER (SPECIFY) (A)

_____

_____

DON'T	HOW IT CAN HURT YOU	DO
(PART 2 PROBE: "WHY?")	(PART 2 PROBE: "IS THERE ANY OTHER THING YOU WOULD SAY SO YOUR FRIEND WOULD AVOID THIS PROBLEM?")	(PART 2 PROBE: "WHY?)
____ USE IT ALL (B)	____ POISONOUS/TOXIC (P)	____ BE CAREFUL IN GENERAL (Y)
____ SWALLOW/EAT/DRINK (C)	____ DANGEROUS (Q)	____ READ LABEL/FOLLOW DIRECTIONS (AA)
____ USE NEAR FOOD (NN)	____ HARMFUL IF SWALLOWED (BURNS THROAT AND STOMACH) (R)	____ KEEP IN CHILDPROOF LOCATION (BB)
____ PUT IN FOOD CONTAINERS (D)	____ DAMAGE TO LUNGS, BREATHING (S)	____ KEEP IN ORIGINAL OR LABELED BOTTLE (CC)

Figure C.2   Coding sheet for insect spray responses

DON'T	HOW IT CAN HURT YOU	DO
(PART 2 PROBE: "WHY?")	(PART 2 PROBE: "IS THERE ANY OTHER THING YOU WOULD SAY SO YOUR FRIEND WOULD AVOID THIS PROBLEM?")	(PART 2 PROBE: "WHY?")
____ STORE DILUTED SPRAY (E)	____ EYE INJURIES (T)	____ DISPOSE OF BOTTLE PROPERLY (SS)
____ REUSE EMPTY CONTAINER (F)	____ SKIN DAMAGE (U)	____ WEAR GLASSES/ GOGGLES (FF)
____ BREATHE VAPORS OR SPRAY MIST (G)	____ FLAMMABLE (V)	____ WEAR GLOVES (GG)
____ GET IN EYES (H)	____ HARMFUL TO ANIMALS/ FISH (TT)	____ WEAR PROTECTIVE CLOTHING (HH)
____ USE WHEN WINDY/ SPRAY INTO WIND (I)	____ ENVIRONMENTAL DAMAGE (W)	____ WASH SKIN AND HANDS AFTER USING (II)
____ GET ON SKIN/FACE (K)	____ OTHER (SPECIFY) (X)	____ REMOVE/LAUNDER CONTAMINATED CLOTHING (JJ)
____ GET ON CLOTHES (L)	_____	____ KEEP CHILDREN/ ANIMALS AWAY FROM TREATED AREAS (KK)
____ TOUCH AT ALL (M)	_____	____ STORE IN COOL, DRY PLACE (LL)
____ USE BEFORE HARVEST (OO)		____ CLEAN TOOLS AFTER USE (RR)
____ GET IN LAKES, PONDS WATER SUPPLY (N)		____ OTHER (SPECIFY) (MM)
____ USE FOR OTHER THAN INTENDED USE (PP)		
____ OTHER (SPECIFY) (O)		_____
_____		_____

ANTIDOTES:

____ DRINK LARGE QUANTITY OF WATER (Z)	____ FLUSH EYES (Z)	____ GET MEDICAL ATTENTION (Z)
	____ 15-30 MINUTES (Z)	
____ WASH SKIN/HANDS WITH SOAP AND WATER (Z)	____ INDUCE VOMITING (Z)	____ OTHER (Z)
	____ DO NOT INDUCE VOMITING (Z)	_____

Fourth Stage

In stage 4 the interviewer asks *direct* response questions about what precautionary actions the subject would take to mitigate product risks. In designing the questions, we tried to avoid demand effects, and this severely limited the number of questions we could ask. The questions in stage 4 allow us to determine whether certain precautions are taken (e.g., storing the product in a childproof location) and the level of care that would be taken in using the product relative to other household chemical and pesticide products.

The direct questions on precautionary actions were less discriminatory among product labels because they had to be phrased to avoid "yes" or "no" answers. Also, since this section followed the memory recall section of the questionnaire where several precautions were recalled, the direct response questions were cued by stage 3. As a result we had to rely on the memory recall questions to test hypotheses about the effects of products label and use the direct response questions only to check the relationship between recall of precautions and eventual precaution-taking behavior (as we explained in chapter 5).

Fifth Stage

In stage 5 the interviewer provides information about the frequency of use of toilet bowl cleaners and outdoor insect sprays and inquires about brands the subject uses. This information is later used in the multivariate analysis of the responses to the precaution-taking questions.

Sixth Stage

The interviewer in stage 6 addresses the question of how much the subjects would value the avoidance of the major injuries associated with using toilet bowl cleaner and outdoor insect spray. The interviewer first describes the injuries and their health consequences and then determines whether the subject is familiar with them. For the remaining questions, the interviewer poses a set of paired comparison questions that requires the subject to contrast two similar products that differ only in their probabilities of injury. (The responses to the questions on the premia that subjects would pay to purchase the safer products are discussed in chapter 3, and chapter 4 explores the extent of any altruistic motivation behind the risk valuations.)

Seventh Stage

In the final stage the interviewer asks demographic questions. These questions are used as possible explanatory factors for variations in the injury valuations and precaution-taking responses.

Interviewer's Name _____   Products:

Date _____   TBC _____

Time _____   Insect. _____

Subject's Name _____   Bleach _____

Telephone # _____   Verification: _____

Form B _____

Telephone Questionnaire

Stage 1: Introduction and Screening

Hello, my name is _____. I am doing marketing research for a Duke University project and need your help in answering some questions. They will take about 5 minutes to answer.

1.1 Are you 21 or older?

Yes ____   No ____
(go to 1.3)   (go to 1.2)

1.2 Is anyone at home who is at least 21 years old?

Yes ____   No ____
(greet and go to 1.3)   (thank and exit)

May I speak with him/her?

1.3 Have you used an outdoor insect spray for plants or lawns in the last year? (Roach or indoor bug sprays do not qualify.)

Yes ____   No ____
(go to 1.7)   (go to 1.4)

1.4 Is there anyone at home, 21 or older, who probably has used an outdoor insect spray in the last year? May I speak with him/her?

Yes ____   No ____
(greet and go to 1.3)   (go to 1.5)

1.5 Have you used a toilet bowl cleaner within the last year? (Cleanser, in-tank cleaners, and general household cleaners (Fantastic) do not qualify as toilet bowl cleaner.)

Yes ____   No ____
(go to 1.7)   (go to 1.6)

1.6   Is there anybody at home, 21 or older, who has probably used such a product in the last year? May I speak with him/her?

Yes _____   No _____
(greet and go to 1.5)   (thank and exit)

1.7   Have you used a household bleach within the last year?

Yes _____   No _____

(Ask insect spray questions (stage 2) or toilet bowl cleaner questions (stage 3) depending on which product subject has used. If subject has used bleach, ask bleach questions. ALWAYS ask bleach questions second.)

Stage 2: Insecticide Usage Questions

2.1   For which of the following insect control problems do you use insect spray? Identify as many as apply.

A _____ Ornamental plants such as roses, camellias, azaleas, and chrysanthemums

B _____ Fruit trees such as apples, pears, peaches, and cherries, or fruit plants such as grapes and strawberries

C _____ Vegetable plants such as broccoli, beans, tomatoes, squash, and lettuce

D _____ Kennels pens, yards, and lawns to control fleas on dogs and cats.

(Ask the next question only if the subject checked more than one use above.)

2.2   Which one of these four uses of the insect spray is your most likely one?

A _____ Ornamentals

B _____ Fruits

C _____ Vegetables

D _____ Fleas

2.3   Do you use insect spray for any tasks other than those we have mentioned?

Yes _____   No _____   NA _____

If yes, explain _____.

2.4   Do you apply the insect spray to your pet's coat in order to kill fleas?

Yes _____   No _____   NA _____

2.5   Do you currently have any containers of outdoor insect spray at home?

Yes _____   No _____
(go to 2.6)   (go to 2.7)

2.6   What brand?

_____

2.7   Where do you store outdoor insect sprays?

(All we want to know is if the location is childproof. Do not ask. If necessary,
probe with:
Is that location above or below the counter?
How easy is it to reach the product in that location?
Is the storage shed locked?
Is the location in your basement?)

CHILDPROOF?   Yes _____   No _____

2.8   Approximately how many bottles of insect spray does your family use in a given year?

Bottles of insect spray per year = _____

To which size bottle are you referring?

_____ 8 ounce   _____ 1 quart = 16 ounces
_____ 1 gallon = 64 ounces

2.9   When was the last time you used insect spray?

A _____ Within the week
B _____ Within the month
C _____ Within the year

2.10 Do you take more or less care with insect spray than with general weed killer such as Round-Up?

More _____   Less _____   Equal _____   Don't know _____

2.11 Do you take more or less care with insect spray than with ant killer such as chlordane?

More _____   Less _____   Equal _____   Don't know _____

2.12 Insect spray compared with tree insect spray such as Lindane?

More _____   Less _____   Equal _____   Don't know _____

2.13 Insect spray compared with poison ivy spray, such as 2-4-D?

More _____   Less _____   Equal _____   Don't know _____

(If subject used bleach, go to stage 4; otherwise, go to stage 5.)

Stage 3: Toilet Bowl Cleaner Usage Questions

3.1   Where in your home does your household store toilet bowl cleaner?

(All we want to know is if the location is childproof.
Probe with: Is that location above the counter?
                  How easy is it to reach the product in that location?
                  If in a low cabinet, is that cabinet locked?)

CHILDPROOF? Yes _____   No _____

3.2   Do you currently have any toilet bowl cleaner in your house?

Yes _____   No _____
(go to 3.3)   (go to 3.4)

3.3   What brand(s):

_____

(continue with 3.3b)

3.4

3.5   Do you normally use liquid or crystal toilet bowl cleaner?

_____ Liquid   _____ Crystal

3.6   When was the last time you used toilet bowl cleaner?

A _____ Within the past week
B _____ Within the past month
C _____ Within the past year

3.7   Approximately how many bottles of toilet bowl cleaner does your household use per month or year?

Bottles of toilet bowl cleaner per year = _____
Bottles of toilet bowl cleaner per month = _____

3.8   Do you take more or less care with toilet bowl cleaner than with window cleaner?

More _____   Less _____   Equal _____   Don't know _____

3.9   Do you take more or less care with toilet bowl cleaner than with bleach?

More _____   Less _____   Equal _____   Don't know _____

3.10   More or less care with toilet bowl cleaner than with lye?

More _____   Less _____   Equal _____   Don't know _____

3.11   More or less care with toilet bowl cleaner than with oven cleaner?

More _____   Less _____   Equal _____   Don't know _____

While using toilet bowl cleaner in your home, do you ever:

3.12   Mix it with other cleaners or chemicals, perhaps to clean extra dirty toilets?

Yes _____   No _____   NA _____

3.13   Use it to clean your bathtub/shower?

Yes _____   No _____   NA _____

3.14   Use it to clean your sink?

Yes _____   No _____   NA _____

3.15   Use it to clean bathroom tile?

Yes ___   No ___   NA ___

3.16   Use it to clean anything else?

Yes ___   No ___   NA ___

_____ (Explain)

(Go to stage 4 if subject used bleach; otherwise, go to stage 5.)

Stage 4: Bleach Usage Questions

While using bleach in your home, do you ever:

4.1   Use it to clean dirty sinks?

Yes ___   No ___   NA ___

4.2   Use it to remove mildew from walls?

Yes ___   No ___   NA ___

4.3   Use it to clean floors?

Yes ___   No ___   NA ___

4.4   Add to your laundry for stubborn stains?

Yes ___   No ___   NA ___

4.5   Add to toilet bowl cleaner if toilet is badly strained?

Yes ___   No ___   NA ___

4.6   Add to ammonia or ammonia-based cleaners for particularly dirty jobs?

Yes ___   No ___   NA ___

4.7   Do you currently have a container of bleach in your home?

Yes ___   No ___
(go to 4.8)   (go to 4.9)

4.8   What brand? _____

4.9   Where do you normally store bleach?

(Probe to determine whether or not the location is childproof. Do not ask directly. Acceptable probes are: Is the cabinet above the counter? Is the cabinet locked?)

CHILDPROOF?   Yes ___   No ___

4.10   When was the last time you used bleach?

A ___ Within the past week

B ___ Within the past month

C ___ Within the past year

4.11 About how many bottles of bleach does your household use in a given month or year?

Bottles a month ____
Bottles a year ____

4.12 To which size bottle are you referring?

Quart ____ Half-gallon ____ Gallon ____

(Go to stage 5.)

Stage 5: Demographic Questions

I now want to ask you some questions to help us group your responses with the responses of others.

5.1 How many people live in your household?

_____

5.2 Have you ever had children?

____ Yes ____ No

5.3 How many people in your household are between the ages of 5 and 18 years old?

_____

5.4 How many people in your household are under 5 years old?

_____

5.5 How often do children under 5 years old, other than your own, visit your home?

A ____ Every day
B ____ 2–3 times a week
C ____ Once a week
D ____ Once or twice a month
E ____ Less than once a month
F ____ Never

5.6 What is your age?

____ years old

5.7 Are you now married?

____ Yes ____ No

5.8 What was the last grade of regular school that you completed? Do not include specialized schools like secretarial, art, or trade schools.

A ____ Grade school or less (0–8)
B ____ Some high school (9–11)

C ____ High school graduate (12)

D ____ Some college or junior college

E ____ College graduate (4- or 5-year degree)

F ____ Post graduate work or degree

5.9   If you are married, what was the last grade of regular school that your *spouse* completed? Again, do not include specialized schools like secretarial, art, or trade schools.

A ____ Grade school or less (0–8)

B ____ Some high school (9–11)

C ____ High school graduate (12)

D ____ Some college or junior college

E ____ College graduate (4- or 5-year degree)

F ____ Post graduate work or degree

5.10   Do you work outside the home?

____ Yes   ____ No

5.11   Are you (or your family) a commercial farmer?

____ Yes   ____ No

5.12   Does your job require you to use chemicals that contain hazard warnings on their labels?

____ Yes   ____ No

5.13   Do you have any formal professional training in the use and interpretation of warning labels on hazardous chemical products (for example, training to become a Certified Pesticide Applicator)?

____ Yes (explain _____)

____ No

5.14   Please tell me which category best describes the total income that you (and your household) earned *DURING 1984 BEFORE TAXES*. This information is completely confidential and *will not* be traced to you in any way.

A ____ Under $10,000

B ____ $10,000 to less than $20,000

C ____ $20,000 to less than $30,000

D ____ $30,000 to less than $40,000

E ____ $40,000 to less than $50,000

F ____ $50,000 to less than $60,000

G ____ $60,000 to less than $70,000

H ____ $70,000 to less than $80,000

I ____ $80,000 and over

J ____ (Refused)

(Is respondent male ＿＿＿ or female ＿＿＿?)

(Ask respondent for name, which will be used *ONLY* for verification and clarification purposes. Record along with phone number on the screening sheet.)

Thank you for helping with our project!

Toilet Bowl Cleaners

Lysol
Vanish
Saniflush
Cling
Snobowl
Swish
Store Brand

Chlorine Gas Poisoning

Chlorine gas forms when toilet bowl cleaner is mixed with bleach or other household products. Breathing this gas causes headaches and burning sensations to the lungs, eyes, and/or nose. These injuries may require hospitalization for several days. There are 15 gas poisonings for every 10,000 containers of toilet bowl cleaner that are used.

Child Poisoning

Swallowing by young children can result in severe and painful burns to the mouth and throat. Normally the child will recover in a few days. In extreme cases hospitalization may be required, and the child may lose a part of his or her stomach. There are 15 such accidents for every 10,000 containers of toilet bowl cleaner that are used.

Current Toilet Bowl Cleaner

Cost per bottle:	$2.00
Injury levels for every 10,000 containers used:	15 chlorine gas poisonings
	15 child poisonings

Eye Burn Injuries

Eye burn injuries can occur if the product is splashed in the eyes. These burns are painful and in some cases result in the loss of eyesight. Treatment often requires several visits to an eye doctor. There are 15 eye burn injuries for every 10,000 containers of toilet bowl cleaner that are used.

Current Toilet Bowl Cleaner

Cost per bottle:	$2.00
Injury levels for every 10,000 containers used:	15 chlorine gas poisonings
	15 eye burn injuries

Income before Taxes

A   Under $10,000
B $10,000 to less than $20,000
C $20,000 to less than $30,000
D $30,000 to less than $40,000
E $40,000 to less than $50,000
F $50,000 to less than $60,000
G $60,000 to less than $70,000
H $70,000 to less than $80,000
I $80,000 and over

Current Insect Spray

Cost per container:	$10.00
Injury levels for every 10,000 bottles used:	15 inhalation poisonings
	15 skin poisonings

Current Insect Spray

Cost per container:	$10.00
Injury levels for every 10,000 bottles used:	15 inhalation poisonings
	15 child poisonings

Insect Sprays

Ferti-lome Malathion Spray
Ortho Malathion 50
High-Yield Malathion

Uses of Insect Spray

Ornamental plants such as roses, camellias, azaleas, and chrysanthemums
Fruit trees such as apples, pears, peaches, and cherries, or fruit plants such as grapes and strawberries
Vegetable plants such as broccoli, beans, tomatoes, squash, and lettuce
Controlling fleas on dogs and cats in kennels, pens, yards and/or lawns

Skin Poisoning

If insect spray is left on the skin for several hours, it can cause muscle twitching, feelings of weakness, headaches, nausea, stomach pains, and diarrhea. Hospitalization may be required. Recovery usually occurs within a few hours but may take over a week if the dose is unusually large. There are 15 skin poisonings for every 10,000 bottles of insect spray that are used.

Inhalation Poisoning

If a large amount of insect spray is inhaled, it can cause tearing, salivating, coughing, and difficulty in breathing, sometimes followed by muscle twitching, feelings of weakness, headaches, nausea, stomach pains, and diarrhea. Hospitalization may be required. Recovery usually occurs within a day but may extend beyond a week if the dose is unusually large. There are 15 inhalation poisonings for every 10,000 bottles of insect spray that are used.

Child Poisonings

If children drink insect spray, it can cause nausea, stomach pains, diarrhea, headaches, blurred vision, coughing, weakness, and, for some children, seizures. Hospitalization may be required. Recovery time varies from a few hours in most cases to several weeks for children who drink large doses of the insect spray. There are 15 child poisonings for every 10,000 bottles of insect spray that are used.

Income before Taxes

A   Under $10,000
B $10,000 to less than $20,000
C $20,000 to less than $30,000
D $30,000 to less than $40,000
E $40,000 to less than $50,000
F $50,000 to less than $60,000
G $60,000 to less than $70,000
H $70,000 to less than $80,000
I $80,000 and over

Changes in a Single Risk

The determination of the effect of changes in one risk alone is relatively straightforward. Let the consumer's expected marginal utility D be defined by

$$D = [(1 - p_1 + \alpha)(1 - p_2 + \beta)U_x^0(B) + (p_1 - \alpha)(1 - p_2 + \beta)U_x^1(B)$$

$$+ (p_2 - \beta)(1 - p_1 + \alpha)U_x^2(B) + (p_1 - \alpha)(p_2 - \beta)U_x^3(B)]. \qquad (G1)$$

Differentiation of equation (G1) yields two basic results:

$$\frac{\partial V}{\partial \alpha} = \frac{(1 - p_2 + \beta)[U^0(B) - U^1(B)] + (p_2 - \beta)[U^2(B) - U^3(B)]}{D} > 0, \qquad (G2)$$

$$\frac{\partial V}{\partial \beta} = \frac{(1 - p_1 + \alpha)[U^0(B) - U^2(B)] + (p_1 - \alpha)[U^1(B) - U^3(B)]}{D} > 0. \qquad (G3)$$

Thus the marginal willingness to pay for a reduction in injury risk 1 is the weighted sum of the difference in the utility between the healthy state and injury state 1 and the difference in the utility of the other injury state 2 and the state with both injuries, divided by the expected marginal utility across all states.

The effect of variation in the extent of risk reduction α on the rate of trade-off $\partial V/\partial \alpha$ is given by

$$\frac{\partial^2 V}{\partial \alpha^2} = -\frac{1}{D^3}\{2[(1 - p_2 - \beta)(U_x^1(B) - U_x^0(B)) + (p_2 - \beta)(U_x^3(B) - U_x^2(B))]$$

$$\times [-(1 - p_2 + \beta)(U^0(B) - U^1(B) - (p_2 - \beta)(U^2(B) - U^3(B))]D$$

$$- (1 - p_1 + \alpha)(1 - p_2 + \beta)U_{xx}^0(B)$$

$$+ (p_1 - \alpha)(1 - p_2 + \beta)U_{xx}^1(B) + (p_2 - \beta)(1 - p_1 + \alpha)U_{xx}^2(B)$$

$$+ (p_1 - \alpha)(p_2 - \beta U_{xx}^3(B)]\} < 0, \qquad (G4)$$

and $\partial^2 V/\partial \beta^2$ is similar.

For the reductions of both risks α and β by an equal increment γ,

$$\frac{\partial V}{\partial \gamma} = \left\{\frac{(1 - p_2 + \gamma)[U^0(B) - U^1(B)] + (p_2 - \gamma)[U^2(B) - U^3(B)]}{D(\gamma)}\right\}$$

$$+ \left\{\frac{(1 - p_1 + \gamma)[U^0(B) - U^2(B)] + (p_1 - \gamma)[U^1(B) - U^3(B)]}{D(\gamma)}\right\} > 0, \qquad (G5)$$

where $D(\gamma)$ is the value of D in the equation (G1) above with both α and β replaced by γ.

Additivity of Risk Avoidance Values

Define the composite utility functions $\bar{U}(x)$, $U^a(x)$, and $U^b(x)$ by

$$\bar{U}(x) = (1 - p_1)(1 - p_2)U^0(x) + p_1(1 - p_2)U^1(x)$$

$$+ p_2(1 - p_1)U^2(x) + p_1 p_2 U^3(x), \tag{G6}$$

$$U^a(x) = (1 - p_2)U^0(x) + p_2 U^2(x), \tag{G7}$$

and

$$U^b(x) = (1 - p_1)U^0(x) + p_1 U^1(x). \tag{G8}$$

Then the baseline level of expected utility W satisfies

$$W = \bar{U}(A).$$

Next define V_1 as the willingness to pay for the elimination of the risk from injury 1; that is, $\alpha = p_1$ and $\beta = 0$ in equation (5) of chapter 3. Similarly define V_2 as the willingness to pay for eliminating injury 2 ($\alpha = 0$ and $\beta = p_2$) and V_{12} as the willingness to pay to avoid both injuries ($\alpha = p_1$ and $\beta = p_2$). Thus the risk avoidance values V_1, V_2, and V_{12} of reducing an individual risk to zero (V_1 and V_2) or both risks to zero (V_{12}) are defined by

$$W = U^a(A - V_1), \tag{G10}$$

$$W = U^b(A - V_2), \tag{G11}$$

and

$$W = U^0(A - V_{12}), \tag{G12}$$

or equivalently,

$$V_1 = A - U^{a^{-1}}(W), \tag{G13}$$

$$V_2 = A - U^{b^{-1}}(W), \tag{G14}$$

and

$$V_{12} = A - U^{0^{-1}}(W). \tag{G15}$$

Consider the special case of $p_1 = p_2$ and $U_1 = U_2$. Assumptions 1 and 2 require that

$$U^0(x) > U^a(x) > \bar{U}(x) \tag{G16}$$

for all x. Assumption 3 requires that

$$U^0_x(x) > U^a_x(x) = U^b_x(x) \tag{G17}$$

for all values of x and assumption 4 requires that

$$U^a_{xx}(x) < 0 \tag{G18}$$

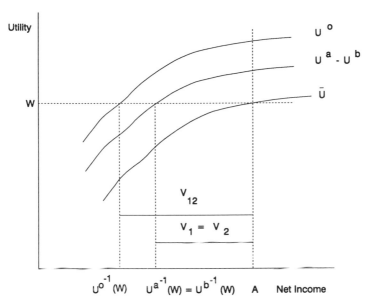

Figure G.1 Special case of $p_1 = p_2$ and $U^1 = U^2$

for all x. In this special case $(V_1 + V_2) > V_{12}$ if $V_1 > V_{12}/2$. As illustrated by figure G.1, the relative slopes (G17) and the concavity (G18) assumptions guarantee that this last inequality holds if

$$\frac{U^0(A) - U^a(A)}{U^a(A) - \overline{U}(A)} \leq 1. \tag{G19}$$

Because this last result may not be obvious to many readers, we record it as a lemma and prove it.

LEMMA 1   When $p_1 = p_2$ and $U_1 = U_2$, $V_1 > V_{12}/2$ if

$$\frac{U^0(A) - U^a(A)}{U^a(A) - \overline{U}(A)} \leq 1.$$

Proof   Equation (3) in chapter 3 and equations (G16) and (G17) imply that

$$[U^0(U^{a-1}(W)) - W] < [U^0(A) - U^a(A)].$$

Thus from (G19),

$$[U^0(U^{a^{-1}}(W)) - W] < [U^a(A) - \overline{U}(A)]. \tag{G20}$$

From (G17) it follows that $U_x^0(A) > U_x^a(A)$, which along with (G18) implies that $U_x^0(U^{a-1}(W)) > U_x^a(A)$. This last inequality and (G18) imply that for all values of x between $U^{0-1}(W)$ and $U^{a-1}(W)$,

$$U_x^0(x) > U_x^a(x + V_1).$$ (G21)

Finally, (G20) and (G21) imply that

$$[U^{a^{-1}}(W) - U^{0^{-1}}(W)] < V_1,$$

which proves that $V_1 > V_{12}/2.$ □

We now use lemma 1 to prove the result in chapter 3 about the additivity of risk avoidance values. From the definitions of the utility functions,

$$\frac{U^0(A) - U^a(A)}{U^a(A) - \bar{U}(A)} = \frac{1}{(1 - p) + p[U^1(A) - U^3(A)]/[U^0(A) - U^1(A)]}.$$

Thus $(V_1 + V_2) > V_{12}$ if $[U^1(A) - U^3(A)] \geq [U^0(A) - U^1(A)]$.

Now consider another slightly more general case in which both injuries are equally probable ($p_1 = p_2 = p$), but the first injury is less serious than the second injury ($U^1 > U^2$). Figure G.2 illustrates this case. Since $U^1 > U^2$, for all values of net income the definitions (G6), (G7), and (G8) require that U^b lie above U^a but that both curves fall between U^0 and $\bar{U}$. The values of V_1, V_2, and V_{12} are defined by (G13)–(G15) and marked in figure G.2.

From assumption 3

$$U_x^0(x) > U_x^b(x) > U_x^a(x)$$ (G22)

for all x. Assumption 4 requires that for all x

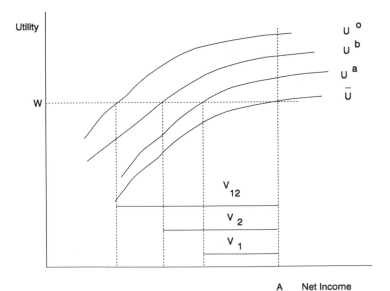

Figure G.2   Special case of $p_1 = p_2$ and $U^1 > U^2$

$U_{xx}^a(x), \quad U_{xx}^b(x) < 0.$ (G23)

Since $U^1 > U^2$,

$U^b(x) > U^a(x)$ (G24)

for all x. Inequalities (G22) and (G24) imply that $V_1 < V_2$. Thus $(V_1 + V_2) > V_{12}$ if $V_1 > V_{12}/2$. From (G22)–(G24) and lemma 1, this last inequality holds if again

$$\frac{U^0(A) - U^a(A)}{U^a(A) - \overline{U}(A)} \leq 1.$$ (G25)

Substitution from the definitions of U^a and $\overline{U}$ yields

$$\frac{U^0(A) - U^a(A)}{U^a(A) - \overline{U}(A)} = \frac{U^0(A) - U^2(A)}{(1 - p)[U^0(A) - U^1(A)] + p[U^2(A) - U^3(A)]},$$ (G26)

which implies the following sufficient condition for subadditivity of risk avoidance values:

$$U^2 - U^3 \geq \frac{(U^0 - U^2) - (U^0 - U^1)(1 - p)}{p}.$$ (G27)

However, in this case of equal probabilities but different injury disutilities, we can construct examples of both superadditivity and subadditivity. Let the state-dependent utility functions be

$U^0(x) = 10x^{1/2},$

$U^1(x) = 9x^{1/2},$

$U^2(x) = 8x^{1/2},$

$U^3(x) = 8x^{1/2},$

with $p_1 = p_2 = \frac{1}{2}$. Then by substituting these functions directly into (G13)–(G15) and using (G6)–(G12), it follows that $(V_1 + V_2) < V_{12}$. By changing the last utility function to $U^3(x) = x^{1/2}$, without any other changes to the example, it can be shown that $(V_1 + V_2) > V_{12}$.

Finally, consider the case of equal disutility from the two injuries ($U^1 = U^2$) but unequal probabilities. Let

$U^0(x) = 10x^{1/2},$

$U^1(x) = U^2(x) = U^3(x) = 9x^{1/2},$

and

$p_1 = 0.9, \quad p_2 = 0.8.$

Then from (G6)–(G15) it follows that $(V_1 + V_2) > V_{12}$. Using the same utility functions but changing the probabilities to $p_1 = 0.2$ and $p_2 = 0.1$ leads to superadditive avoidance values; that is, $(V_1 + V_2) < V_{12}$.

To confirm the univariate results in chapter 6, we constructed several regression equations that include dummy variables for the label groups as well as demographic and product usage information. Table H.1 provides representative examples of those regression equations, with the statistical tests of differences in coefficients in table H.2 and variable definitions in table H.3.

All of the results reported in chapter 6 are confirmed by these multivariate equations. The formatting effect (toilet bowl cleaner labels 3 versus 4) are supported by tables H.1 and H.2. The difference between labels of the combined category of Don't, Do, and Hurt responses is positive (but only of marginal significance), the Don't responses difference and the Hurt response difference are positive and highly significant, and the Do category difference is positive by not statistically significant.

Again the multivariate results fail to clearly support the hypothesis that increasing the proportion of the label devoted to risk and precautions information raises the level of recall of that information (compare the coefficients of toilet bowl cleaner LABEL2 and LABEL3 and the coefficients of insect spray LABEL4 and LABEL5). The hypothesized linkage between print size and recall is also not supported (comparing insect spray labels 2 and 4).

Note that few of the demographic or product usage variables are significant for either the toilet bowl equations or the insect spray equations and that none of the variables is significant for both sets of equations.

Table H.1 Regressions of numbers of responses as a fraction of all possible responses on the labels (except label 1) against label dummy variables, demographic variables, and usage variables by groups of possible responses

Independent variable	Don't, Hurt, Do	Don't (200s)	Hurt (300s)	Do (400s)
A. Toilet bowl cleaner responses				
INTERCEPT	-0.00475	3.895×10^{-5}	-6.363×10^{-4}	-0.0114
	(0.00639)	(1.125×10^{-4})	(1.703×10^{-3})	(0.0156)
LABEL2	$0.00636*$	$1.654 \times 10^{-4}*$	2.931×10^{-4}	$0.0154*$
	(0.00214)	(3.764×10^{-5})	(5.694×10^{-4})	(0.00523)
LABEL3	$0.00825*$	1.778×10^{-4}	$1.229 \times 10^{-3}*$	$0.0195*$
	(0.00213)	(3.754×10^{-5})	(5.679×10^{-4})	(0.00522)
LABEL4	$0.0107*$	$2.410 \times 10^{-4}*$	$2.286 \times 10^{-3}*$	$0.0250*$
	(0.00213)	(3.741×10^{-5})	(5.66×10^{-4})	(0.00520)
FAMSIZE	0.000973	7.308×10^{-6}	3.149×10^{-5}	0.00240
	(0.000648)	(1.141×10^{-5})	(1.726×10^{-4})	(0.00159)
AGE	$0.000162*$	-1.718×10^{-6}	-2.143×10^{-5}	$0.000415*$
	(0.0000629)	(1.107×10^{-6})	(1.675×10^{-5})	(0.000154)
MALE	-0.00264	-3.312×10^{-5}	1.148×10^{-4}	-0.00656
	(0.00214)	(3.768×10^{-5})	(5.701×10^{-4})	(0.000154)

Table H.1 (continued)

Independent variable	Don't, Hurt, Do	Don't (200s)	Hurt (300s)	Do (400s)
EDUC	0.000286 (0.000383)	1.629×10^{-6} (6.736×10^{-6})	1.417×10^{-5} (1.019×10^{-4})	0.000696 (0.000936)
WORK	0.00153 (0.00180)	1.176×10^{-5} (3.175×10^{-5})	5.126×10^{-4} (4.803×10^{-4})	0.00408 (0.00441)
USECHEM	−0.000150 (0.00174)	3.138×10^{-5} (3.055×10^{-5})	1.120×10^{-6} (4.621×10^{-4})	−0.000464 (0.00425)
INCOME	1.783×10^{-7} (1.474×10^{-7})	3.498×10^{-9} (2.594×10^{-9})	6.690×10^{-8}* (3.925×10^{-8})	3.981×10^{-7} (3.606×10^{7})
BLACK	0.00147 (0.00175)	-8.264×10^{-5}* (3.086×10^{-5})	1.062×10^{-4} (4.668×10^{-6})	0.00377 (0.00429)
YEARUSE	0.000151 (0.000116)	-5.948×10^{-7} (2.042×10^{-6})	2.115×10^{-5} (3.090×10^{-5})	0.000361 (0.000284)
LASTUSE	0.000484 (0.000323)	3.142×10^{-6} (5.683×10^{-6})	-9.697×10^{-5} (8.598×10^{-5})	0.00125 (0.000790)
TRAINED	−0.00153 (0.00213)	3.659×10^{-5} (3.741×10^{-5})	-5.871×10^{-4} (5.660×10^{-4})	−0.00346 (0.00520)
CHILD	−0.00195 (0.00188)	-4.659×10^{-6} (3.308×10^{-5})	5.939×10^{-4} (5.005×10^{-4})	−0.00517 (0.00460)
R^2	0.0556	0.0806	0.0374	0.0529
ADJ R^2	0.0375	0.0630	0.0189	0.0347

B. Insect spray responses

INTERCEPT	0.0611* (0.0142)	0.0524* (0.0232)	0.0132 (0.0148)	0.107* (0.0236)
LABEL2	0.0223* (0.00513)	0.0295* (0.00836)	0.00693 (0.00532)	0.0256 (0.00852)
LABEL3	0.0225* (0.00512)	0.0369* (0.00835)	0.0173* (0.00531)	0.0102 (0.00850)
LABEL4	0.0210* (0.00516)	0.0618* (0.00841)	0.00927* (0.00535)	0.00621 (0.00856)
LABEL5	0.0183* (0.00517)	0.0325* (0.00843)	0.00179 (0.00537)	0.0147* (0.00858)
FAMSIZE	−0.000808 (0.00153)	0.000926 (0.00250)	−0.000911 (0.00159)	−0.00268 (0.00255)
AGE	−0.000417* (0.000152)	−0.000376 (0.000248)	−0.00174 (0.000158)	−0.000646 (0.000253)
MALE	−0.00626 (0.00364)	−0.00773 (0.00593)	−0.00418 (0.00378)	−0.00617 (0.00804)
EDUC	0.00142* (0.000714)	0.00196* (0.00116)	−0.0000354 (0.000741)	0.00190 (0.00119)
WORK	−0.00361 (0.00403)	−0.00409 (0.00657)	0.00297 (0.00418)	−0.00799 (0.00669)
USECHEM	−0.00390 (0.00399)	−0.00897 (0.00650)	−0.00288 (0.00414)	0.00104 (0.00662)
INCOME	-1.398×10^{-7} (9.646×10^{-8})	2.199×10^{-7} (1.567×10^{-7})	1.819×10^{-7}	-2.909×10^{-7}*

Table H.1 (continued)

Independent variable	Don't, Hurt, Do	Don't (200s)	Hurt (300s)	Do (400s)
BLACK	−0.00666 (0.00476)	−0.0152* (0.00776)	−0.00993 (0.00494)	−0.00135 (0.00790)
YEARUSE	−0.00000336 (0.00000648)	8.948×10^{-7} (0.0000106)	−0.00000224 (0.00000672)	−0.00000899 (0.0000107)
LASTUSE	−0.00221* (0.00106)	−0.00481* (0.00173)	−0.000829 (0.00110)	−0.000334 (0.00177)
TRAINED	−0.00312 (0.00444)	−0.00955 (0.00724)	0.00242 (0.00461)	−0.0000413 (0.00737)
PRIMUSE2	−0.00516 (0.00667)	−0.0135 (0.0109)	0.00745 (0.00692)	−0.00519 (0.0111)
PRIMUSE3	−0.00319 (0.00424)	−0.00230 (0.00691)	0.00254 (0.00440)	−0.00849 (0.00703)
PRIMUSE4	−0.00673 (0.00403)	−0.00583 (0.00656)	0.000416 (0.00418)	−0.0131* (0.00668)
FARMER	0.00601 (0.00696)	0.00566 (0.0113)	−0.00110 (0.00722)	0.0117 (0.0116)
R^2	0.0170	0.0714	0.0274	0.0244
ADJ R^2	0.0486	0.0490	0.0040	−0.0014

Note: Standard errors are in parentheses. Asterisks denote statistical significance at two-tailed 90 percent confidence level.

Table H.2 Normalized test statistics for differences between all pairs of label coefficients in table H.1

	t-statistics			F statistics[a]		
Response group	Label 2– label 1	Label 3– label 1	Label 4– label 1	Label 3– label 2	Label 4– label 2	Label 4– label 3
A. Toilet bowl cleaner responses						
Don't, Hurt, Do	2.973*	3.869*	5.052*	0.7906	4.2532*	1.3671*
Don't (200s)	4.394*	4.736*	6.442*	0.1094	4.0897*	2.8512*
Hurt (300s)	0.515	2.164*	4.038*	2.7206*	12.3985*	3.4775*
Do (400s)	2.941*	3.738*	4.802*	0.6244	3.4013*	1.1037

	t-statistics				F statistics[b]
Response group	Label 2– label 1	Label 3– label 1	Label 4– label 1	Label 5– label 1	Label 3– label 2
B. Insect spray unprompted responses					
Don't, Hurt, Do	4.340*	4.398*	4.060*	3.540	0.0025
Don't (200s)	3.528*	4.424*	4.976*	3.856	0.8242
Hurt (300s)	1.302	3.260*	1.732*	0.334	3.9913*
Do (400s)	3.010*	1.203	0.725	1.717*	3.4308*

Table H.2 (continued)

Response group	F statistics (cont.)				
	Label 4– label 2	Label 5– label 2	Label 4– label 3	Label 5– label 3	Label 5– label 4
Don't, Hurt, Do	0.0663	0.0948	0.5983	0.6762	0.2602
Don't (200s)	2.1904	0.3515	0.1291	0.2805	1.2255
Hurt (300s)	0.1946	2.3174	0.9374	8.5456*	1.9393
Do (400s)	5.2323*	0.2252	1.6454	0.2820	0.9841

Note: Asterisks denote significance at 90 percent, two-tailed confidence level.
a. Degrees of freedom equals 1,605.
b. Degrees of freedom equals 1,682.

Table H.3   Variable definitions

Variable name	Definition
AGE	Age (year)
BLACK	Dummy variable, equals 1 if the subject is black and 0 otherwise
GHILD	Dummy variable, equals 1 if the subject ever had children and 0 otherwise
EDUC	Years of education
FAMSIZE	Family size (number)
INCOME	Before-tax household income (1985$)
LABELi	Dummy variable, equals 1 if the subject received label i and 0 otherwise ($i = 2, 3, 4, 5$)
LASTUSE	Months since the last use of the product
MALE	Dummy variable, equals 1 if the subject is male and 0 if female
PRIMUSEi	Dummy variable, equals 1 if the subject's most likely use of the insect spray is for use i and 0 otherwise ($i = 1, 2, 3, 4$, where 1 = ornamental plants, 2 = fruit trees, 3 = vegetable plants, 4 = controlling fleas)
TRAINED	Dummy variable, equals 1 if the subject has any formal professional training in the use and interpretation of warning labels on hazardous chemical products and 0 otherwise
USECHEM	Dummy variable, equals 1 if the subject has a job requiring the use of chemicals with hazard warning labels and 0 otherwise
WORK	Dummy variable, equals 1 if the subject works outside the home and 0 otherwise
YEARUSE	Household usage rate of products (quarts/year)

Appendix I
House Description and Home Energy Analysis Input Sheet

An information packet about the house being audited was given to each subject at the start of the experiment. The information was intended to help the subjects make informed decisions about energy conservation investments. It included pictures of the house (figure I.1), a summary of the house's energy characteristics (figure I.2), and detailed information on the house's energy consumption used by the computer to generate audit results (e.g., the Home Energy Analysis Input Sheet in figure I.3). Although not included in this appendix, each subject was given all the additional information provided by Duke Power Company to their audited customers (e.g., standard bid form, contractor list, supplier list, and loan application).

Figure I.1   Pictures of the audited house

House Fact Sheet

House: 1 Story Ranch Style - 1,500 square feet

Rooms: 3 Bedrooms
                1 Baths
                1 Living Room/Dining Room
                1 Kitchen

Age: 7 years old

Heating: Oil

Air Conditioning: Electric Central Air

Oil Costs: Annual   - $676
                Peak Month - $80 (August)

Insulation Levels and General Energy Efficiency

	Existing R-Value	R-Value to be added
Ceiling	14	16
Walls	o	0[a]
Floor	0	11 or 19

Windows: All the windows in the house are single pane glass and none have storm windows.

Doors: None of the doors are equipped with storm doors.

Caulking: Poor[b]

Weatherstripping: Poor[c]

Notes:
[a]If the walls have any insulation, additional insulation cannot be retrofitted with standard techniques.

[b]Poor means most of the caulk is widely cracked, missing or loose.

[c]Poor means the door or window is not weatherstripped.

Figure I.2   House fact sheet

Form 22328 (6-81) (13 page set)

RCS - R330 - A

DUKE POWER

HOME ENERGY ANALYSIS INPUT SHEET

Date:___/___/___
　　　　Mo.　Day　Yr.

Prepared for _____   Phone _____

Address _____ City _____ Zip _____

ID Code |_|_|_|_|_|_|_|
　　　Rep. No.　Cost　Wthr.　Rate Opt.

Analysis Number ___**986**___

GENERAL INFORMATION

Enter "0" when a question is not applicable.

| 4 | 4 | 5 | 5 | 5 | 4 | 4 | 5 | 5 | 4 | # #1 Customer Account Number |

| 2 | 2 | ## | 2. Number of different energy sources

3. Type of energy units:
   1. Electric KWH   7. Electric DOLLARS
   2. Natural gas THERMS   8. Natural gas DOLLARS
   3. Propane GALLONS   9. Propane DOLLARS
   4. Oil GALLONS   10. Oil DOLLARS
   5. Wood CORDS   11. Wood DOLLARS
   6. Coal TONS   12. Coal DOLLARS

4. Prior 12 month total

5. Monthly base

ENERGY SOURCES

	#1	#2	#3	
3	1	4		Energy
4	13520	495		Total
5	700	0		Base
6	1			

6. Dwelling type:
   1. Single family detached, owner occupied
   2. Duplex (two family), owner occupied
   3. Triplex (three family), owner occupied
   4. More than three family, owner occupied
   5. Mobile home, owner occupied
   6. Single family detached, renter occupied
   7. Duplex (two family), renter occupied
   8. Triplex (three family), renter occupied
   9. More than three family, renter occupied
   10. Mobile home, renter occupied

| 7 | 4 | 7. Number of occupants

CEILING

| 8 | 2 | 8. Color of roof:
　　　1. Light   2. Medium   3. Dark

| 9 | 5 | 9. Net square feet of existing attic ventilation openings

| 10 | 1 | ## | 10. Number of ceiling area groups separating living space from unconditioned space

11. Net ceiling area in square feet

12. Existing R-value

13. R-value to be added

CEILING GROUP

	#1	#2	#3	
11	1500			Area
12	14			Existing R
13	16			Add R

WALLS

| 14 | 1 | ## | 14. Number of wall area groups separating living space from unconditioned space

15. Wall type:
   1. Open frame   4. Block/masonry in heated
   2. Closed frame   basement below grade
   3. Block/masonry   5. Closed frame below grade

16. Net wall area in square feet

17. R-value existing

18. R-value to be added

WALL GROUP

	#1	#2	#3	
15	2			Type
16	1084			Area
17	9			Existing R
18	0			Add R

GLASS

| 19 | 4 | ## | 19. Number of glass area groups (consider orientation and type)

20. Glass location:
   1. Window   2. Patio door

21. Orientation:
   1. North   4. Northeast/Northwest
   2. South   5. Southeast/Southwest
   3. East/West   6. Horizontal (i.e., skylight)

22. Area in square feet

23. Present type/shading (enter appropriate 2-digit code)

24. Proposed type/shading (enter appropriate 2-digit code)

	Single	Double	Storm	Triple
Clear	11	12	13	14
Tinted Glass/Film	21	22	23	24
Heavy Drapes/Venetian Blind	31	32	33	34
Reflective	41	42	43	44
Outside Shade/Shade Screen	51	52	53	54
Insulated Shutter/Shades	61	62	63	64

GLASS GROUP

	#1	#2	#3	#4	#5	
20	1	1	1	2		Location
21	1	2	3	2		Orientation
22	25	27	102	40		Area
23	11	11	11	11		Present
24	33	33	33	32		Proposed

DOORS

| 25 | 2 | 25. Number of outside doors (double-wide count twice)

| 26 | 0 | 26. Number of existing insulated or storm doors

| 27 | 0 | 27. Number to be equipped with insulated or storm doors

WHITE - LOCAL OFFICE COPY; CANARY - CUSTOMER COPY; PINK - G.O. COPY

Figure I.3 Home Energy Analysis Input Sheet

INFILTRATION

| 28 | 12 000 | 28. Volume of home's conditioned space in cubic feet |

Enter 1. Good, 2. Fair, 3. Poor, to describe condition of caulking and weatherstripping

29	3	29. General condition of door caulking
30	3	30. General condition of door weatherstripping
31	3	31. General condition of window caulking and putty
32	3	32. General condition of window weatherstripping
33	0	33. Area of Jalousie windows (square feet)

WATER HEATER

| 34 | 1 ** | 34. Number of water heaters |

35. Type of water heater:
1. Electric   3. Propane   5. Wood
2. Natural gas   4. Oil   6. Solar

36. Size of water heater in gallons

37. Thermostat setting:
1. Low (up to 120°)
2. Medium (between 120° and 140°)
3. High (over 140°)

38. Location of water heater:
1. Conditioned space   2. Unconditioned space

39. Should insulation blanket be installed?
1. Yes
2. No - insulation wrap already present
3. No - water heater won't accommodate
4. No - water heater remaining useful life less than three years
5. No - solar water heater
6. No - already energy efficient
7. No - not appropriate

WATER HEATER

	#1	#2	#3	
35	1			Type
36	52			Gallons
37	3			Temperature
38	2			Location
39	1			Blanket

FLOORS

| 40 | 1 ** | 40. Number of floor area groups separating living space from unconditioned space |

41. Floor construction:
1. Over vented crawl space
2. Over closed crawl space or unheated basement
3. Slab on grade
4. Slab in heated basement
5. Mobile
6. Stem wall

42. Area in square feet (unheated basement floor, floor over crawl space, or stem wall), perimeter in linear feet (slab) or skirting square feet (mobile home)

43. R-value existing

44. R-value to be added, level one (N.C. Only)

45. R-value to be added, level two

FLOOR GROUP

	#1	#2	#3	
41	1			Construction
42	1500			Area
43	4			Existing R
44	11			Add R, Level One (N.C. Only)
45	19			Add R, Level Two

HEATING AND COOLING SYSTEMS

| 46 | 7 | 46. Main type of heating system: |

1. Electric central furnace
2. Electric resistance room heaters
3. Electric central heat pump
4. Electric room heat pumps
5. Natural gas central furnace/boiler
6. Natural gas room heaters
7. Oil furnace/boiler
8. Coal furnace
9. L.P. gas furnace
10. L.P. gas room heater
11. Wood
12. Fireplace
13. Solar
14. None
15. Other

| 47 | 1 | 47. Main type of cooling system: |

1. Electric central   4. Evaporative unit
2. Gas absorption   5. Whole house fan
3. Electric window units 6. None

| 48 | 3 | 48. Central cooling unit size (Tons) |
| 49 | 1 | 49. Should clock thermostat be evaluated? |

1. Yes - single setting
2. Yes - double setting
3. No - there is already one present or setting is manually performed
4. No - system will not accommodate one

50	10	50. Degrees setback heating
51	5	51. Degrees setup cooling
52	4	52. Should an electric load management device be evaluated?

1. Yes - control water heating only (LC1)
2. Yes - control air conditioning only (LC2)
3. Yes - control both water heating and air conditioning (LC3)
4. No - not available

| 53 | 0 | 53. Number of load management devices to be installed |

1. One controller inside
2. One controller outside
3. One controller inside and one controller outside
4. Two controllers inside
5. Two controllers outside

| 54 | 0 | 54. KW demand of air conditioner (maximum of 4 KW per 1000 sq.ft. of conditioned space) |
| 55 | 1 ** | 55. Number of duct groups to be entered |

56. Duct location:
1. Crawl space   2. Attic

57. Estimated duct length (linear feet) in unconditioned space

58. R-value existing

59. R-value to be added

60. Ducts used for:
1. Heating system   2. Cooling system   3. Both

DUCT SYSTEM

	#1	#2	#3	
56	1			Location
57	110			Length
58	1			Existing R
59	7			Add R
60	3			System

| 61 | 0 ** | 61. Number of hydronic piping systems to be insulated |

62. Piping system:
1. Steam   3. Heating and cooling
2. Hot water 4. Cooling only

63. Linear feet of pipe to insulate per system

PIPING SYSTEM

	#1	#2	#3	
62	0			Type
63	0			Length

WHITE - LOCAL OFFICE COPY; CANARY - CUSTOMER COPY

Figure I.3 (continued)

| 64 | 2 |

64. Should furnace/oil burner/heat pump replacement be evaluated?
1. Yes - furnace
2. Yes - oil burner
3. Yes - heat pump
4. No - violates code/law or system will not accommodate the installation
5. No - furnace not over five years old or high efficiency burner already installed

| 65 | 66 |

65. Estimated seasonal efficiency of existing oil or gas furnace

| 66 | 77 |

66. Estimated seasonal efficiency of proposed oil or gas furnace

| 67 | 4 |

67. Should flue opening modifications be evaluated?
1. Yes
2. No - already present
3. No - violates code/law
4. No - cannot install
5. No - combustion air taken from non-conditioned space

| 68 | 4 |

68. Should electrical or mechanical furnace ignition system be evaluated?
1. Yes
2. No - already present
3. No - violates code/law
4. No - system will not accommodate installation

| 69 | 1 |

69. Should replacement of central air conditioner be considered?
1. Yes
2. No - violates code/law or system will not accommodate installation
3. No - not over five years old

| 70 | 7.0 |

70. Estimated Seasonal Energy Efficiency Ratio (SEER) of existing unit

| 71 | 7.6 |

71. Estimated Seasonal Energy Efficiency Ratio (SEER) of proposed unit

RENEWABLE RESOURCES

| 72 | * * |

72. If a solar swimming pool heater is to be evaluated, present fuel type is:
1. Electric
2. Natural gas
3. Propane/butane
4. Oil
5. Wood
6. Pool not heated
7. Solar not evaluated - no site exists free of major obstructions
8. Solar not evaluated - pool presently heated with solar

| 73 | * * |

73. Number of months pool heater is used

74. Enter corresponding number for each month pool is heated (e.g., Feb = 2, Dec. = 12, etc.)

MONTHS POOL HEATED

| 74 | | | | | | | | |

| 75 | |

75. Square feet of swimming pool surface

| 76 | |

76. Is a pool cover used?
1. Yes   2. No

| 77 | |

77. Prime solar fraction of solar swimming pool heating system

| 78 | * * |

78. Should an active solar system be evaluated?
1. Yes - domestic water heating only (air system)
2. Yes - active solar space heating system only (air system)
3. Yes - combined active solar space heating system and solar domestic hot water (air system)
4. Yes - domestic water heating only (liquid system)
5. Yes - active solar space heating system only (liquid system)
6. Yes - combined active solar space heating system and solar domestic hot water (liquid system)
7. No - violates code/law
8. No - structure will not accommodate
9. No - no site exists free of major obstructions
10. No - already present

| 79 | |

79. Prime solar fraction for active domestic water heating system

| 80 | |

80. Prime solar fraction for active space heating system

| 81 | |

81. Prime solar fraction for combined active space heating system and domestic hot water system

| 82 | * * |

82. Should passive solar space heating systems be evaluated?
1. Yes
2. No - already present
3. No - violates code/law
4. No - structure will not accommodate
5. No - the living space of the residence does not have a south facing (+ or – 45° of true south) wall or integral roof which is free of major obstructions to solar radiation

| 83 | * * |

83. Number of passive systems evaluated

84. Square feet of gross south wall area available

85. Square feet of adjacent floor

86. Square feet of existing south facing glazing

87. Type of passive system:
1. Direct
2. Indirect - Trombe wall
3. Indirect - water wall
4. Sunspace

88. Orientation of south facing wall in degrees magnetic

89. Glazing tilt (90° equals vertical)

90. Prime solar fraction (PSF)

PASSIVE SOLAR GROUP

	#1	#2	#3	
84				South area
85				Floor area
86				Existing glazing
87				Type
88				Orientation
89				Tilt
90				PSF

| 91 | * * |

91. Should a wind energy device be evaluated?
1. Yes
2. No - does not meet applicability tests

| 92 | |

92. Average annual wind speed corrected to 35-foot height

| 93 | |

93. Roughness character of wind site:
1. Ocean, sand
2. Grass, crops
3. Low woods, rural
4. High woods, suburbs
5. Forest, city

| 94 | |

94. Terrain of wind site:
1. Plains
2. Rolling plains
3. Hills
4. Dense hills
5. Open mountains
6. Mountains

| 95 | |

95. Terrain shelter:
1. Better exposure
2. Typical exposure
3. Slightly sheltered
4. Very sheltered

| 96 | * * |

96. Height of minor wind obstruction

Extra Cost Work Area

Report Item No.	Option 1. Add 2. Replace	Adjustment Amount
_____	_____	_____
_____	_____	_____
_____	_____	_____
_____	_____	_____
_____	_____	_____

	HOME HEAT LOSS BTUH	HOME HEAT GAIN BTUH
Existing	_____	_____
Proposed	_____	_____

Figure I.3 (continued)

Appendix J
Five Formats of the Home Energy Analysis Report

This appendix gives the five versions of Duke Power Company's Home Energy Analysis Report. These five versions are the control case, which is the original Home Energy Analysis Report currently used by Duke Power and the four formats discussed in the report.

Format 1 (figure J.1) is the Duke Power format which is our control case. Format 2 is the control case modified so that the conservation measures are ordered by fastest payback (based on contractor installation costs). The measure with the fastest payback is listed first, and so on. Format 3 (figure J.3) is the control case modified so that the first-year energy-savings column now appears in the first column rather than the last.

Format 4 (figure J.4) involves the greatest modification of the control case. For this format the subjects' reference point is changed. The results of the audit are presented in terms of reductions of energy costs rather than in terms of increases in energy savings (above zero savings). The first-year energy-savings column was replaced by a total annual energy cost column for the house. This latter column represents the annual energy cost of the house if no measures are adopted, less the energy savings of adopting each measure. This column was also moved to the first column. The final modification involved inserting the estimated annual energy cost if no measures were adopted in the upper right-hand corner of the form. Format 5 (figure J.5) highlights the conservation measures that qualify consumers for Duke Power Company's lower RC electricity rate. Figure J.6 shows the notes on the back of the five Home Energy Analysis Report forms.

Each subject was assigned one of the five formats in this appendix by use of a randomization procedure designed to eliminate the systematic effects of any factors, besides information format, on the subjects' conservation decisions.

DUKE POWER

HOME ENERGY ANALYSIS REPORT

Prepared for _____ Phone _____ | 4 | 4 | 5 | 5 | 5 | 4 | 4 | 5 | 5 | 4 | 4 |

Address _____ City _____ Zip _____ CUSTOMER ACCOUNT NO.

ENERGY CONSERVATION MEASURES

Analysis Number 986		CONTRACTOR INSTALLATION d			DO-IT-YOURSELF INSTALLATION			ESTIMATED FIRST YEAR ENERGY SAVINGS e
DESCRIPTION OF MEASURES a		Estimated Cost b	Payback Years Before Tax Credit c	Payback Years After Tax Credit c	Estimated Cost b	Payback Years Before Tax Credit c	Payback Years After Tax Credit c	
1) Ceiling Insulation	f	$ 534	9.3	8.1	$ 360	6.7	5.8	$ 46
2) Attic Ventilation		$ 93			$ 48			$
3) Wall Insulation	g	$			$			$
4) Floor Insulation R-11	h	$ 540	4.9	4.2	$ 210	2.0	1.8	$ 100
5) Floor Insulation R-19	h	$ 810	5.9	5.1	$ 360	2.9	2.4	$ 120
6) Storm/Insulated Windows		$ 1052	11.2	9.9	$ 884	9.8	8.6	$ 71
7) Storm/Insulated Doors		$			$			$
8) Shading Sun Exposed Glass		$ 970	20.2	20.2	$ 582	14.4	14.4	$ 28
9) Caulking Doors/Windows, etc.		$ 183	5.1	4.4	$ 31	1.0	0.8	$ 32
10) Weatherstrip Doors/Windows		$ 428	13.7	12.2	$ 166	6.5	5.7	$ 22
11) Water Heater Insulation Wrap		$ 34	1.2	1.1	$ 12	0.4	0.4	$ 27
12) Clock Thermostat		$ 83	0.8	0.6	$ 77	0.7	0.6	$ 110
13) Duct Insulation		$ 111	2.3	2.0	$ 44	1.0	0.8	$ 46
14) Pipe Insulation		$			$			$
15) Flue Opening Modification		$						$
16) Elec. or Mech. Ignition Systems	i	$						$
17) Replacement Oil Burner	☒ j	$ 314	3.7	3.2				$ 79
18) Replacement Furnace	☐	$						$
19) Replacement Heat Pump	☐	$ 2025	25+	25+				$ 23
20) Repl. Cent. Air Conditioner	k	$						$
21) Load Control Device (LC1)	m	$						$
22) Load Control Device (LC2)	m	$						$
23) Load Control Device (LC3)	m	$						$

See reverse side for notes a through m.

TAX CREDIT CALCULATIONS

The federal government provides tax incentives to encourage the installation of energy conservation products. A tax credit applies to the cost of items installed after April 19, 1977 and before January 1, 1986. Details can be found in IRS publication 903, or by calling your local IRS office.

If a state tax credit is shown in the sample calculation, you may determine more specific information by contacting your local tax office.

The sample calculation provided here applies to item(s) of the analysis. [1, 5, 6]

SAMPLE CALCULATION	l
Cost of measure	$ 2396
Federal Tax Credit	$ - 300
State Tax Credit	$ - 0
Cost of measure with tax credits deducted	$ 2096
Payback years after tax credit	7.4

The results of this Home Energy Analysis and the notes on the back of this form have been explained to me and I have been offered assistance in arranging installation and financing of the Energy Conservation Measures.

Customer Signature _____ Energy Consultant _____ Date _____

ENERCOM ®

Enercom® – A Service To Duke Power

© 1981, ENERCOM, INC.
Tampa #2

WHITE · LOCAL OFFICE COPY · YELLOW · CUSTOMER COPY

Figure J.1   Format 1: The Duke Power format

DUKE POWER

HOME ENERGY ANALYSIS REPORT

Prepared for _____ Phone _____ |4,4|5,5|6,4|4,5,5,4|4|

Address _____ City _____ Zip _____ CUSTOMER ACCOUNT NO.

ENERGY CONSERVATION MEASURES

Analysis Number: **986**

DESCRIPTION OF MEASURES a	CONTRACTOR INSTALLATION d			DO-IT-YOURSELF INSTALLATION			ESTIMATED FIRST YEAR ENERGY SAVINGS e
	Estimated Cost b	Payback Years Before Tax Credit c	Payback Years After Tax Credit c	Estimated Cost b	Payback Years Before Tax Credit c	Payback Years After Tax Credit c	
1) Clock Thermostat	$ 83	0.8	0.6	$ 77	0.7	0.6	$ 110
2) Water Heater Insulation Wrap	$ 34	1.2	1.1	$ 12	0.4	0.4	$ 27
3) Duct Insulation	$ 111	2.3	2.0	$ 44	1.0	0.8	$ 46
4) Replacement Oil Burner i,j	$ 314	3.7	3.2				$ 79
5) Floor Insulation R-11 h	$ 540	4.9	4.2	$ 210	2.0	1.8	$ 100
6) Caulking Doors/Windows, ect.	$ 183	5.1	4.4	$ 31	1.0	0.8	$ 32
7) Floor Insulation R-19 h	$ 810	5.9	5.1	$ 360	2.9	2.4	$ 120
8) Ceiling Insulation f	$ 534	9.3	8.1	$ 360	6.7	5.8	$ 46
9) Attic Ventilation	$ 93			$ 48			
10) Storm/Insulated Windows	$ 1052	11.2	9.9	$ 884	9.8	8.6	$ 71
11) Weatherstrip Doors/Windows	$ 428	13.7	12.2	$ 166	6.5	5.7	$ 22
12) Shading Sun Exposed Glass	$ 970	20.2	20.2	$ 582	14.4	14.4	$ 28
13) Repl. Cent. Air Conditioner	$ 2025	25 +	25 +				$ 23
14)	$			$			$
15)	$			$			$
16)	$			$			$
17)	$			$			$
18)	$			$			$
19)	$			$			$
20)	$			$			$
21)	$			$			$
22)	$			$			$
23)	$			$			$

See reverse side for notes a through m.

TAX CREDIT CALCULATIONS

The federal government provides tax incentives to encourage the installation of energy conservation products. A tax credit applies to the cost of items installed after April 19, 1977 and before January 1, 1986. Details can be found in IRS publication 903, or by calling your local IRS office.

If a state tax credit is shown in the sample calculation, you may determine more specific information by contacting your local tax office.

The sample calculation provided here applies to item(s) of the analysis.   7, 8, 10   **   **

SAMPLE CALCULATION	
Cost of measure	$ 2396
Federal Tax Credit	$ - 300
State Tax Credit	$ - 0
Cost of measure with tax credits deducted	$ 2096
Payback years after tax credit	7.4

The results of this Home Energy Analysis and the notes on the back of this form have been explained to me and I have been offered assistance in arranging installation and financing of the Energy Conservation Measures

Customer Signature _____   Energy Consultant _____   Date _____

ENERCOM®

Enercom® – A Service To Duke Power

© 1981, ENERCOM, INC   Tempe, AZ

WHITE · LOCAL OFFICE COPY • YELLOW · CUSTOMER COPY

Figure J.2   Format 2: Ordering by payback

DUKE POWER — HOME ENERGY ANALYSIS REPORT

Prepared for _____   Phone _____
Address _____ City _____ Zip _____ |4|4|5|5|5|4|4|5|5|4|4|
CUSTOMER ACCOUNT NO.

ENERGY CONSERVATION MEASURES

Analysis Number **986**

DESCRIPTION OF MEASURES	ESTIMATED FIRST YEAR ENERGY SAVINGS	CONTRACTOR INSTALLATION Estimated Cost	Payback Years Before Tax Credit	Payback Years After Tax Credit	DO-IT-YOURSELF Estimated Cost	Payback Years Before Tax Credit	Payback Years After Tax Credit
1) Ceiling Insulation f	46	534	9.3	8.1	360	6.7	5.8
2) Attic Ventilation		93			48		
3) Wall Insulation g							
4) Floor Insulation R-11 h	100	540	4.9	4.2	210	2.0	1.8
5) Floor Insulation R-19 h	120	810	5.9	5.1	360	2.9	2.4
6) Storm/Insulated Windows	71	1052	11.2	9.9	884	9.8	8.6
7) Storm/Insulated Doors							
8) Shading Sun Exposed Glass	28	970	20.2	20.2	582	14.4	14.4
9) Caulking Doors/Windows, etc	32	183	5.1	4.4	31	1.0	0.8
10) Weatherstrip Doors/Windows	22	428	13.7	12.2	166	6.5	5.7
11) Water Heater Insulation Wrap	27	34	1.2	1.1	12	0.4	0.4
12) Clock Thermostat	110	83	0.8	0.6	77	0.7	0.6
13) Duct Insulation	46	111	2.3	2.0	44	1.0	0.8
14) Pipe Insulation							
15) Flue Opening Modification							
16) Elec. or Mech. Ignition Systems i							
17) Replacement Oil Burner ☒ j	79	314	3.7	3.2			
18) Replacement Furnace ☐							
19) Replacement Heat Pump ☐							
20) Repl. Cent. Air Conditioner k	23	2025	25+	25+			
21) Load Control Device (LC1) m							
22) Load Control Device (LC2) m							
23) Load Control Device (LC3) m							

See reverse side for notes a through m.

TAX CREDIT CALCULATIONS

The federal government provides tax incentives to encourage the installation of energy conservation products. A tax credit applies to the cost of items installed after April 19, 1977 and before January 1, 1986. Details can be found in IRS publication 903, or by calling your local IRS office.

If a state tax credit is shown in the sample calculation, you may determine more specific information by contacting your local tax office.

The sample calculation provided here applies to item(s) **1, 5, 6** of the analysis.

SAMPLE CALCULATION

Cost of measure	$ 2396
Federal Tax Credit	$ - 300
State Tax Credit	$ - 0
Cost of measure with tax credits deducted	$ 2096
Payback years after tax credit	7.4

The results of this Home Energy Analysis and the notes on the back of this form have been explained to me and I have been offered assistance in arranging installation and financing of the Energy Conservation Measures

Customer Signature _____ Energy Consultant _____ Date _____

ENERCOM®
Enercom® – A Service To Duke Power
© 1981, ENERCOM, INC Tempe, AZ
WHITE - LOCAL OFFICE COPY • YELLOW - CUSTOMER COPY

Figure J.3   Format 3: Savings column switch

DUKE POWER

ESTIMATED ANNUAL
ENERGY COSTS 1265 *

Prepared for _____   Phone _____

Address _____ City _____ Zip _____ |4.4|5.5|5.4|4.5 5 4|4|
CUSTOMER ACCOUNT NO

ENERGY CONSERVATION MEASURES

Analysis Number 986 DESCRIPTION OF MEASURES	ESTIMATED ANNUAL ENERGY COST WITH INSTALLATION OF MEASURE **	CONTRACTOR INSTALLATION			DO-IT YOURSELF INSTALLATION		
		Estimated Cost	Payback Years Before Tax Credit	Payback Years After Tax Credit	Estimated Cost	Payback Years Before Tax Credit	Payback Years After Tax Credit
1) Ceiling Insulation	$ 1219	$ 534	9.3	8.1	$ 360	6.7	5.8
2) Attic Ventilation		$ 93			$ 48		
3) Wall Insulation	$	$			$		
4) Floor Insulation R-11	$ 1165	$ 540	4.9	4.2	$ 210	2.0	1.8
5) Floor Insulation R-19	$ 1145	$ 810	5.9	5.1	$ 360	2.9	2.4
6) Storm/Insulated Windows	$ 1194	$ 1052	11.2	9.9	$ 884	9.8	8.6
7) Storm/Insulated Doors	$	$			$		
8) Shading Sun Exposed Glass	$ 1237	$ 970	20.2	20.2	$ 582	14.4	14.4
9) Caulking Doors/Windows, etc.	$ 1233	$ 183	5.1	4.4	$ 31	1.0	0.8
10) Weatherstrip Doors/Windows	$ 1243	$ 428	13.7	12.2	$ 166	6.5	5.7
11) Water Heater Insulation Wrap	$ 1238	$ 34	1.2	1.1	$ 12	0.4	0.4
12) Clock Thermostat	$ 1155	$ 83	0.8	0.6	$ 77	0.7	0.6
13) Duct Insulation	$ 1219	$ 111	2.3	2.0	$ 44	1.0	0.8
14) Pipe Insulation	$	$			$		
15) Flue Opening Modification	$	$					
16) Elec. or Mech. Ignition Systems	$	$					
17) Replacement Oil Burner	$ 1186	$ 314	3.7	3.2			
18) Replacement Furnace	$	$					
19) Replacement Heat Pump	$	$					
20) Repl. Cent. Air Conditioner	$ 1242	$ 2025	25+	25+			
21) Load Control Device (LC1)	$	$					
22) Load Control Device (LC2)	$	$					

See reverse side for notes a through m.

* Estimate is based on current cost if <u>no</u> measures are adopted

** Cost is estimated annual energy cost less energy savings from adoption of the measure

TAX CREDIT CALCULATIONS

The federal government provides tax incentives to encourage the installation of energy conservation products. A tax credit applies to the cost of items installed after April 19, 1977 and before January 1, 1986. Details can be found in IRS publication 903, or by calling your local IRS office.

If a state tax credit is shown in the sample calculation, you may determine more specific information by contacting your local tax office.

The sample calculation provided here applies to item(s) of the analysis. | 1, 5, 6 | **   **

SAMPLE CALCULATION	
Cost of measure	$ 2396
Federal Tax Credit	$ - 300
State Tax Credit	$ - 0
Cost of measure with tax credits deducted	$ 2096
Payback years after tax credit	7.4

The results of this Home Energy Analysis and the notes on the back of this form have been explained to me and I have been offered assistance in arranging installation and financing of the Energy Conservation Measures

Customer Signature _____   Energy Consultant _____ Date _____

Enercom® – A Service To
Duke Power

© 1981 ENERCOM INC
Tempe, AZ

WHITE - LOCAL OFFICE COPY • YELLOW - CUSTOMER COPY

Figure J.4   Format 4: Reference point change

DUKE POWER

HOME ENERGY ANALYSIS REPORT

Prepared for _____   Phone _____

Address _____ City _____ Zip _____

| 4 4 5 5 9 4 4 5 5 4 4 |
CUSTOMER ACCOUNT NO.

ENERGY CONSERVATION MEASURES

Analysis Number: 986 — DESCRIPTION OF MEASURES a	CONTRACTOR INSTALLATION d			DO-IT-YOURSELF INSTALLATION			ESTIMATED FIRST YEAR ENERGY SAVINGS e
	Estimated Cost b	Payback Years Before Tax Credit c	Payback Years After Tax Credit c	Estimated Cost b	Payback Years Before Tax Credit c	Payback Years After Tax Credit c	
1) ░░░							
2) ░░░							
3) Wall Insulation g	$			$			$
4) Floor Insulation R-11 h	$ 540	4.9	4.2	$ 210	2.0	1.8	$ 100
5) ░░░							
6) ░░░							
7) Storm/Insulated Doors	$			$			$
8) Shading Sun Exposed Glass	$ 970	20.2	20.2	$ 582	14.4	14.4	$ 28
9) Caulking Doors/Windows, etc.	$ 183	5.1	4.4	$ 31	1.0	0.8	$ 33
10) Weatherstrip Doors/Windows	$ 428	13.7	12.2	$ 166	6.5	5.7	$ 22
11) Water Heater Insulation Wrap	$ 34	1.8	1.1	$ 13	0.4	0.4	$ 27
12) Clock Thermostat	$ 83	0.8	0.6	$ 77	0.7	0.6	$ 110
13) ░░░							
14) Pipe Insulation	$			$			$
15) Flue Opening Modification	$						$
16) Elec. or Mech. Ignition Systems i	$						$
17) Replacement Oil Burner ▣ j	$ 314	3.7	3.2				$ 79
18) Replacement Furnace ☐	$						$
19) Replacement Heat Pump ☐	$ 2025	25+	25+				$ 23
20) Repl. Cent. Air Conditioner k	$						$
21) Load Control Device (LC1) m	$						$
22) Load Control Device (LC2) m	$						$
23) Load Control Device (LC3) m	$						$

See reverse side for notes a through m.   *Implementation of <u>all</u> the shaded measures is required to qualify for the RC electric rate

TAX CREDIT CALCULATIONS

The federal government provides tax incentives to encourage the installation of energy conservation products. A tax credit applies to the cost of items installed after April 19, 1977 and before January 1, 1986. Details can be found in IRS publication 903, or by calling your local IRS office.

If a state tax credit is shown in the sample calculation, you may determine more specific information by contacting your local tax office.

The sample calculation provided here applies to item(s) of the analysis. | 1, 5, 6 | •• ••

SAMPLE CALCULATION	
Cost of measure	$ 2396
Federal Tax Credit	$ - 300
State Tax Credit	$ - 0
Cost of measure with tax credits deducted	$ 2096
Payback years after tax credit	7.4

The results of this Home Energy Analysis and the notes on the back of this form have been explained to me and I have been offered assistance in arranging installation and financing of the Energy Conservation Measures.

Customer Signature _____   Energy Consultant _____   Date _____

ENERCOM ®
Enercom® – A Service To
Duke Power

©1981, ENERCOM, INC
Tempe, AZ

WHITE · LOCAL OFFICE COPY · YELLOW · CUSTOMER COPY

Figure J.5   Format 5: Highlighting the RC rate

NOTES:

a. The consultant preparing this analysis is required to offer you lists of approved contractors, suppliers and lenders. You can then select from these lists for the purchase, installation and financing of the Measures listed.

b. Estimated installed costs are based on average market prices of acceptable products in your community. The prices may vary depending on your selection of contractors and/or the particular product you choose to install. Costs do not include modifications or unique adaptations to your particular home such as adding duct work or special odd-shaped glass.

c. Payback years are calculated by dividing the estimated costs by the estimated annual savings. These savings take into account projected energy cost escalation rates. The actual payback period may vary depending on your selection of products and contractors as well as personal life style and energy use habits. A "25+" indicates that the payback exceeds 25 years. If you wish to only install some of the products, then the lower the payback years, the higher the priority for installation.

d. The choice of an approved contractor or supplier from the lists described in note "a" entitles you to certain benefits. These include a one-year warranty on all products and installations and assurances that products and installations meet government standards. To adequately enforce these standards, the installation of Energy Conservation Measures arranged by Duke Power will be subject to post-installation inspection. You will also have access to conciliation and redress procedures in the case of faulty installations or materials.

e. Estimated first-year energy savings are based on the data recorded about your home and its energy consumption patterns. The procedures used to make these estimates are consistent with Department of Energy criteria for residential energy audits. However, the actual installation costs you incur and energy savings you realize from installing these measures may be different from the estimates contained in this audit report. Although the estimates are based on measurements of your house, they are also based on assumptions derived from regional averages which may not be totally correct for your household. Additionally, the total energy savings from the installation of more than one program measure may be less than the sum of energy savings of each measure installed individually.

f. See ceiling section of input sheet for R value to be added. In conjunction with insulation, the home should have proper ventilation.

g. Only open wall area is considered as a do-it-yourself project for wall insulation. See wall section of input sheet for R value to be added.

h. In conjunction with floor insulation in homes with enclosed crawl spaces, the crawl spaces should be properly ventilated. See floor section of input sheet for R value to be added. Floor insulation in a mobile home also means skirting to enclose the space between the building and the ground.

i. If your home is heated by a source of fuel other than electricity, only the supplier of the other fuel may audit your furnace unless you specifically request us to audit your furnace. Federal law requires that such a request be in writing. If you want us to audit your furnace, although we do not supply the fuel for it, please sign below.

Customer Signature_____

j. Replacement furnace is evaluated only if existing furnace is approximately five years old or older. Burner replacement is evaluated if furnace is less than five years old, and burner is not already high-efficiency type.

k. See analysis input sheet for Seasonal Energy Efficiency Ratio (SEER) of replacement air conditioner.

l. The sample calculation provided assumes that a tax liability exists against which tax credits may be applied.

m. The total credits on any monthly bill on the schedule shall not exceed 20% of the current monthly bill as calculated on this schedule exclusive of such credits.

Figure J.6 Notes on the back of the Home Energy Analysis Report

This appendix contains the protocol used for presenting information to the subjects who receiving format 1 (our control case, the Duke Power format). This protocol was used by the interviewer to ensure consistency of presentation across both subjects and formats. By using this experimental design, interviewer bid (i.e., undue influence of the interviewer on the subject) was minimized. The protocols for the four other formats were very similar to the control case protocol. The differences in these formats reflect the different ways in which the audit information on the house is organized on the Home Energy Analysis Report (see figures J.1–J.5).

Audit Protocol—Control

I am a Research Associate working with Professors Wesley Magat and John Payne of the Fuqua School of Business on a study on residential energy audit programs. I wish to thank you for coming today and participating in the project.

Let me give you a brief summary of the main parts of our study. Due to the increasing cost of generating electricity and other energy sources, utilities have become increasingly interested in ways to conserve energy. Through federal and state mandated programs and on their own, electric utilities have developed energy audit programs for residential customers. Through these audit programs, the utilities provide information to customers on how to conserve energy.

The energy audit is performed by a state certified auditor who checks out the general energy efficiency of one's house. This consists of measurements of the house, of various insulation levels throughout the house, and inspection of the windows and doors. The heating and cooling systems are also examined. All this information is then submitted to a computer especially designed to do energy audits. The computer analyzes the data and provides information to the homeowner on the cost and energy savings of various conservation measures. For this study I will assume the role of the auditor.

This experiment was structured in such a way that it models, as realistically as possible, the way an actual energy audit of a home would be performed by a utility in this state. To assist in this process, we are using the actual forms that would be used by a Duke Power auditor. Though we are using their forms, we are not affiliated with the Duke Power Company. However, the results of our study will be available to them and the other utilities, as well as to various state government agencies. Our prime recipient, however, is the N.C. Energy Institute, the sponsor of this study. It is hoped that the results of this project will contribute to the implementation of more effective energy audit programs.

To achieve this aim, it is very important that your answers are as accurate as possible. For the purpose of this experiment, we want you to assume the role of the homeowner of the house for which I have performed the audit. It is most important that you answer all the questions in the same manner as you would if an actual auditor came to do an audit of your place of residence, the only difference being that you are now to consider yourself the owner of this home. For example, if you are planning to not move for three more years then you are to assume that you would be living in this house for three more years. Your income and financial obligations are to remain unaffected by your assumption as owner of this house. In addition we wish you to consider your mortgage obligations for this house in the following manner: If you are a homeowner, your mortgage payments would be the same for this house as it is for your own home. If you are a renter, your mortgage payment (adjusted for tax deductions) would be the same as what you currently pay for rent. These assumptions are most important in generating valid data. Do you have any questions before we proceed?

The procedure for today's experiment is as follows: First, I will describe the house which has been audited and its condition in terms of energy efficiency. Second, I will go over the analysis of the energy audit step by step and discuss how the audit results were computed. Finally, I will provide you with this information and some additional information. You will then be given a form to fill out which asks you several questions about a set of conservation measures you may choose to acquire for this house that I describe.

Do you have any questions before we proceed with the experiment?

It will be useful to look at the pictures of the house, the house fact sheet, and the definition sheet found in the left side if your packet while I am describing the house.

The house for which the audit was performed is typical of a type of house commonly found in the Triangle area. These are some pictures of the house, which should help give you a feel for the size of the house. It is a one-story ranch-style house with three bedrooms, two baths, a kitchen, and a combination living room/dining room. The total floor space of the house is 1,500 square feet. It is seven years old and has oil heat, electric central air-conditioning, and a 52-gallon water heater. The furnace and oil burner are original with the house. There is some insulation in the ceilings and walls, but less than the recommended amount for new houses. Specifically the ceiling is insulated to R-14, and the walls are insulated to R-9. There is no insulation in the floor.

As you may know, the effectiveness of insulation in resisting heat flow, either out of the house in winter or into it in summer, is measured in R-values, not thickness. The higher the R number, the more effective the insulation. More information on insulation and R-values can be found in the information sheet in the right side of your packet.

The windows in this house are standard single-pane glass without storm windows, and the two doors are not equipped with storm doors. The caulking and weather stripping on the windows and doors are poor. This means that most of the caulk is cracked, missing, or loose, and the windows and doors are not weather-stripped. For the last year the total oil bill was $598, and the electric bill was $676, with peak electric bill of $80 in August. This information, which was gathered in more detailed form during the audit, has already been entered on the input sheet, which can be found in your packet.

The analysis of the data obtained from the measures and inspection of this house was produced by submitting the data to a computer in Rockville, Maryland. This computer was programmed by experts solely to do energy audits by utilities all over the country. For several conservation measures it gives information on estimated installation cost, length if payback before and after federal tax credits on conservation measures, and first-year energy savings. The figures are calculated for both do-it-yourself installation and contractor installation for the various conservation measures. The computer also takes into account the specific climatic conditions for the Triangle area when getting its estimates. Thus the actual cost and savings should provide a good guide for comparison purposes among the various conservation measures listed.

In looking at the actual report itself, you can see that in the left-hand column there are a number of energy conservation measures that you can install that will reduce your electric and heating bills. Any measure with information written in beside it has been audited for. I will explain a number of these measures in depth. If there is a measure that I have not explained which is confusing or if any of the information I present to you is unclear, please feel free to stop me. You will notice that the two measures, wall installation and storm or insulated doors, have not been audited for. The reason for this is twofold. First, since this house already has some insulation in the walls, additional insulation was not audited for due to the difficulty of adding it. Second, it is standard practice for this climatic region not to audit for storm or insulated doors.

The first of the conservation measures listed is ceiling insulation. I audited for an increase from R-14 to an R-30 level. This is the level recommended by the state.

If you had a contractor install the insulation, your cost would be approximately $534 with a payback of 9.3 years before tax credits and a payback of 8.1 years after deductions are made for the federal residential energy credits on purchase of conservation measures. By payback, I mean the length of time it would take for this measure to pay for itself through the energy savings you would achieve every year. So in this case your investment of $534 would pay for itself in 8.1 year, when taking into account tax credits. Now, if you do not have a tax liability, the payback you would want to look at is the payback before tax credits.

If you installed the insulation yourself, the cost would be $360 with a payback of 6.7 years before tax credit and 5.8 years after tax credits. If you either cannot or do not want to install the insulation yourself, then the figures you want to concentrate on are those for contractor installation. Finally, your first-year energy savings for installing the additional insulation is estimated to be $46.

This house does not have sufficient attic ventilation. To increase the ventilation to the proper amount would cost $93 if a contractor did it and $48 if it was done by yourself. As you can see, neither first-year energy savings nor payback are calculated for attic ventilation. The reason for this is that proper attic ventilation contributes to energy conservation through allowing the ceiling insulation to function at peak efficiency. Without adequate ventilation, the insulation will not be working at maximum efficiency, the true energy savings will be somewhat less than the stated value, and the corresponding paybacks will be longer.

For the floor insulation I audited for two different values. An R-11 level is equivalent to a standard fiberglass batt of $3\frac{1}{2}$ inches, while R-19 level is equivalent to a 6-inch batt.

In looking at the figures for insulating the floor to the R-19 level, you can see that the contractor cost for this job is $810. The payback before tax credits is 5.9 years, and the payback after tax credits is 5.1 years. The cost of do-it-yourself installation would be $360 with paybacks of 2.9 years and 2.4 years. Your first-year energy savings would be $120. I audited this house for storm windows on all the windows. The cost of installation would be $1,052 if done by a contractor. The paybacks are 11.2 and 9.9 years. For do-it-yourself installation, the cost would be $884 with these paybacks. The energy saving in your first year is estimated at $71. Jumping to another measure, caulking, you can see that the cost fr a contractor to do this job would be $183 with these paybacks. If you were to do it yourself, the cost is estimated at $31 with these paybacks. First-year energy savings is $32. Insulating the outside of your water heater with an insulation wrap to prevent heat loss would cost you $34 if the contractor were to do it. These would be your paybacks. Doing it yourself would cost $12, and your paybacks would be these. The first-year energy savings would be $27. A clock thermostat which would automatically turn down your furnace or air conditioner at night after you have gone to bed and turn it back up before you get up in the morning would cost $83 if a contractor installed it. The payback would be 0.8 years before and 0.6 years after tax credits. The first-year energy savings would be $110. A replacement oil burner which would increase the energy of the furnace was audited for. The cost of a new burner installed would be $314. These would be the paybacks. The estimated first year energy savings would be $79

On the back of the analysis report I just discussed, you will notice a set of notes that more fully explains the terms and provides additional information. You will also find some additional information in your packet that may be of use to you. This information includes a master list of state-approved contractors, suppliers, and lenders; information on how to pick a contractor, suppliers, and lenders; information on how to pick a contractor and lender; and a form for obtaining financing. I advise you to refer to the sheets in your packet when necessary while filling out the questionnaire.

At this point an actual auditor would leave, and you would be able to decide at your own leisure what, if any, conservation measures you would add to your house. However, we are interested in immediate feedback on what measures you would spend money on, if any, over the next six months if this were your actual house. Please look over the information I have given you and consider what measures you would undertake. When considering the various measures, I want you to take into account your time commitment and the inconvenience and aggravation you may be subject to if you were to actually invest in any of these conservation measures. For contractor installation this would involve obtaining bids for the job, deciding on the contractor, acquiring financing if desired, and monitoring the contractor's work. This would require some time off from work to accomplish, and if the contractor did any work inside the house, someone would need to be there to open and close the house. For do-it-yourself installation this would involve obtaining financing if desired, buying materials, and actually installing the materials yourself. This would also probably require some time off from work to accomplish.

Please look over the questionnaire carefully. Answer the three questions as completely and accurately as possible. Do you have any questions on the information I have presented to you, the sheets in your packet, or the questionnaire itself? I will check in on you periodically if you have any questions. When you finish, let me know.

(Hand questionnaire to subject)

Now I would like to answer a few debriefing questions which will provide us with additional information that is very important for our analysis. All answers will be confidential and will not be associated with you in any way.

(Hand subject debriefing questionnaire)

(Pick up debriefing questionnaire; probe for further answers if necessary)
Thank you for your cooperation.

(Pay subject)

This appendix contains the questionnaires that the subject filled out after receiving the audit results. The energy conservation measures questionnaire (A) was given to the subjects upon completion of the protocol by the interviewer, and the debriefing form (B) was then handed out upon completion of the first questionnaire.

A. Energy Conservation Measures Questionnaire

Please note: These answers should represent, as accurately as possible, what you, as the homeowner of this house, would do in the next six months if presented with the results of this energy audit.

1. Do you intend to invest in any of the conservation measures stated on the Energy Savings Program Report? (circle one)

    _____ Yes   _____ No

    If yes, please list the measure you intend to invest in:

    Do-it-yourself installation   Contractor installation

2. Please rank order the measured listed above in the order in which you would do them. (Place the appropriate number next to each item, e.g., 1 for your first choice, 2 for your second choice, etc.)

3. If you could obtain financing at 18 percent per year, would you finance any of the measures you listed in question 1? If yes, please list those measures below.

B. Debriefing Form

Please note: These questions are very important in providing us with valuable information for our analysis. Please try to be as accurate and complete as possible. All answers will be confidential and will not be associated with you in any way.

1. Please describe the process by which you decided what measures to invest in.

2. Was excessive cost the sole factor in deciding not to invest in any of the measures?

    _____ Yes   _____ No

    If yes, for which ones?

3. Did you have a limit on the dollar amount you would spend on conservation measures regardless of payback?

_____ Yes   _____ No

If yes, what is the dollar limit?

4. How did you choose between contractor installation and do-it-yourself installation for these measures?

5. Did you feel that the personal time commitment and inconvenience necessary to install these measures was an important factor in deciding not to acquire any of these measures?

_____ Yes   _____No

If yes, for which ones?

6. Was the information understandable and presented clearly?

_____ Yes   _____No

If not, what caused the confusion?

7. Did you feel that the audit information was accurate and believable?

_____ Yes   _____ No

If not, what specifically did you find to be inaccurate or not believable?

8 Was enough information provided to make good decisions?

_____ Yes   _____ No

If not, what additional information would you have liked?

9. Would advice or recommendations on the conservation measures listed on the form have been useful?

_____ Yes   _____ No

(Be specific)

10. Did concern about the reliability for competence of contractors or suppliers of conservation measures affect your decisions?

_____ Yes   _____ No

If so, how?

11. If we changed the time horizon from six months to one year so that now you are supposed to determine what measures you would acquire in the *next year*, would your answers to question 1 of the Energy Conservation Measures questionnaire have changed?

_____ Yes   _____ No

If so, how?

12. If the interest from question 3 of the Energy Conservation Measures questionnaire you filled out was changed to 6 percent per year from 18 percent, what measures, if any, would you now finance?

13. If the interest rate from the previous question was changed to 0 percent per year (i.e., a no interest loan), would your answers from the above question have changed at all?

_____ Yes   _____ No

If so, how?

14. If the utilities offered a "turnkey" program through which it would, first, *install* any of the conservation measures you chose, second, provide low-cost financing (at a 6 percent interest rate), and, third, add installment payments for these measures to your monthly utility bill, what measures, if any, would you choose?

15. What is your race?

    a.   American Indian, Alaskan native

    b.   Asian, Pacific islander

    c.   Black

    d.   Hispanic

    e.   White

    f.   Other (specify) _____

16. What is your age? _____

17. What was the highest level of schooling you completed?

    a.   No high school   b.   Some high school

    c.   High school degree   d.   Some college

    e.   College degree   f.   Graduate work

18. What is your *family* income? (if greater than $50,000 so state)

_____

The following questions refer to *your* place of residence.

19. Do you live in a house, condominium or apartment?

    a.   House   b.   Condominium

    c.   Apartment   d.   Mobile home

20. Do you own or rent?

    a.   Own   b.   Lease with option to buy   c.   Rent

21. Which best describes where you live?

    a.   City   b.   Suburbs

    c.   Country

22. How many people are living at your current residence?

_____

23. How long have you lived at your current location?

    _____

24. How much longer do you intend to live there?

    _____

25. What temperature do you keep your residence at during

    Winter? _____   Summer? _____

26. What type of heating do you have in your home?

    _____

27. What was your total heating bill (or electric bill if you have electric heat) and the peak monthly bill last winter November 1–February 28)? (estimate if necessary)

    Total bill _____   Peak monthly bill _____

28. What, if any, conservation measures have you added to your house or already have?

29. Have you had an energy audit done to your place of residence?

    ____ Yes   ____ No

30. In making your decision on the conservation measures, did you consider the effect of these decisions on the resale value of this house?

    ____ Yes   ____ No

31. If you were considering purchasing this house, which measures listed on the analysis report would increase the amount you would pay for the house if they were installed?

Notes

Chapter 1

1. For review of studies of cigarette and saccharin warnings, see the U.S. Department of Health and Human Services (1987).

2. The literature on this class of issues is quite extensive. Among the many contributions to the literature are Camerer and Kunreuther (1989), Kunreuther (1978), Kunreuther (1976), Fischhoff et al. (1981), Zeckhauser (1986), and Viscusi and Magat (1987).

3. A critique of these education campaigns is provided by Adler and Pittle (1984). The disappointing seatbelt experience is also documented by Blomquist (1988).

4. See Viscusi and O'Connor (1984).

5. See Viscusi and Magat (1987).

6. U.S. Department of Health and Human Services (1987).

7. Perspectives other than our own on the development of hazard warning policies are provided by Hadden (1985), O'Reilly (1987), and Smith, Desvousges, Fisher, and Johnson (1988).

8. Use of surveys to analyze valuations of risk is not unprecedented. In addition to our own earlier work, see Berger, Blomquist, Kenkel, and Tolley (1987) and Gerking, de Haan, and Schulze (1988). The latter study draws parallels between the survey results and labor market studies of comparable risks.

9. For another subsequent example of the use of the open-ended memory recall technique to the evaluation of an information provision program, see Bostrom et al. (1990).

10. A detailed exposition of the requirements for effective experimental design is provided by Fischhoff and Furby (1988).

Chapter 2

1. Appendixes D and E provide brief descriptions of the adverse health effects caused by these six types of injuries. These injuries were listed on a card that was read and then shown to the subjects who provided the risk valuations.

2. Since the subjects were carefully screened and randomly selected from a mall frequented by middle-income residents of a medium-sized city, we expect that they are similar to the national population of users of the two products; however, only a much more expensive and time-consuming national survey would provide statistically valid inferences about the national population.

3. Despite efforts to assure interviewer uniformity, some interviewers differed in terms of the number of responses that subjects provided to their interview question. To guard against this source, care was taken to ensure that each interviewer conducted approximately the same number of interviews for each variant of the product labels. This balancing ensures that differences in responses across labels are not due to differences in interviewers.

In addition to the unstructured recall questions that formed the main part of our empirical evidence about consumer responses to labels, we did make limited use of direct responses questions for the validation results described in chapter 7. By adding some direct response questions about precautionary actions to the mall intercept questionnaire after the recall question, we were able to compare the mall sample's responses to the responses of a telephone sample of toilet bowl cleaner and insect spray users who were asked the same questions. This allowed us to test how well the mall sample's precautionary responses to labels match the precautionary actions that product users report they take.

Chapter 3

1. Studies using data other than wage-risk trade-off information have been less numerous. See, for example, Acton (1973) and Viscusi and Magat (1987).

2. Contributions to this literature include Arrow (1982), Hogarth and Kunreuther (1985), Kahneman and Tversky (1979, 1982), Lichtenstein et al. (1978), Thaler (1980), and Viscusi (1985b). Kahneman, Slovic, and Tversky (1982) and Tversky and Kahneman (1981) review much of this work.

3. The fundamental treatment of this theory is Savage (1954).

4. Viscusi (1979) employs the health-state framework. The multiattribute framework in Weinstein, Shepard, and Pliskin (1980) is a variant of the same approach.

5. Subscripts denote derivatives.

6. In the case of a fatality, the utility function can be viewed as the bequest function.

7. This issue arises in the labor market context as well. See Viscusi (1979) for a theoretical analysis of this issue.

8. In the appendix H we show that in general for nonincremental risk reductions, the sum of the willingness to pay for reducing risks 1 and 2 separately may exceed, equal, or fall below the willingness to pay for reducing both risks simultaneously. In the special case of equal probabilities of each injury ($p_1 = p_2$), equal utilities when either injury occurs ($U^1 = U^2$), and utility differences across states satisfying ($U^1 - U^3$) $\geq$ ($U^0 - U^1$), we prove that the risk values are subadditive; that is, $\partial V/\partial \alpha + \partial V/\partial \beta > \partial^2 V/\partial \alpha \partial \beta$. However, if either the disutilities of the two injuries differ ($U^1 \neq U^2$) or the probabilities of the two injuries differ ($p_1 \neq p_2$), then both subadditivity and superadditivity are possible.

9. For a discussion of the impact of anxiety on the theory of compensating differentials, see Viscusi (1979, ch. 4).

10. In their study of individuals' assessment of risks of fatality, Lichtenstein et al. (1978) found that individuals tended to overassess low probability risks of death. They viewed this phenomenon as evidence of a systematic bias in behavior, and it has often been cited as an example of individual irrationality. The analysis presented in Viscusi (1985a) using the same data set suggests that this phenomenon is quite consistent with rational Bayesian behavior. The overassessment of small risks and the underassessment of large risks is exactly what one would expect if individuals revised their probabilistic beliefs toward the true probabilities but did not do so completely because they lacked full information about the risks. What is most important is that there is no risk-related bias in the degree of learning about the true probabilities

11. See Viscusi (1989) for a theoretical model of this reference risk effect. Bell's (1982) theory of decision regret provides another possible explanation for why individuals act as if an increase in a risk above a natural reference point, such as the risk associated with an existing product, is larger than the actual value of the risk increase. Under this theory consumers associate regret with the risk increase but not the risk decrease. Thus they must be paid more to accept the risk increase than they would pay to acquire the risk decrease

12. Although it is feasible to present a given subject with different starting risks in such experiments, doing so may jeopardize the credibility of the experiment to the extent that respondents no longer believe the base value and the experimental scenario

13. All the questions were specifically designed to elicit willingness-to-pay values for risk reductions. Consumers may of course gain some consumer surplus from purchasing the product, but the questions were designed so as not to alter the size of this surplus across questions

Chapter 4

1. Although the willingness-to-pay principle has been used for decades in the literature on benefit-cost analysis, its applicability to risk valuation was first articulated by Schelling (1968, 127–162). His concern was primarily with private rather than public risk valuation.

2. In addition market imperfections such as incomplete worker information could limit the usefulness of this approach. See Viscusi (1983) for a discussion of the importance of these imperfections.

3. For a review of this approach of nonrisk issues, see Cummings, Brookshire, and Schulze (1984).

4. We did not adopt the conjoint approach here because it requires considerably more interviewing time and produces results that are similar to those obtained with more directive questions.

5. For a review of these studies, see Viscusi (1986).

6. See Viscusi and Moore (1987).

7. U.S. Department of Commerce (1985, 43).

8. Ibid.

Chapter 5

1. See Viscusi, Magat, and Huber (1986) for an example of how reformatting the information on product labels can increase consumer intentions to take precautionary actions. Chapter 8 provide an example of how reformatting the information provided by home energy audits can improve the effectiveness of consumer energy conservation decisions.

2. See Viscusi and Magat (1987).

3. Beihal and Chakravarti (1982) also use memory recall patterns to infer the organization of consumer memory; Beihal and Chakravarti (1986) use a free recall task to learn about memory processes in consumer choice.

4. See Russo (1974), Summers (1974), Wilkie (1974), and Staelin and Payne (1976).

5. For another example of a study of the structure of memory, see Scrull, Lichtenstein, and Rothbart (1985). As in our study they provide information to subjects and then test information recall by analyzing the fraction of responses in different categories, the items recalled first, and the order in which the information is recalled.

6. By adding cross product terms composed of the label dummy variables multiplied by the demographic variables (e.g., income and education), we did test whether the demographic variables caused a differential effect of the labels on the number of responses in each category. However, these equations do not show any significant interactive effect with the label dummy variables.

7. With the uncluttered label 2, 48.6 percent of the last two responses given by subjects were Do's responses, whereas with the cluttered label 3 that figure fell to 42.8 percent.

Chapter 8

1. See Energy Division, "North Carolina Energy Conservation Plan" (1978).

2. See Russo, Krieser, and Miyashita (1975).

3. See Brownell and Dunn (1978); and U.S. Congress, Office of Technology Assessment, Residential Energy Conservation (1979).

4. See Yates and Arsonson (1983), Dinan (1987), Hirst and Goeltz (1987–1988), and Hartman (1988). In another review of the literature on household energy use, McDougall et al. (1981) suggest that "With home retrofits offering significant energy-savings potential and a range of home audit programs in existence, it seem particularly useful to attempt to identify the program characteristics that increase householders' conservation actions in a cost-effective manner."

5. See Rosenberg and Lanoue (1980).

6. See Pickels and Audet (1987) and Hoffman (1989).

7. In drawing this conclusion, we ignore any nonpecuniary benefits that households derive from energy conservation and assume that households behave as rational economic actors.

8. The RCS program was required of almost all investor-owned utilities by the 1978 National Energy Conservation Policy Act (1979).

9. This is a subsidized cost. The true cost to the utility is approximately $100.

10. See Kunreuther et al (1978) and Plott (1981). For a systematic treatment of the experimental approach to microeconomics, see Smith (1982).

11. For examples, see Lichtenstein and Slovic (1973), Berkowitz and Donnerstein (1982), and Dipboye and Flanagan (1979).

12. We used the outlier diagnostics in Belsley, Kuh, and Welsch (1980) to identify particularly influential subjects and then analyzed them in detail to determine if they should be used in our analysis. As in most experimental or survey projects, a few of the responses (seven) could not be incorporated into the analysis because the subjects misunderstood the experiment (e.g., they selected measures that were not audited for, did not answer some questions, or did not understand the instructions) or made wholly unreasonable choices (e.g., that they would spend more than 50 percent of their income on conservation measures).

13. We did consider, but rejected, an alternative experimental design. This field-based experiment would have changed the format of the information presented to randomly selected subsamples of consumers who requested RCS audits. While this approach would have increased the outward realism of the experiment, we believed that it would have had little effect on the differences in responses across formats. Further it would have introduced a large amount of additional noise into the responses due to the variation in housing characteristics across households. The major cost of using the approach based on a single house is not in the sincerity with which subjects respond to the task but rather in the inability to learn from the experiment how housing characteristics affect the responses to audits. Since the major purpose of the study was to test differences in responses across formats, rather than making population estimates of the magnitudes of the responses, we judged this cost to be small.

15. It appears that when people are asked to consider the benefits of a technology prior to learning about its risks, they become more accepting or the adoption of that technology than

when presented with the risk information first. Fischhoff, Slovic, Lichtenstein, Read, and Combs (1976).

16. See Kahneman and Tversky (1979).

17. Yates and Aronson (1983) offer the same hypothesis.

18. The procedure was designed to closely follow the protocol of an actual home energy audit. See appendix I for the information packet given to each subject that described the audited home.

19. See appendix K for the written protocols the interviewer used when presenting the information to the subjects.

20. We told renters to answer the audit questions as if they were the owner of the house being audited, explaining to them that their income and financial obligations would remain unaffected by their assumption as owner of the house and that their mortgage payment (adjusted for tax deductions) would be the same as what they currently pay for rent.

21. Only 10 out of the 13 conservation measure choices were examined in the logit analyses because two of them were too infrequently selected to analyze (replacement of central air conditioner and shading sun-exposed glass) and one of them (attic ventilation) should logically be selected primarily when ceiling insulation is installed.

22. This yields 1,464 observations (122 subjects times 12 usable measures). The thirteenth measure, attic ventilation, could not be used since it should logically be chosen only when ceiling insulation is installed.

23. Attic ventilation was not included because no estimate of its first-year energy savings or payback was provided to households by the audit. Also we used seemingly unrelated regression (SUR) to determine if there was a correlation between the error terms of the TOTINV equation [equation (1), table 8.3] and the SAVINV equations [equations (3) and (5), table 8.3], or between the error terms of the TOTINV equation and the EFLOSS equations [equations (4) and (6), table 8.3]. The TOTINV and SAVINV equations have no across-equation convariance; thus there was no efficiency gain over ordinary least squares in using SUR. In the other equation systems [i.e., equations (1) and (4) and equations (1) and (6)], the across-equation covariances were not zero. The coefficients and standard errors differed so little between the OLS and SUR formulations, however, that we report the OLS results to simplify our table of regression results.

24. Several other measures of the relative efficiency of consumer choices could have been used as well. We used EFLOSS because we believe that a percentage measure is easy to understand and we wish to focus on the loss of efficiency in choices.

25. When a logarithmic specification is used, the coefficients of the dummy variables (e.g., FORMAT2) measure the percentage change in the dependent variables caused by a change in the dummy variable and the coefficients of the continuous variables (e.g., AGE) measure response elasticities. For example, format 2 is estimated to result in 33 percent less investment than the control format 1 and consumers 1 percent older investment 0.53 percent more.

26. For example, a variable that indicates a household's decision on whether to select a particular conservation measure is a qualitative variable.

27. Usually one hesitates to draw inferences from any individual coefficient unless it is significant at some reasonably high confidence level, such as 90 or 95 percent. However, we are interested in the effects of format changes on the entire set of choices. Thus we also examine the pattern of signs of the coefficients for any one format variable in all the logit equations, even if some of them are not individually significant, for this pattern suggests whether the format change causes consumer choices to be redirected toward those measures with the

fastest paybacks. Given the relatively small sample size in the experiment, we would expect any individual coefficient to be insignificant at traditional confidence levels unless the magnitude of the format effect was extremely large.

28. See note 21.

29. Only 12 out of the 13 conservation measure choices were examined in the logit analyses because attic ventilation should logically be selected primarily when ceiling insulation is installed. Attic ventilation improves the benefits of ceiling insulation, but its separate energy savings cannot be accurately be estimated.

30. The independence of irrelevant alternatives means that if additional bundles of measures are added to the choice set, they will not affect the preference orderings the consumer has for any current bundles. For example, if A is preferred to B (APB), then inclusion of C to the choice set does not change the preference ordering (i.e., APB is still true). Note that bundles can be single measures. This means empirically that the odds ratio between any two measures is unaffected by the total number of choices. Thus, if an additional measure is added to or dropped from the choice set, it will have no effect on the odds ratio of the other measures. For more information on conditional logit models and this issue, see Maddala (1984).

31. With every subject able to select almost any combination of the 12 conservation measures, the multinomial logit model would require identifying all 13 factorial possible combinations, creating an estimation problem much too large to solve. Even if it could be solved, we would still have to make an assumption about the errors, and independence is not necessarily a more benign assumption for the multinomial model than it is for the conditional logit model. With 122 subjects and no useful way to combine them into homogeneous groups, the fixed effects model with 121 dummy variables is also too large to solve.

32. The magnitude of any violation of the independence assumption of the logit model can be reduced by estimating a separate logit equation for every conservation measure, which we discussed above. As we will see shortly, these results are consistent with those reported in table 8.5.

33. Table 8.5 indicates that equation (1) was estimated using 1,188 observations. This reflects the number of subjects who received formats 1 through 4 (see table 8.1) times 12 measures.

34. Equation (5) was estimated with 216 observations. This reflects the fact that only four out of the five highlighted measures are usable (attic ventilation was excluded).

35. We could have combined the observations for equations (2), (3), (4), and (5) into a single equation, rather than presenting five equations, to obtain slightly more statistical power. However, this approach does not allow for the effects of common variables, such as payback, savings, and the demographic attributes, to vary from one format to another without a significant increase in the number of right-hand side variables

36. Logic equation (1) estimates the log odds of investing in a conservation measure as a linear function of PAYBACK, FORMATS234, PAYBACK × FORMATS234, and some other variables. Thus the coefficient of FORMATS234 measures the change in the vertical intercept and the coefficient of PAYBACK × FORMATS234 measures the change in the slope of the line relating the log odds and PAYBACK

37. Because the estimated increase in the vertical intercept is not statistically significant, the 95 percent confidence interval around the vertical intercept under the new formats contains points below the control format's vertical intercept. However, even it the new formats lowered the intercept, the new formats would have lowered the log odds of selecting measures with slow paybacks more than they would have lowered the log odds of choosing measures with fast paybacks. Thus it would still be true that the bundle of measures chosen under the new formats would be more efficient than those chosen under the control format.

38. Because energy savings and investment cost are so highly correlated, we were unable to use the logit approach to measure the effects of format changes on savings and investment behavior in a manner similar to the way we measured efficiency effects in table 8.3, equations (5) and (6). Crossing the format dummy variables with either savings or investment creates a set of collinear variables, ruling out any inferences from individual coefficients. We used SAVINGS rather than TOTINV to measure the scale effect in equations (1) through (5), table 8.5 because SAVINGS was less correlated with the other right-hand variables.

39. None of the six individual coefficients is statistically significant, but the pattern of the signs of the results is completely consistent with our hypothesis. See note 27 for further discussion of this interpretation.

40. See note 37.

41. This result suggests that residential energy consumers may use decision criteria other than payback for making conservation investments. An explanation may be that consumers lack experience in using payback for conservation investment decision making. See Mazis, Staelin, Beals, and Salop (1981).

42. See note 37.

43. The general hypothesis that the savings column switch causes consumers to save more is rejected. Format 3's coefficient (-4 percent) in the TOTSAV equation (2) of table 8.3 is negative and insignificant. However, the results provide some support for the hypothesis that measures with sufficiently fast paybacks yielding high savings do tend to be selected more under format 2. Floor insulation to the R-19 level offers the largest savings of the ten measures in table 8.4 with a near average payback. Despite the slightly faster payback of R-11 floor insulation, subjects given format 3 instead of the control format usually substituted the higher savings measure (R-19) for the smaller one (R-11). The odds of choosing (R-19) floor insulation increased by 181 percent, while the purchase odds for R-11 floor insulation declined 93 percent. An examination of the summary results in table 8.2 (lines 3 and 4) confirms this substitution effect.

44. Note that equation (5) applies only to the four highlighted measures. Attic ventilation, the fifth qualifying RC measure, was not analyzed because it should logically be selected primarily when ceiling insulation is installed.

45. We suspect that the anomalous positive coefficient on PAYBACK in equation (5) is due to the omission of some important explanatory variables that explain why, out of the four highlighted measures analyzed in the equation, the two with the longest paybacks (ceiling insulation and storm/insulated windows) were chosen by more than twice as many subjects as the second most efficient measure (R-19 floor insulation). With only four measures it is not surprising that some important measure-specific characteristics were not captured in the equation. Two possible characteristics are (1) ease of installation and (2) the fact that households were given the choice of either R-19 or R-11 floor insulation (and roughly twice as many chose R-11). Nonetheless, the positive coefficient is not relevant to our central conclusion that highlighting is insufficient to induce more investment in measures with slow paybacks.

46. It reveals a 150 percent increase in the odds of purchasing duct insulation due to highlighting. Of the remaining six measures only two possess positive coefficients (although each one is insignificant when considered by itself), and one of those positive coefficients (for R-11 floor insulation) could be explained by consumers selecting the less expensive and more cost-effective R-11 floor insulation alternative rather than the highlighted R-19 floor insulation.

47. Application of the collinearity diagnostics suggested by Belsley et al. (1980) shows no significant patterns of collinearity involving AGE, so the AGE coefficient t-statistics in all the regression equations are not biased downward.

48. Collinearity diagnostics reveal that INCOME is uncorrelated with any of the other explanatory variables in the EFLOSS equation (6) but is correlated with EDUC in the SAVINV equation (5). Since the coefficient on income is insignificant in both efficiency equations, the collinearity in the SAVINV equation (5) should cause little hesitancy in concluding from both equations that INCOME creates no significant efficiency effect. In equations (1) and (2) INCOME was also found to be correlated with EDUC, causing deflated t-statistics for the two INCOME coefficients. Thus the statistically significant effects of INCOME on both TITINV and TOTSAV are all the more noteworthy.

49. The strong correlation between EDUC and the intercept is caused by the low variability in EDUC.

50. From table 9.1, the efficiency loss (EFLOSS) was 1.33.

51. It is interesting to contrast our results with the conclusion of the review by Winett and Kagel (1984) of the literature on energy conservation. Both studies show that information formatting changes can produce substantial impact on consumer decisions about energy use. However, our results indicate that these changes primarily affect the efficiency of the consumer choices rather that the quantity of energy savings. Winett and Kagel (1984) found that daily feedback on energy usage can save as much as 30 percent of the cost of energy, although the information programs they surveyed did not allow a direct trade-off between energy savings and the efficiency of achieving those savings. This difference in conclusion indicates that the distinction between the efficiency effect and the total usage effect of format changes in information provision regulatory programs may be an important one for the entire class of programs. It suggests, as well, that the relative magnitudes of the two effects may differ considerably across programs, even among those directed at similar targets.

52. Preliminary results on low-interest financing reported in Brucato (1988) suggests that interest-rate subsidies can substantially increase the amount of conservation investment households are willing to finance and therefore increase their total investment and energy savings.

Chapter 9

1. See Cal. Health and Safety Code 25249.5–25249.13 (Deering 1986).

2. See Cal. Health and Safety Code 25249.6.

3. See State of Cal., Health and Welfare Agency, Notice of Emergency Rulemaking (Feb. 27, 1988 [effective date]). These regulations were issued on February 16, 1988.

4. This is the focus of the Food Industry Safety Council which is headed by George Burditt, Esq., of the law firm of Burditt, Bowles, Radzius and Ruberry, Ltd.

5. See Cal. Health and Safety Code 25249.8, 25249.10.

6. See Ca. Health and Safety Code 25249.6.

7. See Cal. Health and Safety Code 25249.11(c).

8. See Cal. Health and Safety Code 25249.6.

9. See Emergency Regulations, Article 7, to be codified at Cal. Admin. Code Title 22, 12701–12713 (1988).

10. See Emergency Regulations, Article 7, 12703(b), to be codified at Cal. Admin. Code Title 22, 23703(b).

11. The only additional assumptions involved in making the calculations were (1) the implicit value of life ($4,000,000), (2) the length of life (70 years), and (3) the real rate of interest (2 percent).

12. See Emergency Regulations, Article 7, 12703(a), to be codified at Cal. Admin. Code Title 22, 12703(a).

13. For a critique of this type of risk assessment approach see Nichols and Zeckhauser (1986, 13–14).

14. This ordering is the generally accepted hierarchy. See, for example, American National Standard Institute, Specifications For Accident Prevention Signs, ANSI Z35.1–1972, at 8 (1972).

15. See Cal. Health and Safety Code 25249.10(c).

16. See Emergency Regulations, Article 6, 12601(b)(1), to be codified at Cal. Admin. Code Title 22, 12601(b)(1).

17. See Emergency Regulations, Article 6, 12601(c), to be codified at Cal. Admin. Code Title 22, 12601(c).

18. See Emergency Regulations, Article 6, 12601(1)(B), to be codified at Cal. Admin. Code Title 22, 12601(b)(1)(B).

19. See Travis (1987).

20. See Schucker (1983).

21. For early evidence of this type see the Gallup Poll Survey #449-K (Dec. 17, 1949) which found that 52 percent of respondents who smoke and 66 percent of nonsmoking respondents believed that "cigarette smoking is harmful."

22. One of the high estimates of the role of cigarette smoking as causing 25 to 40 percent of all cancer deaths is that of Doll and Peto (1981).

23. See Emergency Regulations, Article 6, 1260(b)(1)(B), to be codified at Cal. Admin. Code Title 22, 1260(b)(1)(B).

24. See Adler and Pittle (1984).

25. The saccharin cancer risk of 40/100,000 or 1/2500 appears as entry 100 at Travis (1987), p. 417.

26. This number is simply the perceived lifetime risk of 0.12 divided by the 0.58 cigarette pack equivalent.

27. See Viscusi and Magat (1987, 93–96).

28. See Emergency Regulations, Article 6, to be codified at Cal. Admin. Code Title 22, 12601.

29. See Ames, Magaw and Gold (1987, 273).

30. See Emergency Regulations, Article 6, 12601(b)(1)(D)(1), to be codified at Cal. Admin. Code Title 22, 12601(b)(1)(D)1l).

31. See Emergency Regulations, Article 6, 12601(b)(1)(A)–(C), to be codified at Cal. Admin. Code Title 22, 12601(b)(1)(A)–(C).

32. See Emergency Regulations, Article 6, 12601(b)(1)(C), to be codified at Cal. Admin. Code Title 22, 12601(b)(1)(C).

33. See 29 Code of Federation Regulations 1910.1200(1987).

References

Acton, J. P. 1973. *Evaluating Public Programs to Save Lives: The Case of Heart Attacks.* R-950-RC. Santa Monica: Rand Corporation,

Adler, R., and D. Pittle. 1984. "Cajolery or Command: Are Education Campaigns an Adequate Substitute for Regulation?" *Yale Journal on Regulation* 2: 159–194.

Ames, B., R. Magaw, and L. Gold. 1987. "Ranking Possible Carcinogens." *Science* 236: 271.

Arrow, K. J. 1982. "Risk Perception in Psychology and Economics." *Economic Inquiry* 20: 1–9.

Beihal, G., and D. Chakravarti. 1982. "Informational-Presentation Format and Learning Goals as Determinants of Consumers' Memory Retrieval and Choice Processes." *Journal of Consumer Research* 8: 431–441.

Beihal, G., and D. Chakravarti. 1986. "Consumers' Use of Memory and External Information in Choice: Macro and Micro Perspectives." *Journal of Consumer Research* 12: 382–405.

Bell, D. 1882. "Regret in Decisionmaking under Uncertainty." *Operations Research* 30: 961–981.

Belsley, D., E. Kuh, and R. Welsch. 1980. *Regression Diagnostics: Identifying Influential Data and Sources of Collinearity.* New York: Wiley.

Berger, M., G. Blomquist, D. Kenkel, and G. Tolley. 1987. "Valuing Changes in Health Risks: A Comparison of Alternative Measures." *Southern Economic Journal* 53: 967–984.

Berkowitz, L., and E. Donnerstein. 1982. "External Validity Is More Than Skin Deep: Some Answers to Criticisms of Laboratory Experiments." *American Psychologist* 37 (March): 245–257.

Bettman, J. R. 1979. *An Information Processing Theory of Consumer Choice.* Reading, MA: Addison-Wesley.

Bettman, J., J. Payne, and R. Staelin. 1986. "Cognitive Considerations in Designing Effective Labels for Presenting Risk Information." *Journal of Marketing and Public Policy* 5: 1–28.

Blomquist, G. C. 1988. *The Regulation of Motor Vehicle and Traffic Safety.* Boston: Kluwer Academic Publishers.

Bostrom, A., B. Fischhoff, and G. M. Morgan. 1982. "Characterizing Mental Models of Hazardous Processes: A Methodology and an Application to Radon." *Journal of Social Issues,* forthcoming.

Brownell, W. A., and L. Dunn. 1979a. "Federal Energy Conservation Plan." North Carolina Department of Commerce, Raleigh. June.

Brownell, W. A., and L. Dunn. 1979b. U.S. Congress, Office of Technology Assessment, Residential Energy Conservation, 1, Washington: GPO.

Brucato, P. F., Jr. 1988. *Essays in the Economics of Information and Property Rights.* Ph.D. dissertation. Duke University.

Calfee, J. 1985. *Cigarette Advertising, Health Information and Regulation before 1970.* FTC Working Paper 134.

Camerer, C., and H. Kunreuther. 1989. "Decision Processes for Low-Probability Risks: Policy Implications." Risk and Decisions Processes Center. Wharton School Discussion Paper.

Carlsmith, J. M., P. C. Ellsworth, and E. Aronson. 1976. *Methods of Research in Social Psychology.* Reading MA.: Addison-Wesley.

Cummings, R. G., D. S. Brookshire, and W. D. Schulze. 1984. "Valuing Environmental Goods: A State of the Art Assessment of the Contingent Valuation Method." Draft Report Prepared for the U.S. EPA.

Dinan, T. M. 1987. "An Examination of the Consumer Decision Process for Residential Energy Use." *Energy Systems and Policy* 10, 4: 345–371.

Dipboye, R. L., and M. F. Flanagan. 1979. "Research Settings in Industrial and Organizational Psychology: Are Findings in the Field More Generalizable Than in the Laboratory?" *American Psychologist* 34: 141–150.

Doll, R., and R. Peto, 1981. "The Causes of Cancer." *Journal of the National Cancer Institute* 60: 1193–1265.

Energy Division. 1978. "North Carolina Energy Conservation Plan." North Carolina Department of Commerce, Raleigh. July.

Fischhoff, B., and L. Furby. 1988. "Measuring Values: A Conceptual Framework for Interpreting Transactions With Special Reference to Contingent Valuation of Visibility." *Journal of Risk and Uncertainty* 1: 147–184.

Fischhoff, B., P. Slovic, S. Lichtenstein, S. Read, and B. Combs. 1976. "How Safe Is Safe Enough? A Psychometric Study of Attitudes Towards Technological Risks and Benefits." Eugene, OR: Decision Research. January.

Fischhoff, B., S. Lichtenstein, P. Slovic, S. Derby, and R. Keeney. 1981. *Acceptable Risk.* Cambridge: Cambridge University Press.

Freiden, B. J., and K. Baker. 1983. "The Market Needs Help: The Disappointing Record of Home Energy Conservation." *Journal of Policy Analysis and Management* 2 (Spring): 433–448.

Gaeth, G. J., and J. Shanteau. 1984. "Reducing the Influence of Irrelevant Information on Experienced Decision Makers." *Organizational Behavior and Human Performance* 33: 263–282.

Gerking, S., M. de Haan, and W. Schulze. 1988. "The Marginal Value of Job Safety: A Contingent Valuation Study." *Journal of Risk and Uncertainty* 1: 185–200.

Grether, D., and L. L. Wilde. 1983. "Consumer Choice and Information: New Experimental Evidence." *Information Economics and Policy* 1: 115–144.

Grether, D., A. Schwartz, and L. L. Wilde. 1985. "The Irrelevance of Information Overload: An Analysis of Search and Disclosure." *Southern California Law Review* 59: 277–303.

Hadden, S. G. 1985. *Read the Label: Reducing Risk by Providing Information.* St. Paul, MN: West View.

Halvorsen, R., and R. Palmquist. 1980. "The Interpretation of Dummy Variables in Semilogarithnic Equations." *The American Economic Review* 70 (June): 474–476.

Harrell, F. 1980. "The Logit Procedure." *Statistical Analysis System (SAS) Supplemental Library User's Guide.* Cary, NC: SAS Institute.

Hartman, R. S. 1988. "Self-Selection Bias in the Evaluation of Voluntary Energy Conservation Programs." *Review of Economics and Statistics* 70, 3 (August): 448–458.

Hausman, J. A. 1979. "Individual Discount Rates and the Purchase and Utilization of Energy Using Durables." *The Bell Journal of Economics* 10 (Spring): 33–54.

Hirst, E., and R. Goeltz. 1987–88. "Recommendation and Installation of Residential Retrofit Measures in the Hood River Conservation Project." *Energy Systems and Policy* 11, 4: 297–309.

Hoffman, D. R. 1989. "Managing the Demand/Supply Side System Peak Effectively." *Transmission and Distribution* 44, 3 (March): 134–142.

Hogarth, R., and H. Kunreuther. 1985. "Ambiguity and Insurance Decisions." *American Economic Review, Papers and Proceedings* 75: 386–390.

Jacoby, J., D. Speller, and C. K. Berning. 1974. "Brand Choice Behavior as a Function of Information Load: Replication and Extension." *Journal of Consumer Research* 1: 33–42.

Jacoby, J., D. Speller, and C. A. Kohn. 1974. "Brand Choice Behavior as a Function of Information Load." *Journal of Marketing Research* 11: 63–69.

Jones-Lee, M. W. 1976. *The Value of Life: An Economic Analysis.* Chicago: University of Chicago Press.

Jones-Lee, M. W., M. Hammerton, and P. R. Philips. 1985. "The Value of Safety: Results of a National Sample Survey." *Economic Journal* 95: 49–72.

Kahneman, D., and A. Tversky. 1979. "Prospect Theory: An Analysis of Decision under Risk." *Econometrica* 47 (March): 263–292.

Kahneman, D., and A. Tversky, 1982. "The Psychology of Preferences." *Scientific American* 246: 160–173.

Kahneman, D., P. Slovic, and A. Tversky. 1982. *Judgment and Uncertainty: Heuristic and Biases.* Cambridge: Cambridge University Press.

Kassarjian, Harold H. 1977. "Content Analysis and Consumer Research." *Journal of Consumer Research* 4: 8–18.

Keller, K. L., and R. Staelin. 1987. "Effects of Quality and Quantity of Information on Decision Effectiveness." *Journal of Consumer Research* 14, 2: 200–213.

Knetsch, J. L., and J. A. Sinden. 1984. "Willingness-to-Pay and Compensation Demanded: Experimental Evidence of an Unexpected Disparity in Measures Value." *Quarterly Journal of Economics* 94: 507–522.

Kruglanski, A. W. 1975. "The Human Subject in Psychology Experiments: Fact and Artifact." In L. Berkowitz (ed.), *Advances in Experimental Social Psychology*, vol. 8. New York: Academic Press.

Kunreuther, H. 1976. "Limited Knowledge and Insurance Protection." *Public Policy* 24: 227–262.

Kunreuther, H., R. Ginsberg, L. Miller, P. Sagi, P. Slovic, B. Borkan, and N. Katz. 1978. *Disaster Insurance Protection: Public Policy Lessons.* New York: Wiley.

Lichtenstein, S., and P. Slovic, 1973. "Response-Induced Reversals of Preferences in Gambling: An Extended Replication in Las Vegas." *Journal of Experimental Psychology* 101 (November): 16–20.

Lichtenstein, S., P. Slovic, B. Fischhoff, M. Layman, and B. Combs. 1978. "Judged Frequency of Lethal Events." *Journal of Experimental Psychology: Human Learning and Memory* 4: 551–578.

Maddala, G. S. 1983. *Limited-Dependent and Qualitative Variables in Econometrics.* Cambridge: Cambridge University Press.

Magat, W. A., J. W. Payne, and P. F. Brucato, Jr. 1986. "How Important Is Information Format? An Experimental Study of Home Energy Audit Programs." *Journal of Policy Analysis and Management* 6 (Spring): 20–34.

Magat, W. A., W. K. Viscusi, and J. Huber. 1988. "Consumer Processing of Hazard Warning Information." *Journal of Risk and Uncertainty* 1: 201–232.

Malhotra, N. K. 1982. "Information Load and Consumer Decision Making." *Journal of Consumer Research* 8: 419–439.

Mazis, M. B., and R. Staelin. 1981. "Using Information Processing Principles in Public Policymaking." *Journal of Marketing and Public Policy* 1: 3–14.

Mazis, M. B., R. Staelin, H. Beals, and S. Salop. 1981. "A Framework for Evaluating Consumer Information Regulation." *Journal of Marketing and Public Policy* 1: 3–14.

McDougall, G. H. G., J. D. Claxton, J. R. B. Ritchie, and C. D. Anderson. 1981. "Consumer Energy Research: A Review." *Journal of Consumer Research* 8 (December): 343–354.

National Energy Conservation Policy Act of 1978. U.S. Department of Energy: RCS Final Rule Federal Register, vol. 44, no. 217 (November 7, 1979).

Nichols, A., and R. Zeckhauser. 1986. "The Perils of Prudence: How Conservative Risk Assessments Distort Regulation." *Regulation* 10: 13–24.

O'Reilly, J. T. 1987. *Product Defects and Hazards: Litigation and Regulatory Strategies*. New York: Wiley.

Payne, J. W. 1982. "Contingent Decision Behavior." *Psychological Review* 92 (September): 382–402.

Payne, J. W., M. L. Braunstein, and J. S. Carroll. 1978. "Exploring Pre-decision Behavior: An Alternative Approach to Decision Research." *Organization Behavior and Human Performance* 22 (October): 17–44.

Pickels, S. J., and P. Audet. 1987. "Second Generation Conservation Programs with an Increasing Utility Initiative." *Public Utilities Fortnightly* 20, 13 (December 24): 9–13.

Plott, C. R. 1981. "Experimental Methods in Political Economy: A Tool for Regulatory Research." In A. R. Ferguson (ed.), *An Agenda for Regulatory Research in the 1980's*. Cambridge, MA: Ballinger.

Redinger, R., and R. Staelin. 1980. "Payback as a Means of Predicting Product Choices." Unpublished manuscript. GSIA Carnegie-Mellon University.

Roberts, R. 1984. "A Positive Model of Private Clarity and Public Transfers." *Journal of Political Economy* 92, 1: 136–148.

Rosenberg, M., and R. Lanoue. 1980. *The Costs and Benefits of Utility Operated Residential Conservation Programs*. Boston: Technical Development Corporation. August.

Russo, J. E. 1974. "More Information is Better: A Reevaluation of Jacoby, Speller, and Kohn." *Journal of Consumer Research* 1: 68–72.

Russo, J. E. 1977. "The Value of Unit Price Information." *Journal of Marketing Research* 14 (May): 193–201.

Russo, J. E., G. Krieser, and S. Miyashita. 1975. "An Effective Display of Unit Price Information." *Journal of Marketing* 39 (April): 11–19.

Samuelson, W., and R. Zeckhauser. 1988. "Status Quo Bias in Decision Making." *Journal of Risk and Uncertainty* 1: 7–60.

Savage, L. J. 1954. *Foundations of Statistics*. New York: Wiley. Reprint, Dover Publications, 1972.

Schelling, T. C. 1968. "The Life You Save May Be Your Own." In S. Chase (ed.), *Problems in Public Expenditure Analysis*. Washington: Brookings Institution.

Schucker, R. E., R. C. Stokes, M. L. Stewart, and D. P. Henderson. 1983. "The Impact of the Saccharin Warining Label on Sales of Diet Drinks in Supermarkets." *Journal of Public Policy and Marketing*: 46–56.

Scrull, T. K., M. Lichtenstein, and M. Rothbart. 1985. "Associative Storage and Retrieval Processes in Person Memory." *Journal of Experimental Psychology* 11, 2: 316–345.

Silverman, I. 1977. *The Human Subject in the Psychological Laboratory*. New York: Permagon.

Simon, H. A. 1957. *Models of Man*. New York: Wiley.

Smith, A. 1937. *The Wealth of Nations*. New York: Modern Library.

Smith, R. 1979. "Compensating Differentials and Public Policy: A Review." *Industrial and Labor Relations Review* 32: 339–352.

Smith, V. K., W. Desvousges, A. Fisher, and F. R. Johnson. 1988. "Learning about Radon's Risk." *Journal of Risk and Uncertainty* 1: 233–258.

Smith, V. K., and W. H. Desvousges. 1987. "An Empirical Analysis of the Economic Value of Risk Changes." *Journal of Political Economy* 95: 89–114.

Smith, V. L. 1982. "Microeconomics Systems as an Experimental Science." *The American Economic Review* 72 (December): 923–955.

Staelin, R., and J. W. Payne. 1976. "Studies of the Information-Seeking Behavior of Consumers." In J. S. Carroll and J. W. Payne (eds.), *Cognition and Social Behavior*. Hillsdale, NJ: Lawrence Erlbaum, pp. 185–201.

Summer, J. O. 1974. "Less Information Is Better?" *Journal of Marketing Research* 11: 467–468.

Thaler, R., and S. Rosen. 1976. "The Value of Saving a Life: Evidence from the Labor Market." In N. Terleckyj (ed.), *Household Production and Consumption*. New York: Columbia University Press.

Thaler, R. 1980. "Towards a Positive Theory of Consumer Choice." *Journal of Economic Behavior and Organization* 1: 39 60.

Travis, C. C., S. A. Richter, E. A. C. Crouch, R. Wilson, and E. D. Klema. 1987. "Cancer Risk Management: A Review of 132 Federal Regulatory Decisions." *Environmental Science Technology* 21: 415–420.

Tversky, A., and D. Kahneman. 1981. "The Framing of Decisions and the Rationality of Choice." *Science* 211: 453–458.

U.S. Department of Commerce, Bureau of the Census. 1985. *Statistical Abstract of the United States: 1986*. Washington: GPO.

U.S. Department of Health and Human Services. 1987. *Review of the Research Literature on the Effects of Health Warning Labels, A Report to the United States Congress*. Washington: U.S. Department of Health and Human Services.

Viscusi, W. K. 1979. *Employment Hazards: An Investigation of Market Performance*. Cambridge: Harvard University Press.

Viscusi, W. K. 1983. *Risk by Choice: Regulating Health and Safety in the Workplace*. Cambridge: Harvard University Press.

Viscusi, W. K. 1985a. "A Bayesian Perspective on Biases in Risk Perception." *Economic Letters* 17: 59–62.

Viscusi, W. K. 1985b. "Are Individuals Bayesian Decision Makers?" *American Economic Review, Papers and Proceedings* 75: 381–385.

Viscusi, W. K. 1986. "The Valuation of Risks to Life and Health: Guidelines for Policy Analysis." In J. Bentkover, V. Covello, and J. Mumpower (eds.), *Benefit Assessment: The State of the Art*. Dordrecht: Reidel.

Viscusi, W. K. 1989. "Prospective Reference Theory: Toward an Explanation of the Paradoxes." *Journal of Risk and Uncertainty* 2: 235–264.

Viscusi, W. K., and C. O'Connor. 1984. "Adaptive Responses to Chemical Labeling: Are Workers Bayesian Decision Makers?" *American Economic Review* 74: 942–956.

Viscusi, W. K., and W. A. Magat. 1986. *Analysis of Economic Benefits of Improved Information: Project Period 2 Report*. Report to the U.S. EPA under CR-811057-02-0.

Viscusi, W. K., and W. A. Magat. 1987. *Learning about Risk: Consumer and Worker Responses to Hazard Information*. Cambridge: Harvard University Press.

Viscusi, W. K., and M. Moore. 1987. "Workers' Compensation: Wage Effects, Benefit Inadequacies, and the Value of Health Losses." *Review of Economics and Statistics* 69, 2: 249–261.

Viscusi, W. K., W. A. Magat, and J. Huber. 1986. "Informational Regulation of Consumer Health Risks: An Empirical Evaluation of Hazard Warnings." *Rand Journal of Economics* 17: 351–365.

Weber, S. J., and T. D. Cook. 1972. "Subject Effects in Laboratory Research: An Examination of Subject Roles, Demand Characteristics, and Valid Inferences." *Psychological Bulletin* 77: 273–295.

Weinstein, M., D. Shepard, and J. Pliskin. 1980. "The Economic Value of Changing Mortality Probabilities: A Decision-Theoretic Approach." *Quarterly Journal of Economics* 94: 373–396.

Wilkie, W. L. 1974. "Analysis of Effects of Information Load." *Journal of Marketing Research* 11: 462–466.

Winett, R. A., and J. H. Kagel. 1984. "Effects of Information Presentation Format on Resource Use in Field Setting." *Journal of Consumer Research* 11 (September): 655–667.

Yates, S. M., and E. Aronson. 1983. "A Psychological Perspective on Energy Conservation in Residential Buildings." *American Psychologist* 38 (April): 435–444.

Zeckhauser, R., 1986. "Behavioral versus Rational Economics: What You See Is What You Conquer." *Journal of Business* 59: S435–S450.

Index